THE
NECESSITY
OF
EMPTY PLACES

THE
NECESSITY
OF
EMPTY PLACES

▷ ◁

PAUL GRUCHOW

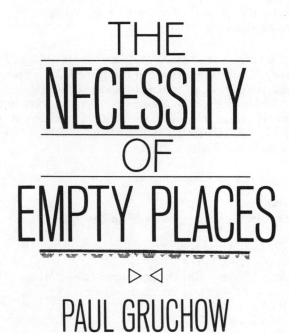

ST. MARTIN'S PRESS
NEW YORK

Chapters 2, 17, 20, and 21 originally appeared in earlier
versions in *Minnesota Monthly*.

Library of Congress Cataloging-in-Publication Data

Gruchow, Paul.
    The necessity of empty places / Paul Gruchow.
        p.   cm.
    "A Thomas Dunne book."
    ISBN 0-312-02198-4
    1. United States—Description and travel—1981–
    2. Landscape—United States.   I. Title.
    E169.04G78 1988
    917.3—dc 19   88-11597

Design by Glen M. Edelstein

10 9 8 7 6 5 4 3 2

A Thomas Dunne Book

For Jim and Florence Vance, who have
made my work as a writer possible

CONTENTS

BOOK 1

BOOK 2

BOOK 3

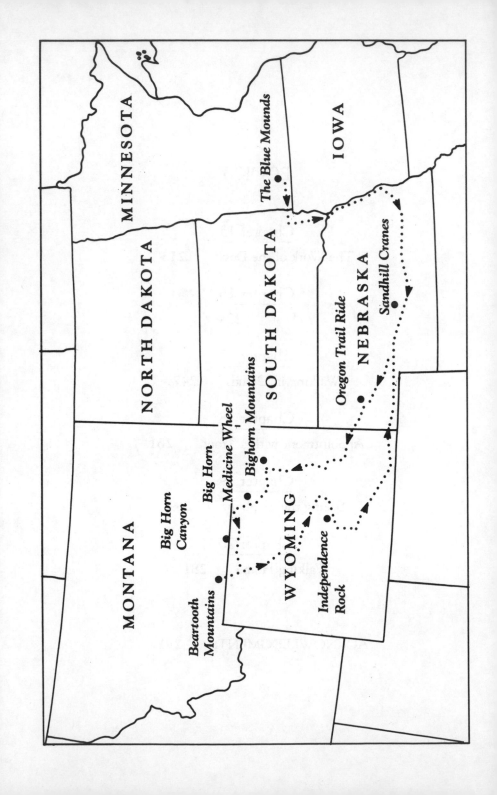

BOOK

1

1

The Blue Mountains of Minnesota

◁ ▷

$\mathbf{M}$Y young son calls them the Blue Mountains. They aren't blue, actually; they are red and brown. They aren't mountains either, not even hills. The Blue Mounds we adults, stunted of imagination, call them. A red cliff, not scarlet, but Indian red, an earthen color tending toward purple, rises abruptly out of the prairie, like a row of teeth, and above it a tongue of brown prairie recedes into the west.

Let them be mountains. A mountain is a perception as much as anything. The mountains gather, Annie Dillard says, the waters disperse. Here, thirty miles west of my gray house, of my brown chair, the west begins to gather,

3

the earth begins to collect for the climb toward the clouds. Go another hundred miles and there will be real hills, another three hundred miles and there will be sandstone buttes, another four hundred miles and there will be snow-covered granite peaks. But these cliffs, the footstool of the plains, will also do. Let them be mountains. And let them be blue. From a distance, and early in the morning and in the long shadows of the twilight, I suppose they are blue enough. Blueness is a state of mind, a habit of seeing.

A stone something-or-other extends for about twelve hundred yards from novelist Frederick Manfred's former backyard to the cliffs of the Blue Mounds. Manfred has contended for years in spirited letters and articles that the construction is prehistoric. The line of stones, looking like the tailbones of a dinosaur, runs true east and west, or close to it. It marks the spot on the horizon where the sun rises at the spring and fall equinoxes. Perhaps, Manfred suggests, the fence figured in the astronomical rites of an ancient Indian people. Or maybe, he says, it steered stampeding buffalo over the cliffs to their deaths, an old way of hunting farther west.

The reactions of the several scholars who have examined the site near Luverne in southwestern Minnesota have ranged from respectfully to tartly skeptical. No corroborating evidence can be found that the Blue Mounds were ever an astronomical site, they say. That the fence runs east and west is no surprise, they add: It follows within a hundred feet of the historical property line. Neither has anyone uncovered bone deposits to suggest a killsite. Even if the bones had all been carried away by the earliest settlers, it seems someone would surely have written about it, but the written records are silent. And preliminary tests suggest that the earth beneath the stones may have been disturbed relatively recently. The latest guess from academic quarters is that the stones were part of a farm fence.

The argument endures in the pages of esoteric journals. Occasional crossfire still erupts. There are much better places on the Blue Mounds for observing the sunrise or for running buffalo, one side says. What fool farmer would build a fence a hundred feet inside his property line, and with stones, and then not make it high enough to keep anything in? the other side asks. In truth, you might well walk right over the fence and not realize it. It is not, after all, Stonehenge.

The central issue—historic or prehistoric—could probably be settled in two strokes: by undertaking a thorough soil study and by identifying the lichens that grow on the rocks. How recently have the soils been disturbed? And if the lichens are a relatively rapidly growing species, the fence could be historic; if not, it isn't. Answers are possible. But I like the ambiguity. It is a place worthy of mystery.

I went there once, years ago, at the cold, clear dawning of autumn. I perched on a stone at the upper edge of the fence in the darkness and waited for the new season to rise. The stars fell, the moon went down. On the eastern horizon the light, doubtful and far away, began to collect like liquid in a pool. The light gathered intensity. In the town below the cliffs, the noises of automobiles started. I sat on my stone, rapt and cold.

Red and pink light began to stream from a place below

5

the horizon in the east like the notes of a silent fanfare. For a long time the sun lingered just below the horizon, like a performer behind a curtain. A mourning dove cried in a bur oak tree. Suddenly the sun burst into view and the whole world was radiant with the new light of autumn. A killdeer arose, screaming ecstatically. The sun paused at the horizon, exactly along the line of the fence—an optical illusion, since the rising sun is not precisely where it appears to be. It began to climb, taking command of the day.

Manfred's theory of the fence prompted me to go to the Blue Mounds. It was my first visit. When the sun rose where Manfred promised, when the mourning doves cried and the killdeer screamed, and when the sunbeams streamed through the tortured branches of the oaks and began to melt the frost at my feet, to render the silver gossamer in the grass invisible, I felt myself in the footsteps of an ancient soulmate watching a similar sunrise centuries ago. I knew then that I didn't care whose fence it was, and that I was coming back.

I can't explain the royally plural name. The Blue Mounds are singular, in both senses of the word. The mounds are a mesa, a table. Ice carved the table out of the Sioux quartzite bedrock. Its edge is a two-mile-long line of sheer cliffs a hundred feet high, split in many places by the ravages of weather, pulled apart by the muscular forces of roots, rent by deep, narrow canyons. It is a vast ruin, all tumbles of talus and crumbling chimney spires.

In the shadow of the cliff and along its upper edge a bur oak savanna prospers and fruits flourish: wild plums, chokecherries, mulberries, raspberries, gooseberries, grapes. Woodland flowers bloom there: violets, false spikenard, trillium, bloodroot, false Solomon's seal.

While the Dutchman's breeches blossom in the outer crevices of the cliff in the springtime, the dark, chill interior crevices still embrace drifts of snow. Bathed in the perpetual quarter-light of shadow, they give rise in late spring to enormous ferns, giant flowered trilliums, and other plants unaccustomed to life in southwestern Minnesota. Climbing down into one of them is like falling in a dream into a dark northern forest.

The table is covered with a cloth of grass and set with plates of water. God forgot Rock County, in which the mounds are situated, when He doled out Minnesota's fifteen thousand lakes. It possesses only the two artificial ones at the north end of Blue Mounds State Park. But the Creator compensated with an abundance of shallow basins in the rock itself. They collect meltwater in the spring and rainwater in the summer. Bright green mosses grow in them, algae multiply there, pond snails graze their pink bottoms, and water striders skate on top of them.

Stockponds also dot the surface of the high table, a reminder of recent days when it was the province of cattle and gumweed. Cattails rim the ponds now. Ducks drop into them on their journeys north and south. Salamanders and frogs overwinter in them. In the evenings white-tailed deer come down to drink from them, and so many smaller creatures leave their footprints in the mud that it is sometimes impossible to tell one from another.

Deer watch over the park's visitors from a discreet distance, like agents of a Secret Service. Often, I will be walking across the mounds and will sense that I am observed and, turning, will see a big doe, her eyes intent upon me. When our eyes meet, she turns and disappears silently over the rim of the horizon.

A few buffalo still roam the Blue Mounds, a remnant of the great prehistoric herds, ghosts of the lost world of the prairies. The fences that contain them remind us of all that once was and might still have been, of the prairie chickens that no longer boom, of the pelicans that roost elsewhere, of the wolves that have ceased to howl in the night.

You can drive to the buffalo enclosure, mount a wooden platform, and view them at pasture. But you approach them best on foot from the opposite end of the park, so that your first glimpse of them is at a distance that obliterates the fences. If you are lucky, it will be a hot summer's day, the clouds will billow above you, a stray breeze will pass like a damp cloth across your brow, and the buffalo will be standing in profile on the ridge of the pasture against the blue sky, all head and chest, like a pride of lions. Or it will be rutting season, and you will hear a bull roaring like a lion.

East of the buffalo pasture lie two small lakes, rectangular, one above the other, set at right angles and connected by a creek that twists through a deep, rock-walled, treelined ravine. You can fish in the shade of a cottonwood tree at the upper lake, or cool your ankles in the water that falls from it into the creek, or sit on the quartzite ledge above the ravine and plot a murder with some of the poison from the roots of the water hemlock plants that grow there, or swim in the lower lake, or cross the dam of the lower lake and bathe in the sunlight beside a puddle of rock-gray water fed by a trickle from one of the hillside springs.

But I have forgotten to mention the oceans of purple phlox in the springtime, and the blazing yellow blossoms of the pear cactuses in July, and the acres of amber goldenrods in the fall.

And I have neglected the grasses: the big bluestem, taller than a man and the color of wine in September; the needlegrasses with their twisted seedpods sharp as pins that corkscrew themselves into the earth; the bearded plumes of the Canada wild rye; the feathery spires of the Indian grass; the tufts of blue grama grass, their flowers shaped like Asian eyebrows.

And what about the sedge meadow below the rim of the cliffs, a treachery of mucks and hillocks? Red-winged blackbirds warble there all summer long, and spiders in a dozen brilliant colors weave their complicated webs from reed to reed, and in the fall the gentians radiate the deepest and purest, the most ravishing color of blue in all the world.

Have I uttered a word about the snakes: the garter snakes, the fox snakes, the bull snakes, the grass snakes? Have I said how many times I have wondered at the magic of a snake, seen it glide before my eyes into a clump of grass, reached down for it, and found that it had altogether vanished?

Where are the meadowlarks in April? The bobolinks sounding like plucked metal strings in July? The nighthawks buzzing overhead on an August night? The pigeons cooing in the crevices of the old quarry in January? The great horned owls on the nest in February? The red-tailed hawks cruising the cliffline at sunset?

And I have slighted the rocks themselves, a billion and a half years old, smothered in green and orange lichens,

9

rubbed smooth on the corners by the itching rumps of centuries of buffalo, etched with the tracings of glaciers. They are pink, or maroon, sometimes almost black, cool in the summer, warm in winter, a relief of hardness, an intrusion of angles into the rounded softness of the prairies.

But I meant to remember a night in August when I crossed the mounds in the blue light of a half moon. I stood above the lakes near a place where I had once found an arrowhead. Fireflies sparked and sputtered in the darkness like struck matches. Crickets sawed in a million houses of grass. Everything shimmered. As I stood there, a pair of coyotes began to yip and cry, a wild and ancient song. It was like that spring morning at the stone fence, a moment when time stops, when centuries fall away, and you briefly glimpse the glory of forever.

The Blue Mounds carry a precious melody from the regions of forever to the present, the song of diversity. About 220 species of birds have been sighted on the Blue Mounds. Perhaps 250 species of plants take root there, including thirty-five or forty kinds of grasses alone. There are perhaps thirty kinds of mammals, at least five kinds of snakes, two kinds of turtles, two kinds of salamanders. Who knows how many varieties of insects frequent the Blue Mounds? Some of them have probably never been named. The sedges have never been cataloged, nor the bryophites, nor the varieties of microscopic flora and fauna. At the least, thousands of varieties of life thrive on the Blue Mounds, their exact number and the intricacies of their coexistence still as mysterious as anything yet to be discovered in the depths of the heavens.

10

Perhaps more mysterious. We know approximately how many stars there are in the Milky Way (a hundred billion) but not even to the nearest order of magnitude how many species of organisms there are on earth. About 1.7 million species have been named since 1753, when Linnaeus unveiled his binomial system of classification. In 1964 British ecologist Carrington B. Williams suggested, on the basis of intensive local samples and mathematical extrapolations from them, that there might be as many as three million species of insects alone. Later studies gave some scientists reason to speculate that the number might actually be as high as ten million. Then, in 1982, entomologists from the National Museum of Natural History developed a way of collecting intensive samples of insects from the previously inaccessible canopies of tropical rain forests. The results exceeded every expectation. Terry L. Erwin did a new extrapolation based on them; there might be, he decided, as many as thirty million *species* of insects. We know even less about many other kinds of organisms: epiphytic plants, roundworms, mites, fungi, protozoans, bacteria. The most basic thing about life on earth, how many kinds of it there are, remains anybody's guess.

Nor are we likely to know anytime soon. There is, for one thing, nobody to do the work. There are more retirees in Jacksonville, Florida, than there are systematists, as the scientists cataloging the earth's diversity are called, in all the world, Edward O. Wilson recently noted to his fellow scientists in a plea for action. Fewer systematists than soldiers in the standing army of Mongolia, he said. And while the species aren't being counted, they are rapidly disappearing. The current extinction rate is four hundred times that of the recent geologic past and climbing.

It is an odd irony that the places we call empty should retain some memory of the diversity of life, while the places we have filled up grow emptier and emptier. If we knew what we were getting rid of, we might have some premonition of the things we are going to miss. The Blue Mounds survive as a tiny remnant island of the old tall-grass sea. A century ago the sea still existed. What stories did it contain? What secrets to the nature of life? What clues about our own standing in life? It is no more read-able now than the ashes of a manuscript of which only the title page remains. The thing unimaginable is how we can be so lacking in simple curiosity.

From the top of the Blue Mounds, I look out across the countryside of southwestern Minnesota and see a land-scape that has been reduced to its simplest terms. On a clear day I can see for fifteen miles or more in any direc-tion. I see the contrails of the jets in the sky, and I hear the roar of truck traffic on Interstate 90. Below me I see the city of Luverne, and beyond it the elevators of Magno-lia, and then the water tower that sits on the knoll at Adrian. In between I see hundreds of square miles of corn, interrupted here and there by the windbreaks of trees around the farmsteads.

Standing on the cliff at night, I have the sensation of being suspended in midair: The stars twinkle in the Milky Way above, and the yard lights on the farmsteads twinkle like stars below. But every time I return the sen-sation dims. Fewer and fewer of the lights are lit any-more.

With every passing decade, the variety of species

that the farms support dwindles. By now we are pretty much down to corn and soybeans and pigs. With every passing year, the struggle to stay on the farm intensifies. As the farms die, the towns die. One of the endangered species on the prairie is *Homo sapiens.* The day is coming when we will have simplified even ourselves out of the picture.

2

The Nebraska Sandhills:
THE FLIGHT OF CRANES
◁ ▷

THE travel alarm sounded at 4:30 A.M. and wound down before I could find it on the unfamiliar night stand in the cheap motel room in Grand Island, Nebraska. I fought consciousness as a drowning man does water. Then I remembered where I was and why. I massaged my eyes with my knuckles, switched on the blinding light, got up, stumbled toward the bathroom. I dressed warmly—jeans, woolen socks, insulated boots, heavy shirt, sweater, winter jacket, stocking cap, gloves—and went out onto the balcony. Stars glimmered through the haze of city lights. The day promised to be hot—temperatures in the high eighties were predicted—but it was still freezing, and I knew I would be grateful for my heavy clothes. I headed my car westward, stopped for a cup of coffee, put the lights of the prairie town and what little traffic there was behind me. I was in search of sandhill cranes.

At the first slumbering village I took a country road south, past the bright lights of an Interstate 80 truck stop. The road arched over the highway, a new river running in place with the old, and descended into a region of bottomlands, of meadows, of gravel mines, of willow and cottonwood thickets, a closed-in place more reminiscent of Missouri than of wide-open Nebraska. I crossed a skinny bridge. The channel of water it spanned was not the main channel of the South Platte. Its flow was too narrow, too direct. But in the faint light of the new day, I could see cranes downriver, emerging from the water like the pilings of some abandoned, improbable ruin.

I pulled onto a meadow road at the far edge of the channel, shut off the engine. Scarcely had I cracked the window glass when the primeval sound rushed in, halfway between a croak and a song, the music of dry bones rattling. It surged and fell in a regular rhythm, like waves of water washing against a shore. I had last heard the cranes a year before in another place, but it seemed as if their rattles had never completely dissipated. The sound of the sandhill cranes is like the roaring of the sea in a conch shell; when you have finally heard it, you recognize that you have always known it. It is like the cry of a loon or the howling of wolves or the warning rattle of a snake, an article in the universal language.

The blades of last year's grass were stiff with frost. They cracked underfoot like plastic trinkets. It was almost too early for birdsong. The river gurgled and sucked. The

15

cranes, standing halfway to their knees in the frigid water, cried and cried. As it happened, it was Good Friday. My ears heard cranes, and my heart heard lamentations.

The main channel of the Platte was still nearly a mile away, but I could hear the cranes there too, in far greater numbers. At the rim of the horizon, the sky began to lighten. The sound of the birds was hauling up the curtain of day. Blackbirds trilled in the willows. A crow cackled. A pair of wood ducks flew low over the water, their wings squeaking against the air underneath. In the hayfield, a meadowlark sang a song as crisp as a bugle call. Matins on Good Friday morning. At the edge of the river, in an eddy around the roots of a cottonwood tree, the carcass of a raccoon rocked gently back and forth in a cradle of death. It was beginning to be light enough to see the yellow blush of life in the supple trunks of the willows.

The cranes stood like a congregation in the shallows of the river. I could see their long necks now, could watch them stalk about as if on tiptoe, could observe them stretching and settling their wings. Already some of their brethren from the sandbars farther south had taken flight, heading from the river to the fields nearby to feed for the day. They showed the characteristic profile of the cranes, necks straight out, legs tucked in, feet trailing behind like rudders. The morning approached when they would have fed long enough along the Platte, when they would rise into the air and not descend again until they had reached their nesting grounds on the tundra.

Behind me, car doors slammed. I turned from my crouch in the shadow of a cottonwood tree. Three persons, a man, a woman, and a boy, stood at the edge of the road, binoculars dangling from their necks, their bare

16

hands tucked into jeans pockets. This arrival stirred the nervous birds, and the volume of their calling intensified. Half a dozen of them stretched their wings, took to the air, and circled the flock in the river below, beckoning the rest. But most of the cranes stuck to the roost.

We were gathered at a great transcontinental cross-roads. The wide and many-channeled river, running from west to east, from the mountains to the Missouri, defined one axis, the highway of the sun. The cranes, traveling from south to north and back again, from the Gulf to the Arctic, defined the other, the highway of the winds. Here at the center of the continent the two great streams of traffic met and mixed.

The way west cut across the grain of the continent, across its mountains, across the Mississippi running down its midsection. It had long been the way of humans. The Pawnees followed the river before the Europeans came, and when the new settlers headed west, their roads also followed it, as ours do now. The four of us were standing on Mormon Island, named for the trail, just to the north of us, that the disciples of Brigham Young took to Utah. Just to the south ran the old Oregon Trail, the river of the westward movement, of the gold rush, of Manifest Destiny. Later, the Pony Express route ran that way, then the railroads and the telegraph wires. The roar of traffic along a modern interstate highway a mile away, carrying even above the wild sound of cranes, continued a stream of traffic that began centuries ago and has run unabated, although increasingly swiftly, ever since. Overhead, the contrail of a jet arced westward.

The continent itself stretched along the north-south axis, the way of the winds, and the way of the great animal migrations, the way of songbirds, of water birds, of monarch butterflies, of bison, of polar bears, of whales, of sandhill cranes, of creatures great and small moving in concert with the seasons, which also followed the northward and southward tiltings of the earth on its axis.

For every century that humans have traversed the mile-wide Platte, there has been a millennium of crane flight. In the few centuries of our intersection, we have, it seems, been moving not only in counterdirections but also at cross-purposes. The differences lie neither in the nature of cranes nor in that of humans, but in our different ways of occupying and using land. The flyways of the cranes are the paths of nomads. Our highways are the routes of settlement or, more precisely, of occupation.

The nomad is a visitor, but not a stranger, whose visit is a kind of embrace. I do not mean that it is innocent or without consequences but only that it is temporary. It is a way of taking hold of the land, even of exploiting it, without altering its essential character. The nomad lives necessarily within the limits of the land and cannot take more from it than the land itself offers at the moment of the visit. The nomad receives the fruits of the land as a gift.

Occupation, on the other hand, is a form of exclusion, and it is possible to practice exclusion without limits. The occupier receives the land not as a gift but as a commodity, as a right rather than a privilege. To the extent that the occupier recognizes limits, they are primarily practical. Morality has proved, with respect to the land, at least, a less powerful restraint than necessity.

When we gave up our nomadic ways, we gained a certain freedom from the limits of the land, although it may yet prove to have been illusory. In his youthful vision, the

Dakota prophet Black Elk correctly saw a river of occupation running from east to west, and he saw that it was the
color of spilled blood. The blood, of course, was that of
his own people, but it was also the blood of the bison,
upon which his people utterly depended. He saw instinctively, as we do not, that the death of the land and the
death of the culture were inextricably linked.

The four of us stood our respectful distance and watched
the ancient race of cranes at their morning rituals, at their
nervous dancing, their strutting, their preening and re-
pairing of feathers, their raucous chattering. The sun rose.
It popped up abruptly as it always does along distant horizons on the prairies or at sea. Suddenly the long reach of
the sun fell upon us, warm as a heat lamp, and cast shadows far behind us. The crystals of frost on the blades of
meadow grass sparkled. Everything was bathed in the
warm backlight. The fields were golden, the waters like
willow-plate china, the willows as brilliant as the appendages of the yellowlegs.

The other three onlookers shivered and retreated.
Doors banged. The car's engine turned and caught. The
machine sped away in a spray of gravel. They had taken
no notice of me, and I had paid scant attention to them,
but I was glad they were gone.

Half of the cranes took to the air noisily, circled above
the river, and headed north into pastures and cornfields
on the far side of the highway. I lingered briefly, but with
the sun the spell of the birds had melted. Alone, I re-
sented the earlier company all the more. I felt as if I had
been interrupted at prayer.

I got into my own car and returned to the city. Its in-
habitants rushed toward places of commerce, running

19

yellow warning lights, honking, yielding their hard-earned places in the pack to no one. I could no more comprehend the impatient daily migration of my own kind than I could the ageless flight of the cranes.

I headed west in the heat of day toward North Platte, 180 miles upriver. The road followed the river flats through a succession of farming towns along the edge of the Nebraska sandhills. The sandhills stretch a hundred miles to the north, an almost unknown region of dunes and grazed grasses and of the yucca plant called soapweed. They are one of the empty places in the North American landscape, the largest unstabilized complex of sand dunes on the continent.

The dunes were formed during the last major period of glaciation, the Wisconsin, which ended in Nebraska about twenty thousand years ago. Strong westerly winds carried the fine, glacier-ground loess soils eastward, creating the foundation for what is now the fertile corn belt, and leaving behind the heavier deposits of sand and gravel. The sands make, in western and central Nebraska, a sensuous landscape, tan and rounded like a succession of bellies, supine. Driving it is like riding across a chart of brain waves. In the hills the road signs mark ranches, not towns. To the south, across the river, rises a line of taller, blue hills, and beyond them lay the wide, flat plains, inclining imperceptibly toward the Rocky Mountains.

For the first sixty miles, until I reached Lexington, the sky was dotted with cranes riding the spring thermals. The fields were speckled with them. After Lexington, the cranes disappeared. The Platte River runs 330 miles across Nebraska. All of it was once familiar ground to the sandhill cranes and to their nearly extinct cousins, the whooping cranes. But the cranes now stop along only eighty miles of the river, the sixty miles from Grand Island to Lexington, and the twenty miles west from North Platte to Sutherland.

For centuries, each springtime, the meltwaters of Wyoming surged down the Platte, scouring it of trees and brush and creating wide, clear channels of water and fresh islands of sand on which the birds could roost at night, safe from the preying of coyotes, foxes, and, in more recent times, dogs. To feel safe cranes need channels at least two thousand feet wide, sandbars free of vegetation, and roosts where the water is no more than six inches deep. Once too the river was bounded by extensive meadows rich in crane forage: in snails and snakes, frogs and worms, the tubers of marsh plants. A crane needs to gain a pound of weight on the Platte to make the next leg of its journey to the Arctic for the summer nesting season.

But 70 percent of the water that once poured down the Platte in the springtime is diverted these days before it ever reaches Nebraska. Some of it goes into reservoirs, some into irrigation canals, some is claimed to manufacture electrical power. Only west of North Platte and again west of Grand Island, where a portion of the diverted water reenters the river, does the Platte retain a semblance of its historical character and offer resting and feeding places suitable for cranes.

The heat descended as promised. I remembered driving across these same plains once farther south in Kansas in August when the whole land from South Dakota to the Gulf was caught in the grip of a suffocating drought. Sparks from the wheels of every passing train set off a grass fire somewhere. Some of the golden wheat still stood. Other fields had already been reaped, and the windrows of yellow straw blazed like the ruins of a battlefield. Smoke and the sweet smell of ashes blanketed everything.

I remembered happening upon a settlement on a knoll. It was scarcely even a village. A few houses, an elevator, a gas station. Mostly it was given over to an enormous cemetery. The striking thing about the cemetery was not that there were so many graves, but that the spaces between them were so wide. These people needed as much elbow room in death as in life. Not only was the cemetery extravagantly spacious, but the wide avenues of grass between the gravestones had been cut and cured and stacked. The stacks looked like loaves of bread. I could not tell whether I was seeing a cemetery that had been harvested or a hayfield with burial markers. And the accumulation of graves did seem incredible. How could so many have died in a place where so few had lived?

Back in Nebraska, the rays of sun streamed through the windshield and concentrated in the car. Inside, it was like August. The heat reminded me of that cemetery in Kansas, and so did the little towns I passed through, weedy, unpainted, boarded up, more like cemetery towns than living organisms. I rolled up the windows, turned on the air conditioner, and sped on toward North Platte, bored with the road and eager to be settled in for the night. It was already dark by the time I had checked in, unpacked and napped, too late for watching cranes, but I got into my car and headed west again anyway. I needed to be reassured that I could find them where I always had.

I passed the bright lights of the biggest rail switching yard in the nation; here trains from the east divide before

they tackle the Rockies. At the sign advertising the pot-
ter's studio, I turned right toward the river, which I could
sense but not see. I missed the next turn and found myself
stopped in the narrow lane by several cows that had escaped their fence. They were transfixed by my headlights.
I flicked the lights, cranked down the window, shouted at
them, honked the horn. They were uncontrollably curious, as cows always are, and completely unintimidated,
the opposite of the nervous cranes. They stared at me,
moonfaced, and would not budge. I was resigned to getting out and forcibly shooing them away when they finally
relented, casting sideways glances at me out of their dole-
ful eyes, ambled slowly into the ditch, and permitted me
to pass.

At the farmyard just up the way I pulled in and circled
back. A German shepherd with a savage bark bounded out
of the darkness and gave fierce chase. I was glad to be
encased in metal. The night was taking a sinister turn. I
had come searching for the reassurance of something ancient and had gotten myself entangled instead in the complicated mesh of civilization.

I found the right intersection, and the next one, saw
the familiar house standing too high on its foundation,
passed it to the place where the road curves along the
canal, shut off the engine, turned out the lights, and
opened the window. The prehistoric rattle of sandhill
cranes at roost filled the night air. I could not see them. I
didn't need to. I knew exactly where they were, and
where they would be tomorrow, and where they would be
next year at the same hour. I search out the cranes every
spring for precisely this reason: because they can be
counted upon, because their lives are predictable, their

movements regular, and their habits ordered. It is as comforting to know that the cranes have come back to the
Platte in March as to feel the blood pulsing through the
veins in my own wrists. It is a tangible sign that all is still
well with the world.

One of the habits of naturalists is the keeping of phenologies. A science can be made of the meticulous map-
ping of patterns of climate against coinciding cycles of
biological phenomena. I know by consulting my own
charts that the leopard frogs migrated from Mudhole Bay
on Lake Okabena at Worthington, Minnesota, on the
night of April 6, 1986, about two weeks later than the
muskrats emerged from their winter dens and about two
weeks earlier than the thirteen-lined ground squirrels first
appeared. Seven frogs were killed that night by passing
automobiles along the road dividing the two bodies of
water. Were I to keep similar records over decades, I
might be able to say something definitive about the life
and population cycles of leopard frogs at Worthington,
Minnesota, as they relate to climate, and it is possible that
this information could contribute in some unforeseen way
to a clearer understanding of life in general. Charles Darwin, after all, spent twenty years studying the life histories
of English barnacles before he was ready to write his theory of the natural selection of species, and Alfred Kinsey
needed what he had learned from an exhaustive study of
the taxonomy of North American grasshoppers in order to
undertake his revolutionary examination of the sexual
practices of North American humans.

But I do not keep phenologies in the cause of science.
Or drive the length of Nebraska every springtime and go
to exactly the same place along the Platte River to watch

the sandhill cranes because I am under the delusion that in doing so I will learn something undiscovered about them. If I were after information not already known to me, I would stay home, visit the library, request a computer printout of the references in the technical literature. I would try for a grant, proposing to study the role of the lesser sandhill crane in the life cycle of some parasite of the pond snail, *Stagnicola elodes.* I would learn to operate a radio homing device and prepare to follow the sandhill cranes north to their nesting grounds. I would do something, anything, systematic. There is nothing systematic about driving to North Platte, Nebraska, even repeatedly, and rolling down the car window.

You may record the phenology of frogs and sunflowers and cranes, but it is not possible, as naturalist Ann Zwinger has said, to keep phenologies of your children. Their lives are not cyclical, as lives in nature appear to be. Your children do not come back in the same form to the same places season after season. The best you can expect from children, the thing you hope for, pray for, is that they will grow and change, that each year will be for them new and different, an advancement. We live out our lives along a linear progression we cannot forecast.

But I am confident that there will be sandhill cranes along the Platte River during the second week of March in 1999, and I would confidently predict that there will be sandhill cranes along the same river in the same month of 2099, as there have been these past millions of years, were it not for human beings and their unpredictable interventions.

As for myself, I cannot say with any degree of certainty where I will be in March of 1989, or what I will be doing, or why. My own life does not seem to me inevitable. It is not orderly. It has never been logical. But we want logic and order in our lives. We long to see the structure in things. We search for patterns, for constancies.

I have been visiting a friend who has Alzheimer's disease. One morning she came into the living room, looked at a brass teapot sitting on the mantel of the fireplace, where a beam of morning sunlight was striking it, and said, "Oh! Isn't that a beautiful teapot!"

"Yes," I said. "Where did you get it?"

"Get what?"

"The teapot."

She looked puzzled. "What is a teapot?" she asked.

I pointed it out to her, but it was no use. She had already forgotten the connection between the word "teapot" and the object shining so brightly on the fireplace mantel. Still, it is possible to have transitory conversations with her. The present may be a constant bafflement, but sometimes she can be drawn into memory.

We ourselves seldom comprehend the moment at hand. So we turn to history, the one element of our lives it is possible to fix on. Or we turn to principle. Or we turn to nature. There we find, amid the silence and mystery, order and structure, the sense that life is not simply random. The sun always rises in the east and sets in the west. Pasqueflowers bloom in April and prairie gentians in September and never the reverse. The spiral of the shell of the right-handed pond snail is always logarithmic. In March the sandhill cranes always return to a certain meadow northwest of North Platte, Nebraska. These are truths we can depend upon.

The next morning, Holy Saturday morning, I returned

to the meadow. It was all familiar to me: the narrow canal and its dry bed of sand, thick with the footprints of creatures that had traveled it in the night; the thicket of dried sunflowers along the banks of the canal; the red-winged blackbird warbling on the fence post; the line of cottonwoods at the edge of the river in the distance; the woodpile in which I had hidden in years past; the sweet song of the meadowlark; the morning air; the long meadow, trim as a golf course, striated with thin puddles of water in which the feathers of cranes floated; the congregations of cranes gathered like drifts of gray snow at the center of the meadow, their voices rising not in one continuous clatter but in waves, like the cheers of a crowd.

I brought a spotting scope. The cranes are loners, nervous and shy. In the Arctic they have been seen to chase full-grown caribou from their nesting grounds. In Nebraska they will flee a human invader while he is still thousands of yards away. They are constantly vigilant. When you can scarcely see them, they have already been long aware of you. Many birds are accustomed to cars and will allow you to approach quite close in one. But cranes in a cornfield will sometimes flee even at the approach of an automobile. They take no chances. In the air a sandhill crane is somewhat more secure. One will occasionally fly so low over your head that you think you might reach up and touch it. But the only way to get close to a roosting crane is to resort to mechanical contrivances, to a blind or a long lens.

In the reach of the glass, I pulled the cranes toward me, singled out one standing at the edge of the crowd, focused on it. I felt like a woman shrouded in a veil, permitted to approach, but not on equal terms. From a distance a sandhill crane is all a mass of gray, impressive for its size—six or seven pounds, three-and-a-half-feet high, wingspan as wide as an average adult male is tall—but rather colorless and awkward, like a pewter pitcher on stilts. In the tiny, round field of the telescopic lens, the bird revealed its fierce ornaments: a mouse-colored wash along the bone line and on the feather tips of its wings; a scarlet cap running from its hooked beak around its eye and across its forehead (the older the bird, the redder the cap); and an eye the color of a raw wound with a piercing black iris.

In the glass too you can see the crane's angular features, its sinewy neck, its scaly legs. It is an archaic bird—the fossil evidence for it dates back fifty-five million years—and it looks as alien, as sinister and otherworldly as that last vestige of the dinosaur age, the crocodile. In fact, the brain of a sandhill crane more closely resembles a crocodile's than any mammal's. The architecture of the crane's brain is one of the reasons for believing, as scientists do, that cranes, indeed all birds, have descended from reptiles.

The evidence of the link between birds and reptiles is the fossil Archaeopteryx, first discovered in 1861 in a limestone quarry in Bavaria, one of five known specimens. Archaeopteryx lived 160 million years ago and was a flying reptile, a crow-sized creature with feathers exactly like those of modern birds and with the wishbone of birds, but with the skeletal features of a reptile: the skull of a dinosaur, a jaw with reptilian teeth, a long bony tail, abdominal and cervical ribs, clawed fingers. (Even now on rare occasions a vestigial claw will appear on the wings of some birds, among them cranes.) "Birds are intense, fast-living creatures—reptiles, I suppose one might say, that have escaped out of the heavy sleep of time, transformed fairy creatures dancing over sunlit meadows," Loren Eiseley said.

The morning had come while I was unawares. I stood, stretched my legs, shook the kinks out of my back. The thousands of cranes in the meadow shrieked in alarm and rose into the air as one body, the force of their wings sounding against the weight of the air like the rolling of a thousand snare drums. They fanned out until they filled the sky and churned forward, their wings wheezing, parting in a circle around us. I stood agape, like the women at the empty tomb. When no sound remained but the champagne music of the redwings, I went to breakfast.

Thinking about it over biscuits and gravy, I realized how wrong I had been. I did in fact know where I would be next March. I would be along the Platte River with the cranes, as much compelled by my own nature to return as they. Perhaps I would be dead by then, of course, but so might they. The odds were that I would be coming to see cranes at this place long after every one of these particular representatives of the species had perished. On average, a human lives at least fifty years longer than a crane.

I find structure in the life of cranes but not in my own life or in the lives of my children, I realized, because I see cranes in communities but I think of humans individually. The paradox of Easter is the paradox of rebirth. Yet the death and rebirth of a community is not paradoxical. An individual sandhill crane is born, matures, and dies; but the community of cranes returns century after century to the same meadow at the foot of the sandhills along the North Platte River in southern Nebraska. It is this truth, the transcendence of the species over the individual, the way in which a community endures and accumulates a history despite the frailties of the creatures who inhabit it, that we celebrate when we stand in awe before the great seasonal migrations. The story of Easter is not paradoxical either if we will think of it in the same way: If we will think not of the individual existence, which is fleeting, but of the continuities in the human community—the continuity, despite everything, of human life, of culture, above all, of faith.

Easter morning arose like a dream. I emerged from my room in the hour before dawn, my eyes raw around the edges, taut with the unfulfilled desire for sleep, and found myself bathed in an untimely darkness. The moon had already fallen and the stars were nowhere to be seen. They were hidden behind great banks of cloud scarcely higher than the tops of the trees, showing a satiny sheen in the gauzy lights of the city. I had driven only a mile or two beyond it when huge crystals of wet snow began to flutter against the windshield like pieces of confetti, driven on a gentle northwest wind.

By the time I had reached the river plain, the snow was falling, or rather raining, in a continuous sheet and everything was shrouded in it, the dried fluorescences of the sunflowers, the soft layer of sand in the bottom of the canal, the tops of the fence posts, the limbs of the cotton-woods. It was damp but not bitterly cold. The soft snow feathered the gray landscape. It looked pristine and smelled freshly washed. I felt veiled once again.

Although dawn was near when I had taken my custom-ary place along the bank of the canal, I could not distin-guish the gray cranes from the gray shadows. Their voices rose, muffled by the breeze, and fluttered down like the flakes of snow. For a long time I sat immersed in the sound. It seemed to be everywhere and at the same time a long way off. Minute degree by minute degree the intensity of the light gathered. The sun rose, invisible behind the thick curtain of clouds. Gradually the faint outlines of the birds emerged from the fleecy shadows through the mists of snow. They were restless. Small groups of them took briefly to the air, settled again. The snow collected on my collar, on the backs of my hands, gathered in my eyebrows, feeling wet and cold, like the muzzle of a dog. The longer I sat watching the cranes while the snow drifted over me, the more mysterious their presence seemed.

Why this congregational movement? I understood the principle of safety in numbers, how the cranes as a species were secured from the ravages of predation by moving this way en masse. And I understood the influence of place, how the Platte River, so ideally suited to the needs of cranes in migration, should come to serve as a common staging ground. But two subspecies of sandhill cranes, the Mississippi and the Florida, do not migrate at all. How does it benefit their cousins to make such a long journey, and so collectively? How did it start? What encouraged it to continue? Why did they not, like their cousins, settle down in a single place where they could both live and reproduce? What, exactly, is the long-term gain to the sandhill cranes in this incredible expenditure of energy every spring and fall? What justifies the risks involved in making the trip? And why should the spring migration be so much more regular and concentrated than the fall one? Why don't I see the same spectacle on the Platte River in September and October that I do in March and April?

I noticed too that despite their great numbers, the sand-hill cranes do not flock on the roost, as other birds do. They spread out along the river in a vast, thin line, in most places no more than two or three birds deep. Why, particularly in this snow, likely to blow into a full-fledged spring blizzard, do they not huddle together, for warmth if nothing else?

And why the continuous racket? What is the advantage in this clamoring from dawn to dusk? What message are they conveying? I notice that as the dawn approaches, the intensity of the singing escalates, reaching its peak as the birds take to the air for the day. It sounds nervous, and the closer the daylight is, the more like an incantation of excitement the singing sounds. I think often when I listen to them of the chorus that emerges in the distance from a schoolyard of children at recess. What is the meaning of this constant singing? When the cranes are on the wing, their language is lower, calmer, somehow more functional-sounding. Some biologists have hypothesized that it is a way of keeping in touch with flockmates who are out of sight. But why, on the ground, should one crane need to keep in constant audio contact with another standing two feet away? It is a great puzzle, this singing of birds.

I drove north, homeward, until noon and then stopped for lunch, still deep in the sandhills but worlds away from the cranes on the North Platte, at the Sherman Reservoir near Loup City. I had left the snow behind. Brilliant sunshine streamed down, but a stiff wind blew, and the air had grown raw and cold. I carried the ice chest to the picnic table, rummaged in it for a sausage and a block of cheese, made myself a sandwich. It was not much of an Easter repast, I had to admit. I had only taken a bite when

I heard, as if it were an echo, the crying of cranes. I disregarded it, took another bite. But the sound of cranes came again, clear, unmistakable. Searching the sky, I spotted them high overhead, distinguishable only as specks, sailing on the winds, headed north.

I was headed north because my clock and calendar told me I must. I had appointments to keep, business to attend. I was reminded as I watched the cranes in my binoculars that they have their own internal clocks, as regular and demanding as mine. Even birds hatched and raised in the laboratory, deprived of any experience with migration, cut off from external clues, subjected, for example, to a lifetime succession of days and nights of exactly equal length and unvarying climate, even such birds show a certain anxiety in the spring and fall when their wild brethren are migrating. They pace nervously in the night. In the fall they choose perches on the south sides of their cages, in the spring on the north side. They molt. They eat more than normal. If released, they take to the air. This behavior, regulated by some genetic timepiece, is called "migratory restlessness." It is, I think, one of the most felicitous terms in the biological literature.

I watched until the cranes disappeared from sight. Buffeted by the wind, I turned toward the car, caught in the throes of my own migratory restlessness. I ached to follow them, to rise up on wings of my own, to fly with them to some wild and unbounded place.

On the radio the next morning I heard reports of the storm in western Nebraska. Eight-foot drifts of snow. Thousands of motorists stranded. Interstate highways closed. All commerce at a standstill. I was glad to be safe at home. The cranes were safe too, I knew. The ancient faith of the cranes, which had set out so blindly a month earlier under a warm southwestern sun into the treacherous northern spring, the ancient faith of the cranes had once again been affirmed.

3

On the Oregon Trail

◁ ▷

I headed west again under the high sun of summer to take a tour on the Oregon Trail.

South and west, across the cornfields of Iowa to Sioux City, which, by virtue of its stockyards, claims to be the home of the world's largest manure pile. Down the Missouri valley, a rich green bottom land rimmed by low soft hills, wind-made. The earth is green, a dark, healthy green; the hills are green, paler and yellower than the bottom lands, but green and growing, folds of greenness rising like green breakers against a green beachhead. Overhead the pale blue sky, pure and unblemished. Nothing but these greens and this blue, stretching away endlessly toward the horizons.

West at the intersection of the Platte and the Missouri. As you head west, the greenness fades. Everything thins and becomes spindly: the corn, the cows, the towns. Lushness gives way to weediness. The landscape yellows, and with it the sky. The country takes on a parched and brittle look, the look of old paper. There is something musty and melancholy about it, like the tattered pages of a newspaper several decades old.

You drive and drive through a land that almost does not exist for people outside the region. When Mari Sandoz, the brilliant chronicler of these sandhills, first began writing about them in the 1920s, she encountered editors in the East who doubted that the region she described actually existed. They thought she had made up the sandhills, that she had imagined her own life and the lives of her neighbors. She had to insist that she had documentary evidence and the fact of her own life to the contrary.

In far western Nebraska, nearing the Wyoming border, the first limestone buttes emerge from the withered grasslands like tan castles with thatched roofs. Suddenly one has passed from the real world into a fairyland. This is where the West begins.

I pulled into a parking lot next to a cluster of low log buildings along the Platte River south of Bayard, Nebraska. Behind me the three-hundred-foot spire of Chimney Rock rose like a monstrous tan oil can, one of the most famous of the landmarks on the way West.

An uncertain milling about.

The realization that this was not going to be an ordinary tour: The hosts issued tents and ordered the guests to put them up. White canvas tents with plastic floors and flaps that hook rather than zip shut, cumbersome and drafty. No instructions. Just "Here it is. Pick a site over there on the grass." I dragged my tent to the grass, erected it stealthily, hoping no one was watching to see how clumsy I was. A cold drizzle had oozed down all day. It had been like that for almost two weeks. The prospect of a long, drippy ride across the Nebraska plains was daunting. On an actual trek across the Oregon Trail, there might have been many weeks like this when it was impossible to find anything dry to burn, when the wheels of the wagons mired repeatedly in the mud, when your sodden clothes never completely dried, when there was never a warm place to sleep.

We put up our tents, began to get acquainted, took a jolting wagon ride through camp, situated along one strand of the Oregon Trail. The trail was not a single rut, like a dirt road, but many trails spread across the river valley and converging only at natural obstructions, at river crossings, narrow mountain passes, along certain routes through steep hills.

Our wagonmaster was Gordon Howard, pudgy, rosy-cheeked, bright-eyed, and with a booming voice—a perfect Santa Claus. He was dressed for the nineteenth century: boots, brown button-front pants held up by suspenders, a leather vest, a calico shirt, a gingham hand-kerchief, a crumpled brown leather hat, round wire-rimmed glasses. He sported a long, gray beard. His wife, Patti, petite, bursting with smiles, wore a long calico dress, high-topped boots, and a flowered bonnet. She might just have stepped out of a sod shanty.

There was work to be done. The females were busy making bonnets while the males greased the wheels of a wagon, a daily task. You slipped an enormous iron wrench over the wheel nut and wrenched it loose. Then the jack was shoved under the axle, kicked into position. The jack was short-handled and operated in a single, downward thrust; there was no way to notch it up a step at a time. I tried it. I crawled under the wagon, took hold of the jack handle, braced my feet, pulled and pushed until my face was the color of raw meat, but I could not budge the wagon. I retreated, feeling weak and childish. A bigger and stronger man raised the axle. The wheel was slipped off. The exposed bearing was painted with a stick dipped into a pot of thick green grease. Several of us hauled and heaved the wheel back into place. On went the nut again. Down came the wagon. We were to run a four-wagon train. Only fifteen more wheels to go.

Afterward there was square dancing. None of us knew anything about it, and nobody seemed very eager to learn, but we paired off, made two circles, and plunged in. The fiddler fiddled, the caller called, we dancers pranced right when we were supposed to allemande to the left, promenaded when we were supposed to circle, circled when we were supposed to swing our partners round and round, and fell giggling into a messy heap on the soggy grass, happy as pigs in a puddle. After that, dinner: sourdough bread, steaks, creamed beans, potatoes, and homemade vanilla ice cream.

Then singing and storytelling around a big campfire. While we waited in a dense fog, Howard fiddled at getting the fire started. But the wood was soaked, the kindling was damp, and not so much as a wisp of smoke curled up from the fire ring. "Aw, hell!" he said finally. He disappeared, returned a minute later with a gas flame-thrower big enough for a war. He turned on the propane, lit the flue, and blasted a campfire into existence while we all cheered. Sometimes there are better things than verisimilitude. The story was a version of Cinderella in which the initial letters are switched: Rindercella and the slass glipper. The singing was in rounds. Then lingering conversations in the fog-bound night. One by one the guests slipped off to their tents. In the darkness, sometime after midnight, the fog began to lift and we caught a glimpse of Chimney Rock, *floodlit*, of all things, there in the middle of nowhere, looking as if it were some misadventure in fiberglass.

My mess, the Bullwackers, was in charge of breakfast, so we rose early. Breakfast consisted of several pounds of bacon, a couple of pounds of link sausages, several dozen fried eggs, and mountains of buttermilk pancakes, all cooked in gigantic cast-iron skillets over an open fire. Although there were only nineteen of us, the food miraculously disappeared, washed down by gallons of campfire egg coffee, one of the staples of the original trail.

We headed for the wagons, four of them, three to carry us and our goods and one of them equipped with a chemical toilet, one of the concessions to the demands of modern travelers. We hung slices of salted and peppered beef from the ribs of the wagons, the way jerky used to be made, and dangled a can of cream from the axle of one of the wagons, where it would joggle and slosh all day until it turned to butter. (In fact, it would do nothing of the kind. Rather, the cream pail would catch on a yucca plant and overturn, spilling every last drop of our potential butter, probably the most realistic thing that happened all day.)

Before we set out, we were lectured about the dangers of the trail: kicking horses, wagon wheels, and rattlesnakes, principally, and the need to drink lots of water to prevent dehydration. There would, of course, have been other dangers a century ago: human violence, disease, the hazards to women in pregnancy, shortages of good water. But even a modern, well-organized, three-day trek through settled country would not be, we were pressed to understand, completely risk-free.

Some of the guests arrived on airplanes traveling hundreds of miles an hour, others in cars traveling sixty. Now we rumbled across the landscape at two miles an hour or less, hoping to make twelve or thirteen miles in the day. The vastness of the American landscape was being reduced for us to human scale. Or rather it was being multiplied for us to human scale: The effect of moving across it at human speed is to lengthen distances, to deepen valleys, to heighten every hill. Approached in this way, the landscape looms as the major character in the journey, and the humans are reduced to minor players upon it.

The first few miles of the trail were principally on established roads, but nevertheless they were along the Oregon Trail. It survives now in places in farm roads and highways. Roads are one of the historical continuities: Animal trails, following the natural features of the landscape, became foot trails, and foot trails became wagon trails, and wagon trails became dirt roads, and dirt roads were graveled, and then paved. We are guided in ways that we do not fully appreciate by the land itself.

Some of us went in the wagons, some on foot, some on

horseback. All were once means of getting west. Each presents rigors, we discovered, for which we were not well prepared. Riding a horse stresses knee and thigh muscles and makes you, after a while, acutely conscious of your hip bones. We don't much walk great distances any longer. And riding in a wagon is like riding in a butter churn.

By about eleven o'clock in the morning the sun had burned away the haze and the sky had begun to clear. It is difficult to be precise about times because I was carrying no watch. We had begun to live in the world of sun time, of getting up at dawn and going to bed at dark, that vague and shadowy world in which there are no appointments, no schedules, in which one responds to the natural rhythms of light and darkness, to the pangs of the body, hunger and thirst and weariness, rather than to the dictates of artificial time. This means, as a practical matter, that the days grow longer. You find yourself doing what you can in a day, rather than what you can do in eight hours of it. One of the consequences of keeping time is that you limit yourself to less than you can actually do. There come to be two worlds, the world of work and the world of free time. In sun time, there is a single world, the world of all that is possible today.

We stopped to look at a buffalo wallow, visible in a pasture as a particularly green and vigorous ring of vegetation. It has been a century since buffalo wandered freely in that country, but their ghosts linger in the grass.

The temperature rose to perhaps eighty or eighty-five degrees once the sky was clear, but it felt much hotter than that; the climate in which your feet move is, of course, warmer than the one in which your head moves. On the open plains the difference can be as much as a

41

dozen degrees. The difference in microclimates became all the more apparent when it was your turn to mount one of the scout horses. You found, from the vantage of a seat four feet higher up, not only cooler temperatures but the presence of a breeze that was not apparent when you were on foot. But no matter where you were, on foot, on the back of a horse, or seated in the rumbling shade of a wagon, the heat, damp as it was, soon began to extract its toll. It parched you, shriveled you, seemed to burn from somewhere inside your skin outward. I began to imagine the awful consequences of traveling the prairies with unreliable supplies of water, with water so alkaline that it was nearly undrinkable, or with no water at all. I have experienced dehydration, the dizziness and nausea, the feverish headaches and weakness that it brings, and it is an experience I have absolutely no desire to duplicate.

Indeed, the only natural body of water we encountered on our trek was at the place where we stopped for lunch, a shallow pothole, sparsely vegetated, marked by the bleached root of a dead willow and ringed with a white crust of alka. The only plant that grew in the meadow surrounding it was salt grass, a short, wiry variety, characteristic of the deserts farther west, that even hungry livestock won't touch. I was grateful not to have to quench my thirst in that water.

For lunch, cold cuts of ham, beef, and corned beef on slices of sourdough bread. Also carrot sticks and pickles and barrels of cookies and chips. The pickles and the cold meats, Howard told us, might well have been part of a typical prairie meal. The first travelers along the Oregon Trail fended for themselves, he said, but by the time the westward migration was in full swing, the route along the

Platte River was well settled. Immigrants encountered a ranch about every seven miles, and provisions of every kind, including cured meats, could be purchased at any of them.

As the afternoon wore on, we paused to look at wildflowers. There were blazing stars, buffalo burs, gumweed, sunflowers, asters, rubber rabbitbrushes, and two plants bearing huge and spectacular white flowers with yellow stamens, the pale evening primrose and the bluestem prickly poppy. There were also clumps of little bluestem, already turning the burgundy of autumn.

But more and more as the day stretched out, we longed for the end of the trail, which we had been told would be near a corral where there was a water tank for the horses, who had had nothing to drink all day. A corral came into view. We approached it endlessly and then passed on by. Nobody said anything, but you could almost feel the disappointment in the air. We passed over a hill into a little swale and suddenly Howard started the wagons into a circle.

We joyously dragged the tents out of the bus, hidden over the next knoll, and pitched them along the sandy ridges above the campsite. Patti Howard had arrived at the camp before us and had already started supper: a big pot of sassafras tea, a batch of sourdough bread, and a buffalo tongue boiled with onions, salt and pepper. Howard added a big pot of beef stew, a wonderful, peppery dish containing huge chunks of beef, potatoes, and carrots. Making stew is a man's job, he declared. Women invariably ruin it by cutting everything into dainty pieces. For dessert there were slices of apple bread made with sourdough that had been flattened, sprinkled generously with sugar and cinnamon, covered with dried apples, rolled up and baked over the coals.

Some of us took the horses to the corral to be watered. The horses drank noisily and long, in two batches because the wagon horses dislike the scout horses and kick at them if they try to share the same tank. I wondered if this were an instance of animal envy; there is no doubt that the wagon horses have a tougher lot than the scouts.

While we were awaiting dinner, drinking cups of tea and sitting on blankets in the shade of the wagons, four Indians made an appearance on the hillside above us. Howard made a show of firing a pistol into the air, and one of the Indians made a couple of passes at us, flinging first a rubber tomahawk and then a rubber arrow. This thoroughly unconvincing bit of theater culminated in the chief advancing and making a speech in Lakota, translated by Howard. All the buffalo were gone, the chief said, and he and his family were hungry. They were invited to dinner, and they came, three young Sioux boys; the chief, a rancher named Myron Taylor; and a woman who farms three miles from where we were camped. Taylor gathered us into a circle and passed a beautiful peace pipe, fashioned from a black vein of catlinite quarried at Pipestone, Minnesota, which he had packed with a mixture of commercial tobacco, the inner bark of a red willow tree, and the shavings from a native root. It was the best tobacco I ever smoked. Then he showed us a variety of artifacts, fancy beadwork, a couple of beaded Indian dresses, and his own war bonnet.

After dinner, the Indians danced while Howard beat the drum. As the drum pounded, Lyle Campbell, another trekker, and I slipped away in the light of the full moon and set out across the prairie toward Whiskey Bluff, which we wanted to climb. We had passed during the afternoon through a line of sandy yellow bluffs, very distinctively shaped, that gave this part of Nebraska its character. Two of them, Chimney Rock and Scotts Bluff, were among the most important landmarks of the Oregon Trail, as were two others just beyond our view, Jailhouse Rock and Courthouse Rock. The line of bluffs we passed through included Whiskey Bluff, sometimes called Alcohol Bluff, Table Rock, Steamship Bluff, and Roundtop Bluff. The names describe shapes, except for Whiskey Bluff, which commemorates an incident in which a group of traders lost their wagon in a mishap and concluded to forge ahead on pack horses. They didn't have enough room for all their cargo, so they hid the kegs of whiskey in the bluff, intending to retrieve them on their return. By the time they got back, the Indians had discovered the cache and heisted it all away.

It was a beautiful night for a walk, windless and clear, balmy. We could hear the beating of the Indian drum as we headed eastward, and, when we had ascended a little, we could see the glow of the campfire in the hollow below us. The moonlight was so bright that the stars dimmed before it. Occasionally we flushed a nesting bird as we walked, and once Campbell almost stepped on one, but otherwise there were just the footsteps of the two of us beneath the vast sky, amid a great stillness. We walked in silence; it seemed sacrilegious to talk. It was easy to imagine that we were walking in another century. We were alert to the possibility of rattlesnakes, knowing their nocturnal habits. The only snake we had encountered during daylight was a foot-long, pencil-thin red racer, which had

45

fled from us into the protective cover of the grass. In places the vegetation was ankle high, in others almost waist deep. Once we passed within view of a herd of cattle, lurking in the distance like big black stones. They did not stir. We headed straight across country, steering by the light of two planets, Venus and Mars. We appreciated then the careful route that the wagon had made, snaking up through the valleys and skirting the big hills, the deep gullies, and the moonlike craters of the blowouts that we encountered on our direct route to the bluff. At times we descended into ravines so deep that we could not see the bluff directly in front of us.

When we had reached the base of the bluff, the moon, its face grinning to the north, was still in front of us, so that we could see the glimmering hulk of the rock itself and then the sharply etched image of it spread out as a shadow upon the grass, like the reverse of the mirror image in a lake. We climbed into the shadow as if we were passing not merely into a different intensity of light but into something substantial, a cave or tunnel of some kind. Within the shadow, the yucca plants were more numerous, and we stumbled over them in the dimness. We also stumbled over boulders of limestone the size of grocery boxes but so light you could easily lift them and so insubstantial they fell apart in your hands. In this eerie world the shadows had weight and the rocks were like shadows.

At the cliff line, it became apparent that we could climb no higher. The boxy spire of the butte, so solid-looking from a distance, proved to be nothing more than a pillar of sand, a pile of limestone that crumbled beneath our feet and fell away in gobs when we tried to grasp it with our fingers. It seemed miraculous that it had stood at all, much less for centuries. We edged our way along the baseline of the cliff toward a buttress of limestone at its northwestern corner, and again we were in for a surprise. The buttress was like a false storefront on a western movie set, a thin, knife-edged sheet, harder in composition than the cliff itself and worn smooth by the rains and the winds, but presenting no more of a surface to sit or walk upon than a two-by-four. We braced ourselves against it and lay back to rest for a few minutes in the awesome, brightly lit stillness of the prairie night. Here and there the light of a farmyard glowed in the distance, and twenty miles away the brilliant lights of Scottsbluff stretched out for an unlikely distance along the horizon. In front of them, along a lower line of cliffs, the red lights of half a dozen radio and communications towers blinked on and off with a faintly sinister force, a rank of sentinels of mythic proportions. But despite the lights, the landscape seemed, in the soft glow of midnight, vast, endless, empty.

"I imagine that this is how the moon looked to its first visitors," Campbell said under his breath, as if the mood of reverence into which we had descended might, in being overheard, shatter like ice; and, indeed, there is the paradoxical feeling of being in the presence of hidden persons in such an open and empty place.

A bird called in the distance. "Hawk," I whispered. The bird received no answer, and it did not call again. But it remained, a silent, unseen, unfelt presence upon the landscape.

We sat in the halo of the moon until the weight of the night began to hang upon our eyelids. Then, by unspoken consent, we rose in unison and started back down the dry slope of the bluff, using our hands and our seats as tripods to ease the way and remembering a lesson often studied in childhood, that it is easier to get up an obstacle than down it.

We made our way westward again, climbing down a long, gentle slope, skirting the deepest gullies, and taking the gentlest slopes down the loping, sandy hills, walking behind our faint shadows in the straw-colored grass, steering by the blinking lights of two radio towers. We believed them, without great conviction, to stand on either side of the hollow in which we were camped. We took it as a triumph when we came over a hilltop, just as we were beginning to suspect ourselves of being lost, and saw the dark hulk of the bus that had carried our tents and provisions for the night.

I smoked a cigar alone in the moonlight, standing on the knoll where I had pitched my tent and looking down upon the circle of wagons and the cluster of canvas tents fifty yards and a century and a half away.

I crawled into my tent, leaving the flap unhooked, undressed, and snuggled into my sleeping bag, wriggling on the surprisingly unyielding sand until I had located a line of minute ridges and depressions that more or less matched the contours of my body. The whiteness of the tent reflected the rays of the moonlight filtering through, and it was warm and cozy in their glow; I imagined that I was sleeping in the glass bowl of a lantern. I had not quite fallen asleep when, from a ridge to the west, a coyote yelped, a single long high-pitched scream as clear as a church bell. There was a second's silence. Then, from several quarters, a dozen coyotes returned the call, a brief, ecstatic, multipitched vocal romp, as complicated and me-

48

lodious as a Bach counterpoint. In thirty seconds it was over. I lay on the ground, from which the sounds of the coyotes seemed to have emanated as from some deep region of my own body, hoping to hear the song again, but before it came, I had drifted into dreams.

Later in the morning—it was nearing dawn—I was awakened by the rattling of my tent flap and by the glare of the last low beam of moonlight. It had grown cold, but not unpleasantly so, and the sweet smell of early morning hung in the air. I tensed, listened sharply, thinking some roaming creature was scratching at my door. The rattle came again, and I recognized it as the sound of the morning breeze beating against stiff canvas. I drifted away again.

I don't know how much later it was, but it was before sunlight, when the rooster we had carried along in a cage on one of the wagons began to crow, a sound that must have reminded many an Oregon Trail traveler of an abandoned home far away, such a long distance away as to seem like a dream. I thought of boyhood mornings in the summertime when I had gone to stay for a week or two with my grandfather and grandmother. There were already voices thick with morning rumbling up from the campfire at the bottom of the swale, but I lingered in my sleeping bag, content to let the day come to me.

When I did arise, a pot of coffee had already been boiled and the mess on duty was preparing to cook bacon and French toast in the monstrous cast-iron skillets. The rooster crowed again lustily. "Isn't that a wonderful sound!" I said brightly. A dozen pairs of disbelieving eyes glowered at me. "I'd like to strangle the damn thing," someone murmured. I got a cup of coffee and sat on a wagon tongue, keeping my mouth shut. The coffee was as stout as campfire brew should be. It reminded me of a cowboy recipe for coffee: Wet some grounds good with water, boil for half an hour over a hot fire, throw in a horseshoe; if the horseshoe sinks, add more grounds.

We set out again after breakfast in the wagons, which had already begun to seem customary. We might as well have been traveling in them for months.

At midmorning Howard abruptly turned his team around so that his wagon was facing the one immediately behind it in the train and ordered the horses to be un-hitched. He called us into a circle. "We seem to have a problem," he said. He looked grim. "We are missing something that we thought might merely have been misplaced, but we have come since to believe it was stolen. So we'll just stop here until we figure out where it has gone. Does anybody want to volunteer anything?" He looked around at us. I hadn't the faintest idea what he was talking about, but I immediately grew apprehensive and began to feel faintly guilty, and to look that way, I suppose.

An embarrassed silence rolled in like a rain cloud.

"Paula, do you want to tell the rest of the folks what you told me?" Howard said. Paula, a cheerful woman from the Chicago suburbs, a police dispatcher in real life, stepped forward. Like most of the participants, she had entered into the spirit of the trip by donning a period costume, a long calico dress and a calico bonnet.

She blushed and began with uncharacteristic shyness. "Well," she said, "I know how I have been constantly misplacing things through this whole trip, but I had a little poke that belonged to my great-grandmother. She traveled this trail all the way to California, I think I've told you. And in part what I want to do on this trip is to get into touch with my family's history, to learn to know it a little better, so I thought I'd bring the poke with me. It's not really very valuable, but it has great sentimental value to me." She choked, looked embarrassed, went on. "Well, I wanted to have it along, but I was fearful of losing it, so I have never brought it out. I just kept it in the bottom of my duffel bag, where it would be safe. After I set up camp yesterday, I wanted to have a look at it, and I couldn't find it. We have hunted everywhere, and I just have to think that maybe somebody, not knowing what it meant to me, has taken it." She paused, looked down at the ground, unable to continue.

Howard's eyes searched the group like an airport beacon. "Does anybody have anything to say?" he asked.

We shifted uncomfortably.

"Is there anybody you suspect?" he asked Paula.

"Oh, I really don't want to accuse anybody," she said.

"You told me you saw somebody, didn't you?"

"Well, I did see somebody, yes."

"Tell us who you saw."

"Well, I know this sounds silly, but I'm quite certain that I saw Bob coming out of my tent yesterday afternoon," Paula said, choking again.

Bob, a mild-mannered, gentlemanly printer from Lincoln, Nebraska, whom we had elected judge a day and a half before largely on the basis of his solid, silver-haired appearance, got a sudden glazed, wild-eyed look in his eyes. His wife, Margery, gave him a little hug. The rest of us began to smell a hoax.

"Did you bring a bag?" Howard asked Bob.

"Um, I think so," Bob said, although we all knew that each of us had been personally issued a duffel bag by Howard, containing, among other things, our dinnerware, and that we had been instructed to bring it with us.

"Didn't you get a duffel bag?" Howard asked.

"Yes, I suppose so."

"Where is it?"

Before Bob could answer, Howard pressed forward. "Didn't you also bring a brown bag?" he asked.

"Yes, I guess so," Bob answered lamely.

Howard turned to the rest of us. "*Now* he remembers," he said. "Sheriff, arrest this man. And get his bags."

The bags were produced and searched. They yielded a little leather poke. Paula declared it to be hers, but we all knew her to be playing a part by now. We began to heckle. "Tell us who framed him," we demanded.

Bob's wife meekly raised her hand. Hoots and jeers.

Nevertheless, Howard called for the jury and demanded a verdict. "Guilty."

Howard, in his capacity as wagonmaster, sentenced Bob to die by hanging in ten minutes, and Bob, grinning, was led away by the sheriff to confess his sins.

Turning, we saw that the tongues of the two facing wagons had been raised and that a noose had been suspended between them. Out from behind the last wagon in the train came a dummy wearing Bob's hat and riding upon a horse. The dummy was led to a position beneath the noose, which was fastened around its neck, and the horse was urged forward, leaving the effigy dangling. End of the lesson in wagon-trail justice.

Lunch a mile or so later at the base of Whiskey Bluff featured slices of roasted buffalo, still warm from its night

of baking in the campfire coals. It was moist, tender, fla-
vorful. It was easy to appreciate why it was so prized in
frontier days.

After the meal, most of us lingered in the shadow of the
wagons, talking and resting. But Maury and Judy, a Minneapolis couple, still energetic, wandered off into one of
the sandy gullies at the base of the bluff. Half an hour
later they returned, Maury grinning triumphantly, with a
large buffalo skull, missing its lower jaw and one horn, but
otherwise in excellent condition. The bone around one of
the eye sockets had been exposed by a recent rainfall, and
unearthing the rest of it from the soft streambank had
proved easy work.

Maury deposited the skull on the dun grass. It gleamed
in the sun. We gathered around it in a circle, as in times
past.

The head of a buffalo is astonishing. It is massive, radically out of proportion to the rest of the animal's body,
majestic. The curve of its short, thick, wickedly pointed
horns, the breadth of its hairy brow, the wide spacing of
its enormous black eyes, the broad sweep of its thick nose,
falling toward huge nostrils, the scraggily thicket of its
short beard: A buffalo looks ancient and wise and all-
seeing from the moment it loses its tan baby hair, although it neither sees very well nor is very bright. In
Plains Indian legend, it is gullible. Old Man and Fox want
to kill four buffalo bulls. Old Man plucks all the hairs from
Fox except a tuft at the end of his tail and sends him
prancing past the bulls. The bulls, seeing naked Fox,
laugh and laugh. They laugh themselves to death. Coyote
challenges Buffalo to a race. He chooses a place near a

cliff, steps aside. Buffalo plunges blindly over the brink. Coyote enjoys dinner.

The skull of a buffalo is as unmistakable as a human skull. It has four strong points, two for the horns and two for the broad plates of bone over the outward-facing eyes, those extraordinarily fishlike eyes. The four points of the buffalo's skull encompass the most sacred number in native American cosmology, the number four, for the four directions, the four winds, the four stages of life, the four underworlds, the four weeks in the lunar month, the four seasons, the Four Grandfathers who hold up the universe, the four phases of the moon.

The four, and the center: The sun was at the center, and the earth was at the center, and life on earth was at the center of the journey through time. In the Sun Dance ceremonies, a four-pointed buffalo skull was placed at the center of the lodge, serving as the altar and representing the earth, from which the buffalo originally sprang and to which they periodically returned. How to explain, otherwise, why there were sometimes buffalo stretching away to the horizons and then again none at all?

When one wanted to summon the buffalo for the hunt, one danced in the disguise of a buffalo skull. When they came, and one had hunted and eaten, one offered some of the meat to a buffalo skull as a sign of appeasement, saying "Eat this."

When, as a young man, one went off alone for four days and four nights to a sacred place to find a guiding spirit and a vision for life, one took along a buffalo skull for a pillow.

The Pawnees said that the father of all buffalo lived in the north at the junction of heaven and earth and that every year he shed a little hair. When the last hair had been shed, they said, life would end.

And so it was. As the buffalo died, so died whole nations and cultures on the Great Plains.

The skull glaring at us in the merciless sunlight from the center of the circle we had made was a bone out of that history, when nations and cultures were dying for want of buffalo.

We spread out then eagerly along the arroyos at the base of the bluff and hunted for bones. Lizards scampered for shelter. Here and there a bird sang. The hot sun scorched the backs of our necks. But the fawn and gray earth kept from us whatever else it was hiding.

4
Approaching the Mountains
◁ ▷

Traveling west again toward mountains.

Before the railroads were built, the way west followed the rivers: west along the Platte into Wyoming, over South Pass, up the Snake River into the Oregon Territory; or up the Missouri through the Dakotas and into Montana, then west along the Yellowstone. It was the easiest but not the most accurate way to see the country. The country looked better or worse from the prospect of the rivers; I can't say which, not having gone that way. But it looked different, certainly, not at all like the high country. There are many reasons why it could not have seemed the same.

A river is an edge, for one thing, and not simply in the cartographer's sense that it divides one piece of ground from another. It is a biological edge. There worlds collide, strangers meet, much business, although not of the monetary kind, is transacted. Edges in the natural world are like cities in human cultures. They are the cosmopolitan places, populous, noisy, gaudy, rich, exciting, where one expects the unexpected and the extraordinary is ordinary. They are altogether unlike the provinces, where the surprises lie not in discovering what is odd or new but in appreciating, at last, what is routine and everyday, a larger accomplishment than one might imagine. The rivers of the earliest westward travelers passed through the provinces, but they revealed a world that was not, in itself, characteristic of them.

Rivers carry water, for instance, but the region of the Great Plains is by its nature arid—not so arid as the deserts, although for a long time the Great Plains were regarded as one, but arid enough to inhibit the growth of trees, except along rivers. You could no more know the Great Plains by canoeing up the Missouri than you could see the Sonoran Desert by rafting down the Colorado. River travelers poled or steamed up the channels by day and fished for supper by twilight. The Blackfeet, the lords of the Plains whom everybody feared, the prairie's most serious students, would no sooner have dined on catfish than we would on a dish of fricasseed sewer rat. The mucus-covered creatures of the muddy river bottoms, the Blackfeet thought, were simply not the best the Plains had to offer; far from being palatable, fish were repulsive, disgusting.

The rivers, moreover, seek the level, that is the low

ground, but the Plains are the province of the big sky. The rivers are always running away to the sea, but the Plains are always rising toward the mountains. They are contrary forces working in contrary directions. The rivers dig in; the Plains surmount. A river closes in, rounds the bend, runs between banks, hides shallows and snags, tumbles over rapids, skirts islands, is forever calling attention to itself, like a trail, which a river inevitably becomes. The Plains, on the other hand, open out, unfold, beg the long and trackless view. The river draws a line; the Plains reveal a space.

It is like the difference between an interstate expressway and a county highway. An interstate is broad and swift and in its own way it keeps to the level. You can drive on an interstate across the most endlessly enchanting of countrysides and encounter only an unrelieved monotony. The expressway exists in its own world, an unwalled tunnel, and moves at its own urgent pace. It has a rhythm and a rigidly regular time quite distinct from the landscape it crosses. It would not serve its purposes in any other way.

The county road, on the other hand, moves in and through the landscape and exists as one more feature of it. Where there is a tree and a sun, the road falls under shadow; where there is a stream, the road follows down one bank, across the water, and up the other bank; where a tall hill intervenes, the road goes around rather than through it and the traveler enjoys the sensation of having moved among hills; at the village, the road unhesitatingly takes it in, and your own pace slows to accommodate the taking in, rather than swooping to the right or left around the settlement at a curve calculated for high-speed safety. A stray cow might cross in front of you, and you will be obliged to stop to let it pass and so you will chance to hear the song of the meadowlark on the fence post. The hay wagon ahead cannot be gotten around; you are forced to reduce your own speed to the local standard, and so you see the marsh hawk circling above a pothole.

The best way to go west, therefore, is the slowest way possible and across country rather than along the rivers, avoiding both the old watery rivers and the new ones of asphalt and cast concrete.

If you head west from my house near the western border of Minnesota, you will begin at the western edge of the tallgrass prairie. You will be on a green and very gently rolling plain—strangers would say that it is flat. It is a region of rich prairie soils; the topsoil is perhaps half as deep as it was a century ago, but it is still very black and as fertile as any soil in the world. The growing season is long enough for corn but not for many fruits (we are in Zone 4 on the horticultural maps), and the twenty-five inches or so of precipitation that falls every year, mostly as rain, is sufficient for feed-grain crops and entirely reliable: We have regular cycles of drought, as everywhere on the prairies, but in 115 years of agriculture, we have never suffered a total crop failure because of it.

When the first white settlers arrived here, there were trees only along the banks of the rivers and streams, and there were very few waterways, although more than now, when so much of our water has been captured and sent running away toward the sea in underground drainage pipes. Once the countryside was dotted with shallow cat-tail-rimmed sloughs. Now it is mostly a region of square fields, but it supports many trees. They line every village street and a grove of them shelters every farmstead. In this

respect, though, we are returning to the original landscape. As the farmsteads fall vacant (we have been
steadily losing farm population for the last thirty-five
years), the neglected buildings weather and cave in; one
day a bulldozer is hired to clear away the ruins and to
uproot the trees, and the piles of scraps are doused in gasoline and set afire. They burn brightly through a night,
smolder for another week, and then there is one less
obstacle for the big machines to maneuver around. We
have always thought of this as the price of progress, although doubts about the value of it are beginning to be
heard. The same fate attends opera houses and school-
houses, gasoline stations and rural churches. Only the
cemeteries, overgrown with lilacs and tattered pines, remain as signs of the civilization that once flourished so
brightly here. In the small towns the Carnegie libraries
have been turned into branches of banks, and the banks
have closed.

It is, nevertheless, still a green place, looking not quite
prosperous but pastoral, a place still cared about and
tended, like a garden. You will see flowers opening in the
yards of the solid country houses, houses recently painted,
as you head west in the warm light of an early summer
morning. Perhaps there will still be a little dew on the
grass and now and then, atop a fence post, you will see a
field stone perched like a totem, put there out of ancient
habit by a careful farmer.

The way west will be steadily uphill, although you will
not be aware of that until you have traveled for most of a
day. The elevation at Sioux Falls, South Dakota, is 1,450
feet; at Rapid City, 3,231 feet; at Gillette, Wyoming,
4,608 feet. The road will never seem to climb, but some-

where beyond Gillette, if you are attentive, you will begin to notice a certain clarity and warmth of light and an unexpected intensity in the blueness of the sky, and these will be signs both of height and of an increasing dryness.

The higher you go, the thinner the atmosphere becomes. The atmosphere, of course, is never void, and this is why light always has color, however mistakenly we tend to think of it as colorless or, perhaps, white. The thinner the atmosphere, the less the color in light is captured or refracted by the particles of dust or moisture in it, and the more intensely yellow or red its hues become; thus they appear to us both warmer and more intense. This explains the depth and clarity of the light at upper elevations. And dust particles are more efficient than droplets of moisture at capturing and reflecting the relatively short, weak rays of blue in sky-light; in dry places, more particles are held in the upper atmosphere, and the sky takes on a deeper intensity of blue than it does in the moist lowlands or along the seacoasts. This is why the Great Plains are more warmly colored than the prairies and the deserts more warmly colored still; and why the sky looks bluer from the summit of a mountain than from its base.

The transformation of the light will not, however, be obvious for a long time, and then only if you are looking for it. The West will first unfold in other equally subtle ways. Somewhere beyond Mitchell, South Dakota, the croplands will take on a ragged and underdeveloped look, and you will notice fewer fields and more pastures. By then you will have crossed an invisible boundary and entered the rain shadow of the mountains, where fewer than twenty inches of precipitation fall in a year, twenty inches being, roughly, the critical number for successful row cropping without irrigation. You will have passed by then from prairie gardens into a wilder and less domesticated place.

Without warning you will suddenly, at Chamberlain, South Dakota, encounter the Missouri River, fat and lazy behind its succession of dams and tucked into a deep and narrow valley beneath dramatic bluffs as naked in their thin raiment of short grasses as newborn bear cubs. Beyond the Missouri lies a new land. In the distance the first buttes appear. Everything is more rugged and endlessly grassy, and the grasses are more brown than green. The few farmyards you pass sit exposed on the hillsides to wind and weather; they are treeless, flowerless; their buildings unpainted; their piles of junk exposed to view. The fence posts are topped not with field stones but with old cowboy boots. There is, nevertheless, a spareness, a wideness, about these unbroken and unadorned hills, an extreme simplicity of line and shape, that gives them a neat and freshly washed look, a pristine and economical beauty.

Then for a long time you will drive through a tedious forest of billboards. Advertisements for the car museum at Murdo, Wall Drug, Reptile Gardens, Crystal Cave, the Borglum Museum near Mount Rushmore will flash incessantly before your eyes, like symbols in a dream from which you are unable to awaken. You will be in the heat of the day, and the first lines of grit will have begun to accumulate in the folds of your neck.

The unearthly spires of the Badlands will loom out of the windswept plains, delicately striped in shades of gray and pink and mauve, and when you think that you have reached the farthest ends of the earth, the Black Hills will appear in the distance, a brief oasis of water and shade, black because of the dark-green color of the Ponderosa pines that cover their craggy granite flanks. You slip quickly through them, the contours of the land soften, the Ponderosas thin and disappear, and the sky billows above you again like the thin blue film of some unimaginably immense balloon.

Somewhere past the Wyoming border in a land that seems uninhabited, the scent of sage begins to fill the sweltering car, the roundedness of the earth gives way to sharp-edged canyons and brushy hilltops, and the dominant color of the brown-green grass is overtaken by the reds and yellows of the rocks. For the first time the yellowness of the warm light is apparent.

Beyond Gillette, mile-long coal trains slither silently across the landscape like enormous black snakes, and then the trains vanish and the earth grows even more rugged, rocky, and red. The sun begins to come down in the western sky, and blue shadows creep across the golden and gray ridges.

You are dizzy with motion, numb with the sound of the wind whistling through the car windows and into your ears, limp with heat. You pull the car over to the edge of the road and get out to stretch your aching legs. The sweet smell of sage hits you like a blast of wind. Gradually the sensation of being in motion subsides. You become aware of the sound of grasshoppers clattering in the bone-dry grass like the sickles of a gigantic mowing machine. You step forward, and a hundred of them take to the air. One lands on your shirt sleeve, another in your hair. You brush them away. Then you sense that you are being watched and looking up into the hills, you see three pronghorn antelopes, as elegantly adorned as a trio going out for a night at the opera, standing on a knoll, as curious as you are numb. Your eyes meet. Suddenly the antelope turn and bound over the hill, their white rumps glittering in the sun. It seems, then, as silent as a cave, and you feel the first hint of the evening chill. You get back into your car. You cannot be far, you know, from mountains.

BOOK

2

◁ ▷

5

The Big Horns of Wyoming

◁ ▷

MY friend John guided me to my first mountaintop. He knew what he was doing. He knew that he was permanently uncoiling my life, forever stretching the reach of my passions. Is there a person who has climbed one mountaintop and not needed to try another? I had been preaching to him the Gospel of the Prairies. He had complained, teasingly, about prairies as the Jerusalem of mosquitoes and of not much else, and I had been determined to show him the Truth. One day, on the way home from a sermon at a prairie fen, he said suddenly, "Well, all right. I admit that there may be something in these prairies."

"Mosquitoes," I said sarcastically.

He ignored the remark. "Now it's time for *you* to see the mountains," he said.

"Fine," I said idly. "Show me the mountains."

So he did. He took me to Rocky Mountain National Park and presented Longs Peak. We were standing at the side of a road near Estes Park when he first pointed it out. "Oh, look at it! What a gorgeous mountain!" he said. I was taken aback. John is, like me, a Midwesterner. We are not given to ecstatic outbursts of such length. I looked at the mountain and tried to be appreciative. He, after all, had stood still for my disquisitions on the marvels of harvester ant colonies, never once uttering a cynical or disrespectful word. "Yes," I said. "It is beautiful." Indeed, it seemed pretty enough. Ten minutes later, though, I couldn't have distinguished Longs Peak from any of a dozen others on the horizon.

We went into training. For several days we climbed in the foothills near Estes Park every morning before breakfast. One day we walked to the summit of Flattop Mountain. It was a pleasant walk, but I have had a good many pleasant walks in my life, more than I could remember, certainly. "Tomorrow, Longs Peak," John said.

I had extremely unpleasant dreams that night. For me, a trip up a stepladder constitutes a brush with death, and I had been reading Kent and Donna Dannen's trail guide. "When we finally leave the seemingly interminable Trough," it said breezily, in the tone of voice that nurses use when something awful is about to happen, "our reward is traversing a section less arduous and more interesting— the cliffs of the West Face. Here we cross The Narrows, a ledge which looks worse than it really is. In some places it is wide enough to walk two abreast, although the long drop straight down certainly discourages such a practice." The Dannens add, quite gratuitously, that the huge rock visible in the depths below the cliffs is named Black Hearse. All night long I found myself falling from narrow ledges and awakening somewhere in mid-drop in a cold sweat.

Fortunately, the night wasn't long. We arrived at the trailhead by 4 A.M., so that we would be well below the summit again by the time the afternoon thunderstorms struck. A flaming red warning, moreover, was posted at the trailhead. We read it in the beam of John's flashlight—a bear had recently, it seemed, been sighted in the area—and then set out through the forest in the darkness, hyperattuned to the breaking of every twig. Which demise did I prefer, I wondered as I trudged fatefully up the trail—a fall, a bear, or a bolt of lightning? With all of them imminent, it was difficult to choose.

The Trough did, in fact, seem interminable; the Narrows were not so awful as they looked but fearsome enough so that I didn't even notice Black Hearse; the altitude at the summit made me dizzy and nauseous; we ran short of water on the long way down and were mildly dehydrated by the time we reached the car on leaden feet twelve hours after we had left it. I went to bed before sunset, my brain bashing wickedly against my skull and every muscle in my body crying lustily for salvation. But the next morning I felt *wonderful*. I had been in High Places. I arose and went out onto the balcony of our cabin. My wife was standing there watching the sun rise over Longs Peak. "Look at it!" I said. "Isn't it gorgeous!"

"Yes, dear," she said in the tone of voice visiting

maiden aunts use with very young nephews, "it's quite nice."

I came upon my first tundra meadow when the alpine sunflowers were blooming. The world of the tundra is Lilliputian. Everything hugs the thin earth for warmth and protection from the drying, chilling winds. An alpine meadow makes a glorious blaze of color for the six weeks or so of its growing season. Alpine plants do not have the luxury of blooming in succession. Everything flowers and fruits at approximately the same time. The striking masses of color are achieved in a multiplicity of blooms, each as proportionately tiny as the plant that supports it. Looking at the tundra is like looking into the painted garden of a delicate teacup.

The alpine sunflowers are also tiny. A single plant stands no more than three or four inches high, enough to elevate it above its neighbors, but just barely, and it consists of a single, thickish, bristled, gray-green stalk supporting a few elongated, almost needlelike leaves. But there is nothing modest about the blossoms of the alpine sunflower. They are two or three inches across, altogether out of proportion to the stems that support them and to everything else that grows on the tundra, big brown buttons with blazing radials of vibrant yellow, always facing east into the rising sun, glowing brilliantly in the backlight of the setting sun, visible from hundreds of yards off.

"They saved my life once," John said. "I was coming down a mountain one day when a blinding snowstorm struck without warning. I was above timberline. It was impossible to see for more than a few feet, and the trail markers had vanished. But here and there an alpine sunflower still showed above the snow. I remembered that they face east, and steered my way by them down into the forest."

How, one wonders, looking at them, could anything so small produce such spectacular blooms in this forbidding environment, and at what price? The answer is that the Old Man of the Mountain, as the sunflower is commonly called, bides its time, husbands its resources, and lives patiently and deliberately toward its moment of glory. For its first few seasons, the plant produces only leaves and roots, which collect energy-rich materials beyond its basic needs. These it stores in large underground tubers until the year comes when it has the resources to bloom. Then the plant calls forth all of its reserves, produces a single magnificent blossom, and, spent from the effort, dies, leaving behind the seed for a new generation.

To the extent that we see ourselves in nature, we see ourselves in animals, not in plants, and especially in the creatures we hunt. There have, it is true, sometimes been close relationships between humans and plants. Our own long and rich relationship to corn, for example. But our relationships with plants in general have been a good deal more distant than those we have developed with certain animals: the wolf, the bear, the fox, the tiger, the bison. It is easier, obviously, for us to humanize animals than plants. We are so much the creatures of our intelligence that we find it hard to make connections with living things we understand to be without sentience. We can imagine a bear talking, even though we know better, but it is almost impossible for us to conceive of a conversational dandelion.

The Old Man of the Mountain surmounts the obstacles

we normally face in trying to relate, as one fully alive being to another, with plants. The life history of the Old Man of the Mountain suggests an earnestness, a steadfastness, a purposefulness, that makes it seem, somehow, moral, like the seed-collecting ant or the spawning salmon. This is, after all, the big distinction we see between ourselves and other living things. We see other creatures as living merely to exist and ourselves as living to some higher order of purpose. We imagine that we can not only live life but improve upon it, and our efforts at improvement, we believe, will transcend mere bodily existence. The idea of evolution lends even to plants something of this transcendence, but it is a hard notion to accept; a plant seems not to command its destiny. It is an open question whether we humans are in any greater command, in the long run, of destiny than, say, the scurf pea, but it seems to us that we are, and the impression matters. The Old Man of the Mountain, gathering and saving and biding its time for its one gigantic moment of glory, for the big production: That seems noble and creative. It seems somehow bent on making a lasting impression, just like us.

John introduced me to the Old Man of the Mountain in a meadow high in the Colorado Rockies. I was charmed by its valiant extravagance of bloom and learned something of its name and of its history, and was smitten, not just by the plant but by the whole community of which it was a part. I wanted to know something more about the kind of place that could give rise to a plant like the Old Man of the Mountain. So, one August, I went walking again with my friend John in mountains.

· · ·

Coming from the east across the middle of the continent, the first mountains that soar are the Big Horns of northeastern Wyoming, a 120-mile-long crescent of granite peaks, bulging toward the east, thirty to fifty miles wide. The Colorado Rockies farther south, the Montana ranges to the north, announce themselves long before you actually reach them, but the high country of eastern Wyoming hides the Big Horns until you are practically in them. You round a curve in the road and you are up against blue peaks looming above the pines like a brigade of white-hatted bandits, daring you to proceed. John and I stopped for the night at the foot of them in Buffalo.

It is impossible to keep your eyes off a mountain you intend to climb. The first step toward a mountaintop is one you take in your imagination, the single giant step from the foothills to the pinnacles, past the pines, past the creeks and waterfalls, past the gleaming snowfields, a leap that assumes none of the intervening steps. In your imagination, the way to a mountaintop is not along earth, over boulders, through bogs, up talus slopes, but a journey as ethereal as the mountaintop itself, a flight through air not to a point on earth but to a place in the heavens. The mountaintop that you see from a long way off is disembodied from its roots in the mantle of the earth, cut off from the mundane facts of ordinary geography by the line of lesser trees and hills. It seems to float like a cloud. Before Icarus fashioned a pair of wings, he surely climbed a mountain, imagining all the way that he was taking flight. And I suppose that the astronauts who first rocketed to the moon studied it the night before they took off in the same way that a climber dreamily examines a mountaintop from a distance before approaching it. We saw the mountains and before we had even reached them, we had already, in our imaginations, climbed them.

The blue and white mountains hovered over us as we slept in a blue and white motel. They lurked in our sleep like the bear eating huckleberries around the next bend in the trail. We rose in the morning and looked out the window, and they were still there, still capped with snow, still floating above the earthbound foothills, keeping company with the clouds in their crowns. It was like waking in a new house and wandering around in the morning, getting acquainted with its corners, with the angles of the morning light in its windows, with its shadows. We pulled open the curtains and gazed at the mountains; paused in the lobby to stare up at them; stopped in the parking lot to study them; stole glances at them at stoplights on our way downtown to buy topographic maps.

The waitress in the motel restaurant had caught our gazes when she brought us breakfast. "Oh, aren't they something," she said. "Some mornings you wake up and they're almost lavender. Like flowers. You can't look at them too many times, that's for sure." She stood looking fondly out the window, having forgotten for the moment our food.

Walkers use the 7.5 minute series of maps published by the United States Department of the Interior Geological Survey, on which five and a quarter inches represent a mile. These maps are marvels of clarity and economy. They are printed in four colors: black for place names, brown for contour lines, blue for water, green for forests.

The contour lines record every forty-foot change in elevation. Where the going gets rough, the brown lines crowd more and more closely together; in the steepest places, they make almost solid bands of brown. The places I look for on the topographic maps are the ones with lots of brown lines and no green. They will prove rugged and rocky, flowerful in summer and swarming with insects, boggy with meltwater in places and still snow-covered in others, ringing with the bright whistles of pikas.

The maps, I suppose, compromise the idea of wilderness even as they help to evoke it. How absolutely wild can a place be that has already been reduced symbolically to the conventions of a topographic map? But the maps reassured us that we were headed, at least, toward houseless, roadless, trailless places, toward empty places.

In empty places life perseveres against harsh restrictions of climate or typography. In a sense they always were empty. The places that survive now as wilderness are by nature demanding, uncompromising, parsimonious. The green and rich wilderness places have long since been claimed for human purposes. I like the brittle and severe qualities of the places that remain empty. I like life that has braved the odds, made the best of little, come to terms with conditions that frustrate life in general.

I see, too, an appealing youthfulness in such places. Most of the places on the maps that remain empty are, by geologic measure, very young. The sparse North American grasslands, the Nebraska sandhills, the Sonoran desert, the tundra-covered mountaintops: all are communities that have developed in the recent geologic past. The alpine tundra community, in particular, is essentially a grassland; and there is a sense in which the grasslands can be said to be a regression toward youthfulness.

We live, that is, in the Age of Flowers. Sometime near the end of the dinosaur era, the first flowering plant emerged, a water lily perhaps, simple in structure, wind-pollinated like the gigantic conifers that then dominated the landscape, but producing a real flower bearing a truly encased seed, like the angiosperms of the contemporary world. Very suddenly then, in a revolution so rapid that it can be properly described as violent—Darwin called it an "abominable mystery"—the earth exploded with flowering plants of many kinds, plants not dependent, as their older relatives were, upon the vagaries of wind or water for pollination; they suddenly had the capacity to entice and exploit animals, particularly insects, into the reliable service of reproduction and seed distribution; they had developed overnight, as it were, a mobility unprecedented in plant life. With this development came the ascendency of mammals and the emergence of the first humanoids from the limbs of trees into the open. "The weight of a petal," Loren Eiseley said, "has changed the face of the world and made it ours." But the grasses, although angiosperms, pollinated though they sometimes are by insects, are still largely dependent upon the winds for their survival, and in this sense they, and the regions they dominate, may be said to recall a more youthful time in our history.

I like too the idea of life lived at the edge. A spruce tree at the upper limits of a mountain treeline, thick and misshapen, shorn of its branches on its windward side, no more than shoulder high although it may be a century old, such a spruce speaks powerfully of the persistence of life. Every person who enters the wilderness goes in search of

76

the same speech. A journey into the wilderness is a test of the will against the odds. Going into the wilderness, any wilderness, is a way of opening yourself to the possibility of danger and to the likelihood of discomfort, at the least. There is the possibility of getting lost, of being trapped in a storm, of confronting an angry animal, of falling. There are the certain hardships of arduous walks, of exposure to cold, heat, wind, rain, of sleeping on the ground, of solitude. To be alone is sometimes the most difficult challenge of all. It is in itself an art, for which we are ill equipped, both by training and by experience. To confront the unknown and to meet its challenges is to be admitted into a permanently enlarged world. Just as the tortured spruce tree at the edge of the upper forest enlarges and frees the world for trees, so our encounters with wilderness widen and free us.

Empty: unoccupied, or uninhabited; unfrequented. We wear our language as blindly as our own faces. Only from the outside can we look into them. Empty is one of those words that reveals unspoken attitudes. Lacking people, it means. No humans equals nothing.

Hence, useless, senseless, valueless, hollow, foolish, without effect or force. The word "empty" inherently expresses contempt for everything that is not human. The old puzzle about the tree falling in an unoccupied forest would not be a puzzle at all in a world where trees and porcupines, say, were assumed to have some justification independent of humanity.

So it is paradoxical, given our culture, to say of an empty place that it is necessary. To do so assigns worth and meaning to something that is, by common definition, worthless and meaningless.

Nevertheless some value and meaning clearly resides in such places, as in all places. Despite ourselves and our beliefs, some among us continue impulsively to seek them out. We go to a mountaintop, or retreat to the desert, or repair to some lonely cove along the wide and empty sea. We are drawn toward wildness as water is toward the level. And there we find the something that we cannot name. We find ourselves, we say. But I suppose that what we really find is the void within ourselves, the loneliness, the surviving heart of wildness, that binds us to all the living earth.

6

Florence Canyon

◁ ▷

MOUNTAINS have a way of insisting on the long view. The first step you take in the morning, if you are practiced and wise, is one measured against the total accumulation of the steps you intend to take before nightfall. In undertaking the first step, you consider the length of the day's walk, the gain or fall in altitude, the burden of your pack, the state of the weather, the frame of your mind, the day to come, the fitness of your body; you balance these considerations against the weight of your experience; work a subconscious sum; and only then do you slowly, deliberately lift a booted foot and carry it forward a single step, a step you expect to be equal in speed and

79

span to the last step of the afternoon. The first time you try this, you feel absurd, as if you were engaged in some kind of play-walking, a theatrical charade or cartoon of a person walking, so slowly and mechanically does the pace unfold.

We are used to running until we run down, but the lesson of the mountains is that the race is to the steady, not to the swift. "In time you'll learn that, generally speaking, the way to hurry is not to hurry but to keep going," walker Colin Fletcher advises in his manual on the subject. "To this end I have two walking speeds: slow and slower." With experience, the right pace for mountains becomes second nature. Take one step and all the others fall naturally into place. The greatest pride in walking in mountains, the badge of maturity, is not in reaching the summit but in reaching it in stride.

There is an intimacy of a special kind in laboring up a steep trail through the long shadows of a forest with forty pounds of unaccustomed weight on your back. Any trail, for one thing, exacts its own discipline. Following one is like driving a car: The road and not the landscape commands your attention. If you get carried away on a trail and let your eyes wander from the route ahead, odd bits of root and the fallen limbs of trees and stray rocks trip you or catch your toes and turn your ankles. A trail eases your way, but it also narrows your focus.

But when you are walking across country, reading the landscape becomes part of the business of walking. You need constantly to be assessing the lay of the land, to be making hundreds of small decisions: which shore of the lake to take, which side of the stream, whether the easiest passage will be along the ridge or farther down the hillside, whether to go around or over the top of a heap of boulders, whether to strike straight up the pass or to tackle it at an angle, whether to climb through the snowfield, whether to wade the river or to cross it on the trunk of the fallen tree. The possibility of surprise attends every decision, the chance that you will find the way ahead impassable; that the summit you have been aiming for is not the summit at all; that the drainage seeming to offer easy passage ends abruptly in a sharp cliff or in a boggy meadow cut with a labyrinth of kettles and treacherous waterways. Off-trail trekking opens you to the rhythm in the landscape itself. It slows your pace, encourages long pauses, requires adjustment to the landscape as it was shaped, accommodation to its essential personality. It is more an exercise in thinking than in walking, more like making a poem than running a machine.

Walking a trail, particularly a steep trail switching up the side of a mountain, is essentially an interior journey. It makes you more like a river than like a mountain. You become less an element of the mountains, one of its pieces moving in harmony with it, than a force resisting the mountain. Indeed, a trail cut across a mountain tears away at it, begins to create its own gully, the humble beginning of a canyon, just as a trickle of running water begins inexorably to impose a new shape upon a mountain. Every step you take up a mountainside trail is a step that reduces the mountain.

You begin easy of breath, full of the challenge of taking possession of the mountain, vibrant with the promise of leaving settled places behind, of approaching high and quiet places where you and the mountain will be alone. "One of the deeply satisfying things about a mountain—

almost any mountain—is the way it can at the same time belong exclusively to so many people," Colin Fletcher once said. You begin to breathe more heavily. You glisten with sweat. The world is gradually narrowed to the requirements of the trail itself, to picking your way step by step among the obstacles in the path, to the measured effort of putting one foot forward and then the other, of advancing from one bend in the trail to the next, oblivious to the forest, to the mountain, to the trickling streams, to the scoldings of squirrels and chipmunks, moving against gravity, against your own limitations, toward a summit that seems to exist only in imagination. You resent giving up gained altitude but are grateful for the chance at every downward turn in the trail to stretch your leg muscles and to straighten the forward incline of your back. You push yourself ahead even when part of you begs to stop, when you have achieved the length of one switchback and are gasping for air and the focus has gone out of your eyes and you despair at the thought of the incline that stretches ahead. You proceed because you know that it takes more energy to get started than it does simply to keep going. Finally the blind progress up the trail in the cloud of your own ragged breath and salty sweat attains a self-sustaining momentum. You are propelled by some force beyond conscious will. Simply to be moving becomes its own comfort. Your thoughts meld into a running, half-perceived daydream made up of forest and mountain, water and heat and air, memory, hope and worry. You crawl in upon yourself as you do in sleep, and are lost to every possibility save the primal sense of being.

To walk easily in mountains is also a matter of music. The right stride returns instinctively to a walker because it is as metrical and regular as the rhythm of a song. The terrain may be smooth in one place and rocky in another; it may rise steeply here and fall gently there. The higher you go the thinner the atmosphere gets and the more you labor under a deficit of oxygen. The trail is firm in one place and unsteady in another. The rate of progress inevitably speeds or slows according to the character of the landscape. As a song moves here in sixteenths, there in whole notes, but in the same number of units per measure, so the progress of a walker speeds and slows in keeping with the underlying rhythm of the walk. As you lose the tune when you lose the rhythm, so you lose the walk. The right pace for a landscape is like the right tempo for a song: It is the one that allows for natural breathing. Walking too fast for conversation is walking too fast.

I try to remember what I have learned about walking in mountains when I go home to the prairies. I try to remember how, as Fletcher says, "The miles come to meet you." I try to aim for the steady accumulation, to have faith in the measured pace, to do what is sustainable. But it is a hard lesson. Sometimes in the evening I will sit down at the piano. I will play the easy passages fast and the hard passages slow, as amateurs do. Then I will remember that I have been walking in mountains. I go back to the beginning of the song and start again, playing the easy passages at a tempo I can sustain when the going gets rough. I remember the right way to make music.

By midafternoon the valley in which we were walking had narrowed, and we could see the crevice leading toward Florence Pass. Its walls looked rocky and barren. We briefly considered stopping for the day, while there were still obvious campsites, but the map showed Medicine Cabin Park ahead, a meadow, and our plan was to reach the summit of Cloud Peak the next day. The closer to it we started, the better our chances. We pressed on. A black bank of altocumulus clouds had rolled in from the west, the direction in which we were moving, trailing gray swirls at their edges. As the days passed, the pattern would prove constant: sunshine in the morning, but always by lunchtime the speeding clouds, the rumble of thunder, the spikes of lightning warning us away from the highest places. The clouds were as powerful as the mountains themselves; towering and massive, demanding caution and respect.

There was something playful about how the mountains hid the clouds, and then the clouds the mountains, a game of the gods from which we mortals were excluded. Under their influence I felt the reality of the earth as a spinning ball. We seemed to be whirling in the direction of the clouds rather than they in ours. I remembered a game we played as children. One of us would take and hold a deep breath and another would squeeze him around the solar plexus, tightly, until he fainted. There was a brief moment of terror when you awakened, flat on the ground, nauseous and confused, the clouds roiling in the sky overhead, not knowing where you were or how you had gotten there.

The trail left the meadow and began to wind like a river up the mountainside. We followed its switchbacks, foreshortened by the narrowness of the ridge, surprised and encouraged at every bend by a fresh view of the heights we were achieving, foot by deceptive foot. About halfway up, at the edge of a stand of tall firs that skirted the valley walls, the clouds opened and a rain of sleet began to fall, straight down and hard, like the sheets of water that descend without warning in the afternoon in the rain forests. The crystals beat on the hoods of our jackets like raindrops on a tin roof. They stung our cheeks, nasty little bullets of multifaceted ice, the next thing to hail, and bounced to the earth, making the rocky path slippery and treacherous. At the next switchback we stopped, unshouldered our packs, and waited out the storm in the dark shelter of a fir thicket, safe, dry, unencumbered, sucking on hard candies from our pockets, breathing deeply of air redolent with the complicated and contradictory aromas of resin, moldering needles, human sweat, and ice. Our muscles slaked their lactic acids and we stopped our thirst with long draughts of sweet water still almost as cold as the mountain stream from which we had drawn it at lunchtime. We waited beneath the dark pines, letting the patter of ice suffice for conversation, savoring the oddly domestic flavor of our respite. Here at the mouth of Florence Canyon, somehow, we felt formally welcomed into the wilderness.

The sleet stopped as abruptly as it had begun. Here and there a ray of sun overran the clouds. We helped each other into our packs, which had already begun to feel like natural appendages, found again the rhythm of the trail, and before long emerged into the canyon, a narrow, steeply walled fissure in the mountain. There the sun was shining brightly. Clear Creek made a bright and babbling ribbon of silver along the southern edge of it, and in its shadow rose a formidable perpendicular wall, more than eighty stories high, of red and tan rock. Rivulets of meltwater ran down its cracks from rocky laps snuggled with snow. Northward, along an earthen ridge, stood a band of spruce trees and behind them another great wall of craggy rock. The floor of the canyon was as wet and green as jade, everywhere studded with the purple, scarlet, and yellow blooms of millions of wildflowers.

The park at first offered no satisfactory place to rest. Its floor was too boggy, its cliffs too steep. But there was a bend in the canyon walls, obscuring from view the western reaches of the park. We crossed the creek and walked around the obstructing elbow, as around the broad bend in a boomerang, and the upper stretch of the park came into view. It terminated in a great rubble of talus, bits and enormous pieces of the canyon split from its glacially carved walls by the heavings of ice. Water flows into the cracks in the rock, freezes, and expands—ice occupies about 9 percent more space than the equivalent amount of water. Something has to give. "Solid as a rock," we say. But it is the rock that gives way to the ice, not inch by inch but tons of it at a time.

Water fell over the boulders, wearing away the rubble the ice had made, and tumbled into the park. Not far below the waterfall, the creek divided, admitting a little island in the shape of a teardrop, a few feet higher than the surrounding park floor. On its rise grew a clump of stunted white-barked pine trees, perhaps fifteen feet high. It looked like home. We headed for it, crossed the northern branch of the creek, a couple of feet wide, on a lovely boulder, flat-topped and placed, it seemed, to receive us, and found what others had before, a dry patch of earth covered with a brown carpet of needles, just large enough to admit a tent and sheltered by low-hanging bows of pine, a place given by some heaven to keep us for the night.

The sun, still brilliant after the sleet, was a long way from setting, but we were reminded, looking at the angle of it against the high rim of the canyon, that, in the mountains, the moment when the sun disappears and the moment when it sets may be radically divided.

On the plains, the day dissolves slowly, seemingly reluc-tantly, into the night. The process extends over hours, a long dance of light against which the darkness unfurls, like a great blanket. First there is the great flatness of mid-day, when what little relief there is in the landscape is suppressed by the weight of the light. As the sun moves toward the western horizon, the rays of light lengthen. Blue shadows begin to emerge, and the world appears more and more extravagantly three-dimensional. In the west, the sky begins to color. The sun grows larger and larger. It mushrooms into a cloud of light, seems to inten-sify, lingers at the horizon, as if teetering on a balance, until it finally falls over the edge. Then it glows up from below the surface of the horizon, like a flaming ember in a molten pot, until finally it is extinguished and darkness comes like dust and the sound of crickets swells or, in winter, the cold glint of ice sparkles in the moonlight. The setting of the sun on the plains seems always a kind of death, and its rising the next morning a resurrection. It is a daily Passion play. If you have lived long enough on the plains, you come to think of this drama as inevitable and universal.

It is alarming, at first, to be in the mountains and to realize that at any moment the sun may precipitously dis-appear, may retreat behind a mountain, never to return, as if giving way without a struggle to the night. The difference is that night on the plains descends from the heavens and in the deep valleys of the mountains it arises from the earth.

"It is curious how the most dismal place after twenty-four hours begins to seem like home," Graham Greene remarked, writing about an arduous journey through a remote region of southern Mexico. "It is, of course, fear of the next step," he said. Perhaps. But I felt no fear that night in Florence Canyon, either of the prospect ahead or of the world at my feet. It seemed as serene and secure, as sublime a place as I had ever known. After a supper eaten standing, after we had savored cups of hot cocoa and done the dishes, John went down to the creek to fish and I set out to admire and make note of the wildflowers.

I remember the flowers, of course, even though I have since lost the notes. A mountain meadow in bloom is not forgettable. There were the white flowers of the American bistort, which look like swabs of cotton and which we might have dined on had we in fact taken up residence in the canyon. The serpentine roots of the plant (it is sometimes called snakeweed) are browsed by black and grizzly bears and were an ingredient in Blackfeet and Cheyenne stews, although they are said to be at their nutty best when roasted over coals. The pink spikes of elephant head, each flower bearing, in fact, a striking resemblance to the head of an elephant, a note of tropical extravagance in the shadow of permanent snowfields. Purple penstemons and mountain asters. Yellow senecios and buttercups. Elegant white-flowered marsh marigolds with golden buttons of stamens, their waxy and vividly green leaves, shaped like hearts, believed to be poisonous to cattle but relished by elk. On the drier slopes, flaming stands of Indian paintbrush, a favorite of hummingbirds, the state flower of Wyoming, a plant flying under deceptive colors in two senses. The paintbrushes would seem to be among the most gaudily flowered of the mountain flora, but in fact their flowers are rather nondescript, tubular, yellowish green. It is the upper leaves and the sepals that blaze so brightly. And the paintbrushes are parasitic. They send down roots until these touch the roots of other species growing nearby, which they then penetrate, a habit so well developed that they can scarcely exist on their own resources. But above all, there were the mountain bluebells, growing in dense drifts along the banks of the creek, lush and robust, waist-high, profusely flowered, so sweetly and powerfully perfumed that they scented the whole valley. Pikas collect them for the winter. Bears eat them. Deer graze them. Elk bed among them, raising their young in their protective cover.

I half-expected to see an elk. When I climbed the ridge leading to the northern rim of the canyon, I found ample sign of them. But if they were present, they eluded me. Still, I felt their company, a ghostly presence, as firmly, as convincingly, as if I had actually set eyes upon them. They were present in the sensation I had of being watched. They were present as rattlesnakes are in the desert or bears in the woods, unseen, perhaps, but there: knowable by the tangible aura of their existence, and not only in the imagination, just as you turn suddenly in a crowd and catch the fleeting glance of someone who has been watching you, as you knew all along.

I had climbed the ridge to get a better view of the snowfield across the canyon, nestled in the lap of a talus pile perhaps two hundred feet high and situated so that much of it lay always in shadow, a permanent patch of winter within bounds of the abundant summer blooming so profusely at my feet. I sat on a boulder of granite and climbed to it in my imagination, as I might have in actuality had not the sunlight, still in play on the other side of the mountain, begun suddenly to take its leave of the canyon. The floor of the canyon had already fallen into twilight while I was not looking, and the shadows had begun to climb the sheer walls of rock. In the extreme angle of the early-evening light, the walls where they were still lit had grown less sheer in appearance and showed themselves now as craggy and deeply etched, split here and there with long rents in which water dripped, blackening the stone. In the rocky dust of the ledges greenery improbably grew, little cushions of alpine plants sending up flowers on stalks, a bold and defiant show of life, of its tenacity and versatility, of its inventive determination.

Now the sunlight put on a pyrotechnical display of its own, flashing here and there among the spires and along the protuberances of the canyon walls, shining now in front of me, now on the walls behind me or down the canyon in long, pure rays, absent the milky, dusty quality of the light on the plowed plains. The features of the canyon walls seemed to come forward, in the spotlight of the sun, like players in a drama, taking their bows at the end of the performance of the day. When the light finally lingered only at the far end of the canyon, marking the places we had already left behind, perhaps forever, glowing like a halo around the darkening trough of Clear Creek, I got up quietly from my seat and made my way down the slippery slope of the ridge, using my hands as well as my feet to keep my balance, collecting the evening dew in the canvas of my shoes. I crossed the river and came to the island we had claimed for the night. John had also returned from the pools in the bends of the creek where the trout hid. We stood together, watching and listening.

Overhead, the evening airplane passed, headed east, low enough so that we could see the lighted windows of its cabin. The plane came first and then, a second or two later, the sound of it, the muffled roar of civilization, like a burst of wind whining in the hollows of the rock. In another minute it was over the rim of the canyon, beyond sight and sound. But it lingered in my mind, obscuring my vision of the canyon itself, as the image of a dream lingers in the eye in the morning in the first blush of awakening, obscuring the reality of the new day. I felt a vivid rush of recollection, a melancholy, a half-guilty vision of the things I had left behind: family, responsibilities, deadlines unmet, business commitments unkept, speeches promised but not delivered. I saw in the gathering darkness an image of the windows of my house, glowing with yellow light like the cabin windows of the airliner, soft and beckoning. Was it right for me to be there? What sort of romantic indulgence was I caught up in? I felt suddenly sad and lonely.

The moment passed, the image of that other world faded. I stood again in Florence Canyon. The waters of Clear Creek murmured at my feet, the aroma of mountain bluebells wafted in the air. I was wearing long underwear, a sweatshirt, a windproof jacket, but it suddenly seemed very cold. I shivered, gathered my flashlight, crawled into the tent, undressed, snaked into my mummy bag, zipped myself in, twisted and turned my stuff-bag pillow until I was comfortable, felt the hard edge of the earth against my hip bone and felt secure in its unyielding embrace. Before the hour was out, there would be stars and the faint light of the moon and the air would be colder still, and in the depths of this star-marked space I would be smaller still, more silent, even more vulnerable; and I liked this feeling, this strange sensation of smallness, this extreme diminishment in the vast body of the unlimited universe. I felt the great, unaccountable luck of being alive at that moment in that place, I who had so little claim on the universe.

It was, I recognized, a gift of the great civilization I had left behind that I felt this joy. It was the gift of contrast, of comparison, the gift of an abundance sufficient to allow me to indulge in the possibility of beauty where there was no commercial utility. When the earth was still largely a wilderness and the rare thing was a place tamed and made safe for human habitation, there was no beauty or joy of this kind in wildness. When every day was still a struggle for survival, there was no leisure for getting away from it all.

Until the eighteenth century nobody visited mountains who could avoid it. Mountains were regarded as hideous places, barren, useless, treacherous. Historian Keith Thomas compiled a list of midseventeenth-century adjectives for them: deformities, warts, boils, monstrous excrescences, rubbish of the earth, wen and unnatural protuberances, Nature's pudenda. The theory of the midseventeenth century was that the earth had been as smooth as an egg until it had been deformed in the

92

deluge. Eighteenth-century visitors to the Alps, Annie Dillard says, wore blindfolds to hide themselves from the hideous irregularities of the earth. As late as the early eighteenth century dragons were said, on good scientific authority, to inhabit mountaintops. As long as one struggled simply to exist, there could be no loveliness, no peacefulness, no serenity in wildness. The earth had to be tamed first.

I thought of the airplane again, and remembered what Sigurd Olson said about hearing the whistle of a train in the silence of a Minnesota pine forest: "Without that long lonesome wail and the culture that had produced it, many things would not be mine—recordings of the world's finest music, books holding the philosophy, the dreams and hopes of all mankind, a car that took me swiftly to the point whenever I felt the need. All of these things and countless others civilization had given me, and I must never forget that because of the wonders it had wrought this richness was now mine."

"No man can lose what he never had," Izaak Walton said. Nor can he find what he has never lost. That is the paradox of the wilderness: It was only when we had already lost it that we could begin to see the value in it.

7
Mistymoon
◁ ▷

IT was a short trek across the green floor of Medicine
Park to the waterfall that had sung gently to us through
the night like a wind in the trees, which I had thought it
was once or twice when I had awakened and was briefly
disoriented. The trail, the Solitude Trail, was built by the
Forest Service in 1920 (the wilderness came under federal
protection in 1897 by proclamation of President Grover
Cleveland). It takes its name from a lake across the range,
one of the largest and most beautiful in the Big Horns.
The standard guidebook describes it as "the emerald of the
Big Horns . . . blue and clear," a nice illustration of the
hazards of ecstatic writing in guidebooks. Lieutenant Gen-

eral Phil H. Sheridan, from whom the epigram "The only good Indian is a dead Indian" derives, visited the lake in 1879 and named it Lake Stager, a name, fortunately, that never caught on, or we might have been walking the Stager Trail or perhaps, given the natural corruption of names, the Stagger Trail. It leads, in any case, up the north wall of the canyon by narrow, sometimes, even in August, snow-covered twists and turns, treacherous enough to be difficult for pack horses, whose manure richly endows easier accesses in the primitive area, transforming many a wilderness walk into a barnyard tramp.

In 1948 the Bureau of Reclamation proposed to dam Lake Solitude, turning it into an irrigation reservoir for the alkali flats west of the mountains, but local opposition stopped the proposal. What the Bureau's engineers failed to accomplish then may yet be accomplished by mounted recreationists, whose iron-shod conveyances are grinding the trails into muddy ravines filled with horse turds that wash into the lakes and streams, none of which any longer carry water safe to drink.

We paused at the top of the waterfall to look back down the green canyon, classically U shaped in the manner of ice-carved valleys, and then set our sights ahead, southwestward, to the tan rubble of rock in which the north fork of Clear Creek ran, sometimes at our feet, sometimes yards below, beneath the tumble of frost-shorn boulders, invisible but always audible, the hollow sound of water falling in a cavern, like the sound of the water running in the storm sewers in the springtime in my prairie town.

On the way up, we met a solitary hiker coming down. She paused, leaning on her walking stick. "Are you enjoying Wyoming?" she asked in the unfailingly polite way of all the natives we met along the trail, discerning without asking that we were not natives.

A friend of mine calls it the Dakota quotient. There is, he insists, a direct relationship between density of population and degree of friendliness, a relationship that might be worked out mathematically if anyone cared to take the trouble. He tells about an annual bike trek across Iowa, an event that attracts thousands. The bikers were met all along the way, he said, by rural Iowans bearing pitchers of ice water. "Which they were handing out for free! To anybody who wanted it! Ten thousand dehydrated strangers, dying for a drink of water, and nobody's charging a red cent! New Jersey, they'd be extracting a buck a glass. Montana, they'd be paying *you* to take it."

The climb up the canyon was steep, and for the first time we had risen above ten thousand feet in altitude, where the air becomes noticeably thinner. We fell to the methodical and absorbing work of simply moving ahead, sometimes gasping for air, our shirts and trousers gradually soaking with sweat. And then, more quickly than we expected, we had passed around the sharp bend of the canyon, narrower than a football field, and into the basin of Lake Florence, icy and deep, green as moss, fed by a spectacular waterfall tumbling out of the Golden Lakes cirque, hidden to the northeast in the peaks above.

Ahead of us rose Bomber Mountain, a blocky 12,840-foot peak named in 1946 by the Sheridan chapter of the American War Dads in memory of twelve army airmen who died in the crash of their B-17 on its southwest ridge on the twenty-eighth of June 1943. The wreckage of the plane lay undiscovered for two years until a couple of cowboys spotted the glint of it in the sunlight. We thought we could spot the glitter of metal ourselves, and, free from our packs, we scrambled up the talus slope on the western side of the canyon for a better view.

The new vantage point proved inconclusive. The reflection we saw might have been from the wreckage, or we might have been imagining things. Whatever, our attention was quickly diverted, first by a stench close at hand and then by what we saw at the waterfall.

You would have sworn there was a skunk somewhere in that talus pile. The smell of a skunk is hard to confuse with anything else. It gradually dawned on us, however, that we had met not with a skunk but with a sky pilot, or rather with a whole community of them. Sky pilot is the common name for *Polemonium viscosum*, a member of the phlox family. It grows in high, rocky places where there is some protection from the winds, an ostentatiously lush and showy plant for such austere surroundings. Its compound leaves are rounded, whorled, and vibrantly green, and each hefty plant sports a profusion of big purple flowers, broadly funnel-shaped, with orange anthers. Nothing could be more handsome. But step on one and you will carry the unpleasant memory of it with you for a long time.

We tend to think of plants, stationary as they are, as unaggressive. In fact they have evolved many devilish strategies for fighting potential enemies: sharp, stiff thorns, poisonous juices, bitter-tasting excretions. The stench of the sky pilot is its admirable defense against being grazed or trampled. Despite the scarcity of good greenery in the regions it occupies, most animals studiously shun it; only domestic sheep are known occasionally to help themselves to it, and domestic sheep are not notably bright.

A merciful breeze blew through the pass, sweeping the odor of bruised sky pilot down Florence Canyon. Our attention was diverted to the great stone wall over which water from the Golden Lakes falls into Florence Lake, a seventy-story tumble down what looks, from a distance, like sheer granite. A group of boys had appeared on the lip of the precipice and were angling their way down it toward the waterfall. The oldest of them looked in the lenses of the binoculars to be high-school aged, the youngest perhaps middle schoolers, members, no doubt, of the Boy Scout troop that was camped in the pass. They moved as recklessly as mountain goats, not merely climbing but leaping and bounding down the boulders, gliding from one foothold to another, or hanging by their fingers from one ledge and dropping through the air to the next. As we watched them from the opposite side of the pass, their progress looked effortless, and because from our perspective the wall appeared flat and featureless, they seemed to have developed the ability to fly.

In no time they had achieved a broad ledge about three-quarters of the way up the waterfall and immediately adjacent to it. Here they paused. Suddenly the two oldest boys stripped off all their clothes, innocent, certainly, of their audience. This, in itself, was bold enough. A raw wind was by now whipping through the pass, and we, bundled in jackets, were shivering against it. I turned my back to it, feeling a vicarious chill.

"My God!" John said.

I turned to see the two naked boys, hand in hand, stepping out onto a narrow, wet, slippery sliver of rock beneath the waterfall and subjecting themselves to the full force of the icy water. They were inches and seconds from death. If one of them flinched in the face of the frigid blast of water, slipping slightly, or being ever so minutely knocked off balance by the force of a ton of water falling twenty stories, both of them would have plunged the remaining fifty stories onto the boulders below. Once when we were four, my twin sister fell into a bonfire. My mother saw her fall and screamed, but she couldn't reach out to rescue her; she was literally frozen in horror. I thought I finally had some understanding of that brief and endless moment in her life. I myself was now frozen in fear. I wanted not to look and couldn't resist looking.

The two boys lingered a few seconds, no longer, and then inched back toward dry stone. The boy in the lead reached it. The other boy slipped. But their hand grip held, and in the next second, they were both back on safe ground, hastening into their clothing. In a minute they were bounding down the wall again.

"Idiots!" we said, feeling as if we ourselves had been resurrected. But when we climbed down the talus slope to the trail again, we took the rocks with a certain youthful facility of our own.

We scrambled southwestward to Mistymoon Lake, following in the path of the West Tensleep Glacier, a Pleistocene river of blue ice and embedded rock that gouged and cut its way westward, leaving behind a chain of lakes, the Fortress Lakes and Gunboat Lake, among them, and a series of mammoth tables, a god-sized staircase.

By noon we had reached Mistymoon Lake, a large and

very beautiful alpine basin at an elevation of 10,236 feet. From a ridge above, we could see the string of lakes stretching south down the West Tensleep valley through forests of lodgepole pines, islands of cerulean blue in a green trough, the polished peaks rising on either side like waves of stone. While we were admiring the view, a tall man, slender as a blade of grass, outfitted in the uniform of Wyoming—denims and a cowboy hat—came up and greeted us. He was carrying a fly rod, and his young son, also outfitted for fishing, tagged behind in his shadow. He elicited the information that we were headed for Cloud Peak and pointed out the way to us. "Two hours up and two hours back," he said. The guidebook we had read before coming suggested planning on at least four hours for the climb up and three hours for the descent, but here was someone who had made the trip a number of times and obviously knew the way well. We wished him good fishing and set out around the lake and headed north up Solitude Trail, light of heart and foot.

Just out of sight of Mistymoon, we heard the tinkling of bells, and, looking up into the hills, we spotted a herd of domestic sheep, part of the two thousand licensed to graze the fragile tundra in this part of the so-called primitive area. The sheep cried out to each other as they made their way down the slope, a strangely pastoral sound after so much walking in what we regarded as wilderness. "Wooly locusts," one-time shepherd John Muir called them. "Poor, helpless, hungry sheep, in great part misbegotten, without good right to be, semi-manufactured, made less by God than man, born out of time and place, yet their voices are strangely human and call out one's pity." The description is from Muir's account of his first summer in

100

the Sierras, toward the end of which he would lament, thinking again of the sheep in his care, "The harm they do goes to the heart, but glorious hope lifts above all the dust and din and bids me look forward to a good time coming, when money enough will be earned to enable me to go walking where I like in pure wildness, with what I carry on my back, and when the bread-sack is empty, run down to the nearest point on the bread-line for more."

Here were the beginnings of a great debate running through the twentieth century, in which we have struggled, for the first time in history, to fashion a public policy that would allow us to have both wilderness and the fruits of the abundance of the land. Muir understood himself to be a Thoreauvian. He believed Thoreau's famous dictum: "In wilderness is the preservation of the world." In his passion for the conservation of wild places, he led the campaign for the establishment of Yosemite National Park, the first park set aside wholly for its wilderness values. He argued for these values as self-justifying: "The universe," he wrote, "would be incomplete without man; but it would also be incomplete without the smallest transmicroscopic creature that dwells beyond our conceitful eyes and knowledge."

Still, he was a realist. He saw his own connection to the breadline and to the economic freedoms of civilization, which afforded him the opportunity to walk alone in wild places, just as Thoreau saw the advantages of living with one foot in civilized Concord and the other in the wild places beyond its boundaries. Both men have been sometimes called primitivists, but they were not: They were social reformers, not social dropouts—Thoreau an abolitionist, among other things, Muir an ardent con-

servationist; they were self-consciously literate men, although Muir experienced popular success on this account
during his own lifetime while Thoreau's success was post-
humous; they were skillful technologists—Thoreau in surveying and the manufacture of pencils, Muir in the design
of farm implements; and they both believed in wilderness
not as an alternative to civilization but as a necessary
complement to it.

Thoreau went to Walden Pond, we are inclined to forget, not to escape Concord—to which, in any case, he
walked every day or two—but to conduct an experiment,
and when the experiment was completed, he promptly
left it. It was not civilized Concord that caused him to
tremble, but the absolute wildness of the Maine woods.
And Muir, who thought Thoreau a bit silly for regarding
the woods around Concord as wild, came to a purist
position about the preservation of wildernesses only by
stages, as he saw the impracticality of the alternatives. In
the beginning, he was a friend and ally of Gifford
Pinchet, another notable conservationist and the archi-
tect of the "multiple use" school of preservation, still
practiced in places such as Cloud Peak Primitive Area,
with its herds of grazing sheep, trains of pack horses, and
sturdy footbridges.

For a while Muir argued, with Pinchet, that sensitive
logging of prime timber in wilderness areas could be com-
patible with their other values. But when Pinchet opened
the forests in 1897 to sheep grazing (and mining as well),
Muir angrily confronted him in a hotel lobby in Seattle,
reminding him that Pinchet himself had admitted that
sheep did a great deal of damage in wilderness areas and
demanding an explanation. Pinchet offered none and did

not back down. The rift between the two men, never repaired, mirrored a rift in the conservation movement generally, one that continues to this day.

Mistymoon Lake in the Cloud Peak Primitive Area is long past its primitive state. The trail to it up the West Tensleep valley is gentle and the scenery along the way is varied and gorgeous. It offers the best views of Cloud Peak in the range and a sampling of everything else the mountains have to give: lush meadows, shaded forests, crystal-clear lakes speckled with trout, the creek crashing through a deep rock gorge, great expanses of brilliantly colored wildflowers, finally the austere and refined beauty of the country above treeline—all within an easy day's walk. Not surprisingly, therefore, it is very heavily used, and the campsites at Mistymoon are in constant demand. Frequently during the summer months the camping population at the lake numbers thirty or more people a night, enough so that either some limits ought to be put on its use or some effort made to accommodate the crowds, not so much in the interests of the campers as in the interests of the lake itself. There are, for example, no toilets at Mistymoon, and all of the available campsites drain into it. How many "cat piles" of human feces need to accumulate in the alpine environment before the lake, the only handy source of drinking water, is completely contaminated?

And what of the sheep? Is it really necessary that we should allow grazing at the central showcase of a designated primitive area in a national forest? Are those few thousand sheep, cutting highly erosive trails into the alpine slopes and pummeling the fragile turf and bawling day and night in the wilderness, really the best use to which this land might be put? In a nation where we subsidize sheep growers because there is an oversupply? We need sheep and sheep ranchers, surely. The world would be incomplete without them, as Muir said. But here? Do we really need them here?

8
The Summit

◁ ▷

WE followed the trail northward around the peak on which the sheep grazed, putting them out of sight and sound, passed a couple of tiny lakes in the Mistymoon drainage, and headed west, climbing until we found ourselves, as the fisherman had said we would, standing above the Paint Rock Creek valley, a broad, picturesque outwash, flat and green, marked by the winding channels into which the creek splits after it has tumbled out of its rocky bed below the southwest ridge of Cloud Peak, the only nontechnical route to its summit.

We climbed down the grassy ridge to a place where the slope flattened sufficiently to allow the pitching of a tent.

A single small clump of pines huddled a couple of hundred yards off, but several accidental boulders of red granite gave the illusion of shelter from the elements. We established camp, shed our packs, scrambled down a loose and gravelly cliff cut by spring floods, and set out across the outwash, a spongy bog, green with sedges and grasses, redolent with wildflowers and swarming with mosquitoes, wending our way through a sinuous maze of stream channels, narrow enough to leap, and around little pockets and kettles of water, pit traps unseeable until you were on top of them. Nowhere was the turf solid; it was like walking in one of those pens filled with plastic balls to amuse children at entertainment parks.

At the northern edge of the outwash we forded the rapidly running main channel of Paint Rock Creek on boulders and followed its bank up the drainage past a roaring waterfall. We switched our way up the wall of the little canyon and emerged in half a mile on a tiny tributary of the creek. This we traced northeastward up a broad slope, grassy, dotted with pools of clear water and the remnants of winter snows. We were ascending a series of ice-carved tables, the footprints of the largest of the glaciers that sculpted the Big Horns, a river of ice 1,500 feet thick. It was an enchanted place, sheltered in the rocky arms of the mountains, bathed in the cool sunlight of afternoon, green and quiet, an oasis of easy walking, of softness, in a citadel of stone.

Cloud Peak is the highest in the Big Horns, the tenth tallest in Wyoming. At 13,167 feet, it reaches a quarter of the distance into outer space. It is massive, squat and flat-peaked in relation to its height, a broad hulk of granite, hefty and muscular.

At the upper limit of the green tables, we faced a wide tan wall of rubble, a great pile of elephantine boulders that obliterated our view of the summit we aimed to achieve. The wall forms one of the mountain's four buttresses. They are like the sinews of a gargantuan arm, carved by three major glaciers and a lesser one. The remnant of one of the glaciers still lingers in the shadow of the mountain's east face. At the base of this drainage the size and character of the mountain, its peak still miles distant although we seemed to be at the heart of it, first became clear to us. We started up the rock pile, following a confusing array of ad hoc cairns; although the summit has been climbed thousands of times in the years since the first official assault in 1887, by W. S. Stanton of the U.S. Engineers, there is still no formal trail to it. Stanton, moreover, found the remains of an Indian medicine bivouac, a spiritual artifact, on the peak when he arrived, evidence of a human history long predating our own.

We were at the widest point on the ridge. To the north lay Wilderness Basin, a treeless and barren-looking bowl of rock dotted with frigid lakes, seldom visited even now; southward, the ridge plunged precipitously down sheer cliffs. We climbed and climbed, our route gradually taking us more eastward and less northward. The trek up these boulders is a journey of about two and a half miles, but its psychic distance is far longer. As we climbed, one steady foot ahead of the other, the journey became not a single assault on the mountain but, as it inevitably does, a sequence of thousands of journeys, each taken a second or two at a time. At this point, when a climb has become infinitely divisible, the magic of a mountaintop takes hold, the allure of the summit grabs you and pulls you into its embrace. Its beckoning is as irresistible as the pull of the magnetic field on the needle of a compass.

We were nearing the neck of the ridge, somewhere above twelve thousand feet, when trouble pounced. We were beginning, for one thing, to realize that we were climbing under false expectations, that we had already been on the trail for more than two hours and that the summit of the mountain was still beyond view; everything in the mountains is always a good deal farther off than it seems, a function of the extreme clarity of the light. I, for another thing, had begun to develop the symptoms of altitude sickness.

Altitude sickness results from oxygen deprivation. Its effects generally first show at altitudes above about eight thousand feet and are exacerbated by the strenuous exercise that inevitably accompanies excursions into the upper reaches of mountains. They include headache, nausea, dizziness, listlessness, loss of appetite, weakness, difficulty in concentrating, a diminished facility for mental work, and sometimes visual or auditory disturbances, among them vertigo.

Susceptibility to the disease varies for reasons not understood, sometimes paradoxical. Young men in the prime of health seem especially vulnerable, for example, but smokers may be less afflicted than nonsmokers. Several things about it are, however, clear. The higher you go, for one thing, the more pronounced the symptoms become and the greater the percentage of persons affected. And the faster you climb, the more likely you will be afflicted. A hiker who drives or flies to an altitude of ten thousand feet and begins to walk has a 20 percent chance, roughly, of being stricken, while the chance is 80 percent for a hiker who drives or flies to an altitude of fourteen thousand feet and then sets out. This is why every good guide to mountain climbing advises you to start at a moderate altitude, take some time to get acclimated, and proceed slowly to higher terrain. There also seems to be some connection between sleeping at high altitudes and susceptibility to illness. Day hikers who return every night to lower ground are seldom stricken. Bad sleep is common to those on high mountain journeys, and it is universal among persons susceptible to acute mountain sickness. You breathe more shallowly when asleep than when awake; the resulting sensation of oxygen deficiency awakens you repeatedly, no matter how tired you feel; you may also be visited by bizarre or unpleasant dreams. Another thing seems clear: Altitude sickness repeats itself. Once stricken, the chances are excellent that you will suffer again.

The symptoms are bearable, for me, at least, but the headaches can be violently painful. My head was beginning a familiar throb. I knew from experience that it would be with me for two or three days, no matter what I did.

While I was regretting the condition of my head, John's thoughts were focused on his alimentary canal. He said that he was having stomach cramps. He made the announcement matter-of-factly, without a hint of complaint. It is unlike him to complain, one of the things I like about hiking with him. The art of wilderness walking is the knack of adjusting your expectations to reality, of taking circumstances as they come. You enter the wilderness expecting to find the expansiveness of space, the intimacy of caverns, the solitude of rocks, the music of birds, the silence of stars, the fragrances of flowers, the depths of waters. And you do. But you also encounter fogs and mists, sudden rain showers, the whining of mosquitoes, the bites of flies, trails that disappear, rocks that stub your toes, the cloying heat of midday, the gnawing cold of midnight, lumpy beds, aching muscles. One gray morning you awaken unrested, pull on your stinking socks, find that the stove won't light, force yourself to eat a nauseating breakfast of cold instant oatmeal, which you remember now that you have always hated and can't imagine why you brought, and, surveying the skies, see that you are going to spend the day walking in a drizzle. This is the litmus test, the moment when you expect a good companion to say, without a hint of irony, "Well, ready whenever you are."

John admitted to stomach cramps, I to a bit of mountain sickness. We took some water as long as we were stopped anyway and went on, following the winding trail of rock cairns up the long southwest ridge of Cloud Peak, grateful for the uncharacteristic brilliance of the afternoon sky. Lightning is the most serious danger of nontechnical climbing, and there was no threat of it, so we had a realistic shot at the summit, despite the lateness of our start. In a few minutes we stopped again. John's cramps had turned into diarrhea. He disappeared among the boulders, lamenting the fact that we had forgotten to bring toilet paper. When he returned, he bore discomfort in his eyes, but he said nothing. We went on.

The ridge grew less steep, and the focus of our efforts now shifted from the long view behind us down the valley, which we could no longer see, to the summit, which had quite suddenly reappeared. John needed to stop again, and then we set out across the narrow neck of the ridge, a rubble of boulders ending abruptly on either edge in the sheer walls of two cirques, the bottoms of which we could not see. We passed over it and onto the desolate crown of the mountain. We were half a mile now from the summit, a few hundred feet away in elevation.

The route turned north. We climbed for another twenty minutes, stopped. We were nearing thirteen thousand feet, and the wind that perpetually blows around mountain summits was bitterly cold. John disappeared into the boulders off the trail again, and I put on a windproof jacket. It was hard for me to think of anything but my head, which ached everywhere to the touch and felt soft and swollen, like an enormous sponge. John returned. He was plainly in agony. We studied the summit. It looked so close that we might reach out and touch it, but we both knew that it was probably half an hour away. We looked at each other.

"What do you think?" he said.

We knew that we had to be down the mountain again by nightfall, that we were running now against time as well as our own bodies.

"No sense in killing ourselves," I said, reluctantly.

We lingered for a long time, the wind whispering in our ears, studying the summit, measuring our resolve against our good sense. Both of us knew what we were going to decide, but neither wanted to declare it. Finally John turned, without a word, and started slowly down the mountain.

Back on the neck of the ridge, we paused to catch our

breath. "Well," I said, "we as good as made it." John kept pointedly silent, refusing to dignify the rationalization with a reply.

We set out again, moving with every weary step against the force of the mountain. Back at camp, we gathered water for the morning and went to bed in the twilight without any supper. Neither of us fell into fitful sleep harboring any delusions, for the moment, at least, about being autonomous forces moving at will through the wilderness.

What could we do in the morning but try the summit again? It summoned us as powerfully as ever, and the day was bright and clear, just a bit cool, a perfect day for a climb. We were feeling our maladies still, but we were both on the mend, and we had all day to make the attempt. So off we set along the waterfall, through the canyon, up onto the great buttress of the mountain, across the bridge, around the snowfields, and over a million boulders—a mountain often seems on closer approach to be nothing more than an enormous pile of rocks—to the top.

The summit of Cloud Peak is rather flat, sagging at its center, about two hundred yards wide from east to west, and slopes gently to the north. It is often, as its name implies, enshrouded in clouds, but on that cloudless day we could see the northern half of Wyoming: to the west the wide, dry bowl of the Big Horn Basin and beyond it the snowy peaks of the Absarokas, and to the east the rugged, empty red-brown expanse of the Great Plains, fading into the haze.

It was as if we were suspended in midair, floating some-

how high above the planet. There seemed no solid connection between the rubble of rock upon which our feet
were planted and the living skin of the earth stretching
away before us, so distant, so mute, to the ends of the
horizon. The wind scratched at our eardrums and clawed
at our exposed skin as we stood in midsummer amid piles
of unmelted snow and glinting plates of ice. A mountaintop is not simply an elevation, but an island, a world
within a world, a place out of place. It has what Colin
Fletcher has called "the self-assurance of diamond
beauty."

Snow, ice, rock, wind. The mountaintop spoke in
terms of hardness, of coldness, of sharp, clean austerity.
No lyricism sounded; there was no embroidery, no embel-
lishment, nothing frivolous, nothing understated. Just this
frank, lofty, elemental simplicity: bold, defiant, perhaps
even arrogant; the irreducible and lifeless residue of the
world making a last stand against the vast surrounding
blue void.

But there was also life and a vision of beauty.

Already black lichens had found anchor among the
rocks, engaging life in its long, heroic battle against the
forces of barrenness. While we stood there, a fly buzzed
past, carried perhaps on the winds, as whole clouds of
grasshoppers sometimes are (a climber in 1936 reported
seeing grasshoppers near the Cloud Peak summit by the
thousands, melting out of a wind-packed drift of snow).
But what brought the ladybug to the base of the cairn
marking the summit and how long could it possibly survive in such a place? (Ladybugs, despite their dainty
name, have unrefined habits. "If I were to eat as the delicate ladybug eats," Annie Dillard remarked, "I would go

113

through in just nine days the entire population of Boys Town.") And how did the pika whistling at us from the center of the summit plateau make its living? Pikas do not hibernate, and they live exclusively on vegetation, which they industriously gather in summer into gnome-sized haystacks. It was hard to imagine how there could be the makings of even a single hay pile out of the paltry spikes of vegetation growing in the protected crannies of that summit. Even if it had gathered enough food for the winter, how did it survive the 200-mile-an-hour blasts of the winter winds? But there it was, whistling at us and scurrying away and whistling again as if it had nothing better to do in the rare afternoon sunshine than to play hide-and-seek with a pair of hopelessly outmatched visitors.

We approached the eastern edge of the mountain, almost as sharp and sheer still as it was on the late ice-age morning when the glacier began to slide down the mountain toward the plains. Peering over the edge, we saw, far below, the remnant glacier that still hides in the shadow of the cliff, a fan of white ice shaped like a scallop shell, its melt-lines delicately and regularly etched and filled with darker debris from the winter snows so that they looked from on high like the ribs of a seashell; and flowing from beneath the sheet of ice a tan fall of water, which entered a turquoise lake and fell from there into an aquamarine lake, and from there into a chain of lesser, sky-blue lakes. It was like looking down into a mountain-sized jewel box.

Then we did what one ritually does on a summit. We ate lunch. The truth is that however much you may need the calories, you are not really very hungry on a mountaintop. Altitude and excitement both kill appetites. But eating together is one of two ways in which we consummate shared experiences—the other, of course, is sex. And so on a mountaintop one makes a meal and, in consuming it, acknowledges the basic needs we share with all living things, however humble or exalted. Anyone even remotely reflective on a mountaintop, at the outer edge of earthly life, must feel with new intensity how we are bound by the common thread of life itself, a thread invisible most of the time, but somehow in high places made plain.

We ate together on the very peak of the mountain and then took our leave of it, pausing one last time on the way down for a last glimpse to remember it by. From the place where we paused, the summit cairn looked already remote and cold. The peak had released its claim on us.

How characteristic, I thought, when we had resumed our descent, that the Absaroka Indians had left there in that high place an altar and the U.S. Engineers, beneath a pile of rocks, a cache of coins. The coins were still there, I imagined, buried in the rubble, corroding slowly into dust.

9

Wilderness Basin:
THE ROBIN
◁ ▷

FROM the air, Wilderness Basin looks as if it had been bitten out of the Big Horns, one gigantic chomp taken by some earth-eating behemoth. It lies at the heart of the wilderness, protected both to the north and the south by rugged ridges, trailless, inaccessible to horses. It is very high; all of it lies above ten thousand feet in elevation. Mostly it is treeless. There are few places in it to camp; the ground tends to be either rocky or boggy. Consequently, it is seldom visited, so seldom, in fact, that it remains one of the places in the lower forty-eight states where the major geologic features—the lakes, the streams, the long waterfalls—have yet to be named. It is not a place you chance upon. Either you intend to go there or you will not find it.

Base camp: a green shelf a story above a narrow lake. Several stunted white-barked pines sheltered us against the winds. We pitched our orange tent upon a carpet of pine needles. Near its door stood a small, nearly flat rock, our kitchen and dining table. To the north, the lake, shallow except along the serpentine channel of the stream running through it; it was actually less a lake than a widening of the stream. Its water was ice cold and clear as air. Across the lake, another stand of pines, and then eighty towering stories of granite. To the south, three or four square yards of alpine meadow, an animal trail, another rock wall seventy-five stories high. To the east and west, waterfalls, tumbling from and leading into lakes.

On our ledge we could watch the trout emerging from the shadows of submerged rocks, gliding along the brown-green bottom, suddenly bursting upward to snatch hatching insects, invisible to us, on the surface. There is some evidence that trout, which have a rather good sense of smell, can catch the scent of their tiny prey. Perhaps they can also hear them. Trout perceive underwater sounds acutely through a series of sonar sensors along their lateral lines, and the nymphs on which they prey pop when they hatch, sometimes loudly enough so that the sound is audible to human ears. The source of the popping noise is the little gas bubble that forms in the nymphal sack just prior to hatching. It serves as a balloon to aid the nymph to the water's surface, and when it explodes there, it also helps the nymph to emerge from its birth chamber.

In the pristine waters of high mountain lakes, you can

see the trout as clearly as if they were swimming in an aquarium. The trout feeding in the lake below our tent site, we could see, were members of a species new to us, *Salmo agua-bonito,* beautiful-water trout, commonly known as golden trout. Once the species was found only in the headwaters of the South Fork of the Kern River in the Sierra Nevadas, to which it was limited by high and inaccessible waterfalls. It has since been transplanted into other streams, but it is still something of a rarity, a creature of very pure, very high mountain pools and rapids. It is among the most beautiful of freshwater fishes, tropical in the brilliance of its coloring: a speckled green along its back, scarlet in its gills and along its lateral lines, splashed with brick red on its belly, which is the color of aspen leaves in autumn, or, as outdoorsman Stewart Edward White, who first saw the fish in its original habitat in 1903, said, the color of "the twenty-dollar gold-piece, the same satin finish, the same gold yellow." "One would almost expect," he said, "that on cutting the flesh it would be found golden through all its substance." It darts through the water like a liquid rainbow.

We were at timberline. On the next step up the glacial staircase, thickets of dwarf willows grew, and above that only grasses, sedges, mosses, and ground-hugging forbs. In terms of latitude, we were at the equivalent of Hudson's Bay. We were soon to be forcefully reminded of this.

John had caught a pair of trout for supper and was thinking of cleaning them when a chill rain began to fall. We hustled into rain gear and had no sooner donned it than the hail came, thick as snow, marble-sized. (These measurements are, so far as I know, standard in hail country: pea-sized, marble-sized, golf-ball-sized, baseball-sized.)

The stones felt as hard as marbles, hurled as they were out of violent clouds and free-falling thousands of feet onto our thin-skinned bodies. One whacked against my forehead, sending tremors through my skull. "Shit!" I said, and then, as if I were still a little boy, I got a good stiff smack for it against a bone in the back of my hand. Above the blasts of the wintry wind I could hear John cursing too as both of us scrambled in opposite directions toward shelter beneath the paltry pines. There we perched like a pair of bedraggled grouse while the hailstones piled up around us. The ice storm, mercifully, did not last long, but the winds continued to gust out of the west, thick with a fine mist of rain.

We schemed to wait the weather out, but it had more energy than we. Eventually John emerged from his tree cave and took the trout down to the edge of the lake to clean them. I, in the meantime, hauled the tiny stove out of a soggy pack, set it up in the shelter of our dining rock, and anxiously nursed it. It sputtered and moaned in the wind but caught hold, the throbbing of its flame making a cheerful roar. John returned with the fillets. "It's so cold," he said, "that that lake water actually feels warm." I fried the fish in a little butter. They curled in the pan, as if they were still capable of fleeing from the heat. We ate them, every tender, succulent flake, under a steady drizzle, our backs turned to the wind, while we stomped our soaked and stiffening feet to warm them. At a fish apiece we dined modestly. Stewart Edward White reported that he and his two companions sat down, the first time they fished for them, to a supper of sixty-five golden trout.

The rain failed to thaw the hailstones, hot chocolate failed to thaw us, and the thick, black storm clouds had imposed an early dusk. We were content to retreat to our sleeping bags. Rain pattered against the tent, billowing and sagging in the gale, but we were warm and cozy and free as the wind. We could not be summoned from anywhere by anybody; not another soul on earth knew where to find us. (My wife, of course, knows the general outlines of these trips: Where I will enter a wilderness and when, how long I expect to be out of communication, and where I plan to end a walk. But beyond this, it is usually impossible to be very specific. She has never thought of coming, with her own enthusiasm for the out-of-doors ending at approximately the last sociable campfire. A week or two of solitude is not her idea of a great time. She sometimes worries, is sometimes faintly bemused, but in general she regards my need to disappear from time to time into some trackless place as an eccentric and incurable disorder, quite manageable between eruptions and therefore tolerable, if mildly unfortunate. It doesn't cost much money to undertake this sort of journey; there are very few boutiques along the way. So the only serious expense is in time, which I, as a freelance writer, have to spend, particularly since I can usually wrangle a magazine assignment at some point along the way or turn some experience en route to the purposes of an essay.) Nothing demanded doing, nothing remained unattended. Our sole obligation, at that moment, was to abandon ourselves to the blustery night. We did so feeling wealthy in everything we had to spend: those dark and secure hours and the whole range of our half-awake imaginings.

In the morning the sun arrived to pay a long visit. It seemed more than fortuitous, beyond the normal course of events, a gift, like a yellow rose in the breadbox. That the mountain did not stand in the way of the sun seemed somehow a concession on its part; and the mountain never makes concessions. It is unforgiving, unyielding, not in the least considerate. It does not care whether you come or go, prosper or fail, find your way or lose it. To the mountain, it is all the same; you respect it or wish later that you had. Either way, the mountain says. Have it as you wish. But in the end it always prevails.

The sun beamed down upon us, seeming benevolent, but the robin nesting in the pine tree just beyond our tent door was furious at the intrusion and voiced its opinion loudly before retreating a discreet distance to await happier developments. Our immediate and permanent departure, preferably.

The robin! Like the story someone is forever telling about bumping into the mailman in a back alley in Budapest or sitting down at a table in the only restaurant in Urubamba and seeing the cousin who hasn't been heard from in twenty years at the table directly opposite, deep in conversation with the Homecoming Queen of 1952, and neither of them looking a day older. A backyard robin, ho-hum. Bob-bob-bobbing along.

Unfair, I know. The robin has become commonplace, adapted to a virtuosic range of habitats, from coast to coast, from sea level to twelve thousand feet or so in elevation, from city streets to remote wilderness regions. But it was not always so. At the advent of European settlement the robin occurred in much smaller numbers and in much more localized populations than it does today. It is by its nature a creature of edges. It prefers to nest in trees, although it will settle for almost any aboveground structure: There is a report in the bird literature of a robin successfully nesting on the boom of a construction crane, even though it was in regular use at the time. The robin, on the other hand, favors relatively open country. So it once routinely avoided vast areas of the continent, the extensive prairies of the midcontinent, and the interior regions of the dense eastern forests in particular.

Robins have suffered serious setbacks since then. In the nineteenth century they were profligately hunted, particularly in the South, as were meadowlarks, bobolinks, and passenger pigeons, among others. No less an authority than James Audubon pronounced them "fat and juicy . . . excellent eating." The toll was so heavy that, at the turn of the century, robins seemed destined to become a rare, if not extinct, species. Not until 1913 did they, and other songbirds, come under protection of the U.S. Migratory Bird Act, and it took years to establish effective enforcement of the law. The ultimately unsuccessful war against Dutch elm disease, fought for a long time with DDT, an extraordinarily powerful and persistent pesticide, also incidentally resulted in an extravagant slaughter, not only of robins and other birds but also of the scavengers of their carcasses. And robins have been subjected to chemical barrages of a more localized sort: A single application of Azodrin to combat potato aphids in Dade County, Florida, in 1972, for example, killed ten thousand migrating robins in three days. Until 1973 blueberry growers in New Brunswick, Canada, to take another example, waged aggressive battle against robins—which happen to be prodigious harvesters of insect pests—until they were brought up short by an equally aggressive public opinion campaign.

Still, on the whole, robins have thrived and prospered,

and in the last couple of centuries they have become nearly ubiquitous in North America. This can be read as a triumph of adaptability, and, indeed, it has been. The most extreme statement of the case, I think, is this one, from the book, *The American Robin,* by Len Eiserer:

> . . . the Robin's many successes in extending its range over precolonial times offer a marked contrast to the achievements of most other native North American populations. Consider, for example, the Indian. With the coming of white civilization, both the American Robin and the American Indian watched the wholesale loss of a great primeval way of life. But it might be suggested (albeit with over-simplification) that while one group compromised, adapted, and consequently prospered, the other group resisted, clung to the old, and was largely destroyed.

Aside from the inherent racism of this incredible statement (there was a Migratory Bird Act, it might be noted, but never, when it would have mattered, a Native American Protection Act), and aside from a certain self-hatred—a willingness to celebrate any circumstance in which another species is perceived as having bested humans, a dangerous and counterproductive strain of environmentalism—this statement follows a trivial and falsely comforting line of reasoning. There is, in fact, little evidence that the robin's success has been due to its adaptability. Rather, the continent itself has been altered on a large scale in ways that replicate conditions the robin already favored before settlement. As the eastern forests have been cleared or thinned, and as the prairies have been plowed and domesticated, the robin's natural range has been vastly extended. The landscape, not the robin, has changed. I doubt whether this is a triumph for nature, even though it has promoted the prosperity of one particular species of bird. On the contrary, it is one more reason to doubt the efficacy of our management of the biosphere.

We now perceive the homogenization of urban America as a truism. The pervasive influence of the mass media of communications and the concentration of economic power have helped to create a society in which many local, or even regional, distinctions have vanished. We all watch the same television programs, read essentially the same newspapers, shop in the same national stores, live in the same houses, and subscribe, mostly, to the same middle-of-the-road politics and philosophy of life. A person crossing the country from one airport or commercial strip or housing development to the next has only the local road signs and certain peculiarities of flora—if there are palm trees in the boulevards, it can't be Ohio—as reliable visual clues to place. This monotony of physical detail has, perhaps, promoted social stability and a certain kind of economic efficiency. But we often rightly wonder what strengths of culture, what resiliency, we have sacrificed in adopting such bland uniformity.

Less often remarked is the phenomenon the robin represents, the parallel homogenization of the natural landscape. As we have drained the swamps and marshes, leveled the forests, farmed the prairies, and diverted the waters of the western rivers for the greening of the deserts, we have done something more pervasive than simply de-

124

stroying a multitude of local habitats. Not only have we undermined the framework for biological diversity, but we have, sometimes deliberately, sometimes unintentionally, substituted look-alike ecosystems for regionally distinctive ones.

In my prairie town, the upland sandpipers and the bobolinks are mostly gone and the meadowlarks become rarer every year, but I now see plenty of robins and eastern bluebirds. White pelicans no longer nest there, but wood ducks do, in artificial nests. The gray wolf is extinct, but the coyote has moved east to replace it. The only elk I have ever seen at home was an escapee from a game farm, but I see white-tailed deer, a woodlands animal, almost every time I go for a walk. The otter has disappeared, but there are plenty of beaver in that formerly treeless landscape. As I write, they are busy cutting down the crabapple trees in the city park near my house. I have no chance of seeing a pronghorn antelope anymore, but opossums are plentiful. Most prairie children do not now encounter any of the magnificent large mammals of their place—the grizzlies, the elk, the antelopes, the bison—until they take a trip to one of the sanctuaries of the intermountain west, to Yellowstone National Park, for example. Their own biological heritage no longer exists at home.

That heritage has so thoroughly vanished, in fact, that it no longer survives even in memory. A few years ago the biology department at the community college in my town set out to turn a vacant corner of the campus into a nature study area. The first step: some magnificent native cottonwood trees were razed and replaced with a planting of Colorado blue spruces! I was furious, but I also found the whole project screamingly funny. I soon learned it was a joke you couldn't share in my town. You always had to explain the punch line. "Well, you see, the cottonwood is natural here, and the blue spruce isn't, and this is a *nature* study area. . . ." The prairie, I discovered, is an arcane subject in my prairie town.

The robin flew angrily from its pine tree next to our tent and perched nearby on a rock in the shadow of a shrubby cinquefoil bush, one of the Potentillas.

We know the Potentillas quite well, of course, in Worthington, Minnesota. A third of the foundation plantings and rock gardens here, I would guess, contain species of Potentilla. Spruces, Douglas firs, mountain ashes, cedars: These we also know well. The nurseries routinely stock them. But suppose you wanted to plant a tree or shrub native to the region. Suppose you wanted a bur oak or a basswood or a hackberry, a chokecherry or a buffalo berry. In that case, you had better think again. There is no ready commercial stock of such species. The same goes for the grasses. We have lots of grass in that former grassland: corn, Kentucky bluegrass, Bermuda grass, lovingly tended, tended to an obsession, sprayed and manicured, raked and fertilized, watered and weeded. Our little prairie lake is choking to death on the chemical residues of our zeal. A good man in Worthington is thrice married: to his wife, to his job, and to his lawn. But big bluestem, or Indian grass, or prairie dropseed? Our affection for grasses stops well short of native species. Of the 400,000 acres in our county, about forty support remnants of the presettlement vegetation.

The point, though, is not that we have radically altered our world, which is not news, but that we have homogenized it. A backyard in Worthington, Minnesota, is no

126

longer distinguishable from one in New Haven, Connecticut, or Great Falls, Montana, or Bend, Oregon. We plant the same trees, tend the same grasses, nurture the same flowers, play host to the same birds. Our backyards have become as regular and predictable as our McDonalds. We have industrialized nature.

From time to time we get some inkling of the folly of our conformity. Every boulevard in Worthington for seventy-five years was planted in American elms. And what an enchanting cityscape they made! We have almost forgotten those graceful tall trees, arching until their crowns met high over sun-dappled streets. Then Dutch elm disease struck and within a decade, our town was naked again, as it was in the beginning. We cut down the arching elms, hauled them to a landfill on the edge of town, burned them, dug out the stumps, and started all over. We planted maples. Do we really doubt that in another seventy-five years we will be battling maple disease? What is it that causes us so passionately to believe that one kind of anything is sufficient?

But that is not exactly what I had in mind either. The point that lies forgotten underneath all of this is that, in industrializing nature, we have squandered our claim to place.

Bruce Chatwin has recently written a provocative novel called *Songlines* about an encounter with the Australian aborigines. The aborigines are, of course, nomads in a land as spare and parsimonious as any upon the habited earth, and so they are obliged to be almost constantly on the move across vast stretches of desert, vast particularly if you consider that they move on foot, carrying all that they possess. They come to know an area of hundreds

127

of square miles down to its minutest detail, every water-hole, every patch of vegetation, every animal lair, and they never lose their way. How do they do it? They have no written language, make no notes, carry no maps. How do they memorize it all and keep it in the memory? The answer is that they sing the landscape. Every landmark in the territory has its own verse, a snatch of melody, a fragment of poetry, and the sum of an aborigine's territory is the accumulation, in sequence, of its songs, its *songline.* Chatwin writes, "Richard Lee calculated that a Bushman child will be carried a distance of 4,900 miles before he begins to walk on his own. Since, during this rhythmic phase, he will be forever naming the contents of his territory, it is impossible he will not become a poet."

Chatwin's point is that we are born, like the Australian aborigines, to wander. He believes the nomadic life is the natural way. I think he is wrong. The real meaning of his story is that even wanderers have found, sometimes with awesome vision and beauty, as in this case, how to make for themselves a place in the world. And his story means, further, that the deepest and most satisfying sense of place comes from the keenest appreciation of its multifold distinctions. When the uniqueness of a place sings to us like a melody, then we will know, at last, what it means to be at home.

But how shall a place sing to us like a melody if we have already rendered it monotonal?

We have lots of utilitarian answers to the question "Why must there be wild places?" But the most important answer is not utilitarian. It is wildly, hopelessly unscientific. It is that except by the measure of wildness, we shall never really know the nature of a place, and without a sense of place we shall never really make a poem, and without a poem we shall never be fully human.

I was disappointed when I crawled from a tent into the bright sunlight of a new morning in the Wilderness Basin of the Big Horn Mountains and encountered a scolding robin whose territory had been invaded. It was not the robin itself that disappointed me, nor the scolding. Both were entirely appropriate to the place and the circumstance. I was disappointed in us for making a world so full of robins that when we finally meet one in its own place, our first thought is that it must be out of place; so many robins at the expense of so many other birds; an embarrassment of robins, which is how a robin, like anything else, begins to be undervalued. It would be better for the world and for robins, I thought, if there were still places in it inhospitable to them.

At the same time, I was annoyed at myself for being disappointed. The truth is, I was also disappointed in the robin for its ordinariness. I went into the wilderness hoping for something more exotic than an engagement with a screaming robin.

When I visited New York for the first time as a young man, I wanted above everything else to see a Broadway play. I didn't much care what the play was or who the players were. It was the experience of being present on Broadway that I was after. I visited a scalper the afternoon I arrived in town. "I want something, anything on Broadway," I said. "Tonight." I was sold a ticket, an excellent seat, to a performance of *A Delicate Balance* by Edward Albee. I no longer remember the name of the theater, but I do remember the price of the ticket, forty-five dollars, which happened to be equal to the sum I was then paying for a month's rent in a student hovel in Minneapolis. And I remember how disappointed I was. Not that it wasn't an engaging play. It was. And not that I didn't find the performance satisfying in every way. I did. I was disappointed because the stars were Hume Cronyn and Jessica Tandy, whom I had already seen on the stage at the Guthrie Theater in Minneapolis. Something I had already seen: How could that be so special?

A robin, I thought. So what?

The robin flew back to the pine tree and stood on a branch scolding me. "Dumb! Dumb!" it seemed to be saying. That, at any rate, was what I heard.

10

Wilderness Basin:
THE OUZEL

◁ ▷

ONE bird that remains splendidly true to place is the water ouzel. Robin-sized, wren-shaped, slate-colored, a chubby bird with a stubby tail, it is, until you see it in action, rather nondescript (*ouzel* derives from the Old English word for blackbird), distinctive in appearance only because of its flashing white eyelid. Perched on a rocky ledge along a crashing mountain stream, the only place you are likely to find it, it is next to invisible.

Its celebrated voice, however, is anything but retiring; on a calm night it can sometimes be heard for a mile. It sings the year around, one of the few birds to do so, in high, clear, fluted tones, lending support to the generalization that the plainest-looking birds sing most sweetly. Its song often leans on long repetitions of a single note, but it is also gifted at improvisation and imitation. Naturalist Edwin Way Teale heard one singing "like the music of the stream." It reminded him, as it has many others, of the mockingbird; then he thought of the song of the brown thrasher; then of the catbird. No, he thought, it reminded him of an oriole. Then he heard intimations of a warbling vireo. Finally, he said, it seemed to him that the ouzel's song was like none of these; it was simply, and incomparably, original. Its inventive evening song puzzled and confused me for several days. I searched the pines in vain for a glimpse of the source of the glorious music that cascaded down upon us every nightfall, never suspecting that it came from the plain bird at the water's edge.

And a water ouzel in motion—there is a sight to see! On solid ground it bobs and bows, a fat gray ball of twittering energy. The twittering is something of a puzzle. It is a habit among many water birds. Two explanations have been advanced, neither conclusively. One possibility is that, given the steady din of the rapid streams these birds frequent, even the clarion song of an ouzel can be difficult to hear; perhaps the bobbing is some form of non-oral communication. Another possibility is that twittering is a strategy for remaining inconspicuous; perhaps the ouzels, and other water birds, have learned to match water motion with body motion. For whatever reason, the ouzel twitters, and then suddenly it lifts from the ledge on which it has been genuflecting and plunges like a kamikaze straight down into the roily waters of the stream and disappears into the froth. You can't believe your eyes. You wait an impossible minute, and then, *upstream*, it bursts out of the water again with a single violent shake of its feathers and lands on its ledge, as if nothing extraordinary had happened.

You know that the current of the stream surges with power. Even at ankle depth, you have felt it threatening to sweep your feet out from under you. And you know that the water is breathtakingly cold. It is just barely liquid. Yesterday it was ice or snow. And you know that the bird, a seemingly ordinary bird, has not only been down under swimming against the current but hunting all the while. It has been catching insects or little water invertebrates or fish fry. It is well adapted for this adventure. It has an unusually large oil gland for keeping its feathers waterproofed, and skin flaps to cover its nostrils when it is submerged, and an extra layer of down next to its skin to keep it warm. When it dives, its heart rate slows by more than half, and the store of oxygen in its blood increases. It has not developed webbed feet, but it does have strong legs, and it has learned how to walk with its head down and its tail end raised, employing the current to counteract its natural buoyancy. Underwater, it uses its half-raised wings to stabilize itself and to propel itself forward. Now it perches on a rock, a bird in Cinderella plumage, passing the time of day. *Zeet, Zeet, Zeet,* it sings. *Zeet, Zeet, Zeet.*

You laugh. You laugh as you laugh with joy for the Chinese acrobat who has just climbed a pair of unsupported parallel ladders balancing a tray pyramided with goblets full of wine on a mouthstick while juggling four white rings. You laugh in disbelief.

As if it hears you, the water ouzel dives again, climbs out of the water upstream, lands on a boulder in the

133

rapids, and preens itself nonchalantly in the spray. You applaud spontaneously and, spooked, it flies over the waterfall and out of sight. You could watch such a bird forever.

The water ouzel was John Muir's favorite bird. He wrote about it in *The Mountains of California* in a passage as unabashedly partisan and adoring as any in the literature of American birds:

> . . . the Ouzel sings on through all the seasons and every kind of storm. Indeed no storm can be more violent than those of the waterfalls in the midst of which he delights to dwell. However dark and boisterous the weather, snowing, blowing, or cloudy, all the same he sings, and never with a note of sadness. No need of spring sunshine to thaw *his* song, for it never freezes. Never shall you hear anything wintry from *his* warm breast; no pinched cheeping, no wavering notes between sorrow and joy; his mellow, fluty voice is ever tuned to downright gladness, as free from dejection as cock-crowing.

Contrast the poor robins Muir observed in the Yosemites in a winter storm:

> I found most of the robins cowering on the lee side of the larger branches where the snow could not fall upon them, while two or three of the more enterprising were making desperate efforts to reach the mistletoe berries by clinging nervously to the under side of the snow-crowned masses, back downward, like woodpeckers. Every now and then they would dis-

lodge some of the loose fringes of the snow-crown, which would come sifting down on them and send them screaming back to camp, where they would subside among their companions with a shiver, muttering in low, querulous chatter like hungry children.

It was, Muir reported, the same story for the sparrows, the nuthatches, the Steller's jays, the woodpeckers, and a solitary gray eagle. Every bird endured the storm in some degree of observable discomfort, save the water ouzel, "who could no more help exhaling sweet song than a rose sweet fragrance."

Birds, of course, do not sing for joy or chatter like hungry children, except, perhaps, in picture books for preschoolers. Let us say that joy is a cultural, not a biological, condition and that it is, therefore, improper to ascribe the emotion to a water ouzel. Even so, we would be right to say that our own reaction to the water ouzel, or John Muir's, is capable of teaching us something about the nature of our own joy. Why, we might ask, does the water ouzel seem joyful to *us*? Never mind whether the bird itself is in fact joyful.

Muir answers that the ouzel seems joyful because it sings in the face of adversity. *To sing in the face of adversity.* That is not a bad definition of joy. It implicitly recognizes the kinship of fear or pain and joy. Kierkegaard, with the same connection in mind, once defined humor as "the joy that overcomes the world."

Joy is a puzzling emotion, little examined from a biological point of view, perhaps because we suspect Stendahl to have been right when he said "To describe happiness is to diminish it." But it seems clear enough that it is, like other emotions, a reaction, that it does not spring to life by spontaneous generation but in response to some sort of release. To be joyful is to be relieved, to be sprung free from anxiety. It then follows that absent real anxiety, neither can there be any real joy.

There is a modest and tentative suggestion in the biological literature of a physical basis for this perception. Stanley Schachter of Columbia University injected subjects with the hormone epinephrine, which is naturally secreted under stress. His subjects responded either joyfully or angrily, depending upon the angry or joyful behavior of a companion. But this is only one experiment with a variety of possible readings.

There are, certainly, plenty of intuitive arguments in the same direction. To stick with the biological possibility for a moment longer, we know of the addictive pleasure of strenuous exercise—of jogging, for example. Runners continue to run—it sometimes seems to us nonrunners helplessly, compulsively—not only because the practice fulfills some need for competition, or because it is ultimately satisfying to have a strong and lean body, or because these are people in search of the Fountain of Youth, but also, perhaps primarily, because they feel *joyful* for having done it. And, it turns out, the same stress hormone, epinephrine, is involved; jogging stimulates its secretion, just as fear does. The pain of running, quite literally, produces the joy of having run. For the same reason, everyone who has done a hard day's physical labor has experienced at the end of it the same blissful sense of serene elation.

It is difficult to think of any moment of real joy that does not come after some incident of physical or emo-

tional stress, whether it be so simple as the successful com-
pletion of a test or so complex as the birth of a child. I do
not mean the basic sense of well-being and security that
every person hopes for in ordinary, day-to-day life. I mean
the occasional feeling of intense happiness that sometimes
visits a person, the sort of feeling that might provoke
tears. It does not seem incidental that we normally cry
only when we are, as we say, unbearably happy or else
when we are profoundly sad. "Weeping may endure for a
night," the psalmist says, "but joy cometh in the morning." This is not merely a statement of contrasts but a
linkage of events intimately related, of a cause and an
effect: Weeping endures for a night; *therefore* joy comes in
the morning.

This suggests one kind of explanation for the spiritual
joy so often ascribed to the wilderness experience. Every
important religious prophet has spent a sojourn in the wilderness and has found there some source of strength important to subsequent belief. What is this source? It is, I
would suppose, the product of having successfully faced
danger and deprivation, of having, in Kierkegaard's
phrase, overcome the world: It is joy.

In cultures that have valued visions, the connection between what I might call ecstatic insight and deprivation
has often been ritualistically cultivated. For example, the
hunters who left behind the medicine bivouac on Cloud
Peak's summit, the Crows, shared with many Plains Indian peoples a belief in the power of spiritual visions to
shape life. A Crow child—I am relying here on the account of anthropologist Robert H. Lowie—grew up under
the influence of the assumption that every success in life
flowed from visions. Boys in particular, although women

also invoked them, were encouraged from an early age—perhaps in some cultures from the age of six or seven—to seek guiding visions for their own lives and for their communities.

Sometimes visions simply visited you wherever you happened to be, out of divine solicitude. But normally a vision had to be sought. You did so by going to a solitary place to fast and pray for four days, either for a general vision or for some specific outcome—the health of a child, for instance, or victory in battle. You suffered, a spirit took pity upon you, and you were delivered of a sign. Among the Crows, you frequently cut off a finger joint of the left hand or mortified your flesh in some other way to attract the sympathy of the spirits. And when, customarily on the fourth day, you saw or heard a sign, you returned to the village, gave an account of it, as you might of a dream, aided in your telling by accounts you had heard of the visions of others, and tried thereafter to live in harmony with what you had seen and heard.

Among certain Dakota nations, this practice reached its extreme in the Sun Dance, a ritual in which young men, after elaborate ceremonies and preparations involving the whole village, were hung from poles on skewers inserted through the skin of the breast and the back. After three increasingly ecstatic dances, the men began to struggle to tear themselves free, an effort that might last well into the night. The greatest honor redounded to those who tore themselves down unassisted, but even those who fainted and had to be extricated by friends had gained considerable stature in the community. When the last man was freed, the Sun Dance was pronounced complete, and there was great rejoicing.

The assumptions of the vision quest or of the Sun Dance may seem so radically at odds with those of our own culture as to preclude comparison, but I think the differences are not so great. Millions of Westerners, after all, including me, regularly partake of a sacrament in which wafers of bread and vials of wine or grape juice, said to be either the actual body and blood of a man who lived two thousand years ago or representations of it, are consumed in the belief that this human sacrifice offers the promise of absolution and eternal life. In both instances the central principles are the same: that there is a higher spiritual power, that it can be invoked by sacrifice, and that its benefits accrue to those who believe.

There are, however, two notable differences. First, native Americans offered themselves personally as sacrifices, while we accept the sacrifice of a substitute. Although there were those to whom no vision ever came, and although there were, therefore, arrangements for buying the benefits of a vision from another, the only honorable course was first to seek your own vision and only when that had failed to purchase into the vision of another. Second, the native American sought a vision in solitude; excepting our prophets, our own searches for spiritual wisdom are characteristically conducted communally.

Royal B. Hassrick, a student of the Dakotas, makes an odd remark about their vision quests. Aware, he says, "that their very existence was dependent upon the natural environment, they sought to gain rapport to an extent that was almost compulsive. Once having accepted the proposition that they stood alone amid the universe, different from the plants and animals and subject to the buf-

139

fetings of physical forces, they seem to have been driven to fit themselves intellectually into its realms." What seems to me odd about this remark is its implication that the Dakotas in particular, and native Americans in general, were unusual, both in their dependency upon the natural environment and in their desire to find, intellectually, a place in nature. It seems to me that this is the universal human condition and that we are all, in one way or another, "almost compulsive," "driven," by the same need to make sense of our standing in the world.

But we will not come to any deep understanding of our place in nature except as we delve into its basic documents, and these documents are our wild places. Decimating a natural environment is, in this sense, exactly like burning all the copies of some book essential to the history of our culture. And when we destroy some entire ecosystem, as we have nearly done with our prairies, for example, it is like eliminating whole sections of our libraries.

Learning is one property that simply must be acquired individually. It cannot be bought or sold on the marketplace, or exercised by proxy, or transferred from one life into another by last testament. Either you have acquired it for yourself at considerable trouble and pain and time, or you will not have it. (It is because it comes at such a dear price that it yields, ultimately, so much joy.) And a sense of one's standing in the natural world is not instinctive, not automatic, and only in the most general way culturally transmitted. In any usable degree it is, like all learning, a personal acquisition, arrived at only by becoming acquainted with the basic texts, with wild places. The Plains Indians, who lived in an essentially wild world and whose existence depended directly upon an intricate and everyday knowledge of nature, nevertheless understood that the deepest communications with the natural world required intensive and solitary concentration and provided routinely for it in their rituals.

We, on the other hand, live out our lives, for the most part, at great distance from wildness. We may still have a keen intellectual sense of the interconnectedness of life in all its forms, and we certainly cannot shed the interior longing to understand this interconnectedness. But the circumstances of our lives keep us apart from the basic texts of nature and rarely provide for real solitude; our spiritual texts are too often interpreted in ways that accent these disconnections. When we grow aware of this, we begin to feel one of the deepest of all human sadnesses, the sadness of standing alone.

One day on a vacation we walk into a wilderness, our muscles singing with disuse, our systems chemically charged with the hormones of happiness, and we come quietly to a place where a stream crashes down a mountainside. The sun shines sweetly or a cold rain barbed with sleet begins to fall, it does not matter which. We lay down our burdens and sit upon the rocks, and from some nearby ledge at the verge of a waterfall the clear, flutelike song of an ouzel sounds, a strange and rare melody. That bird sounds *happy*, we think. In our hearts we begin to sing the same joyous song. We have come, as poet and essayist Wendell Berry has written, "into the peace of wild things/who do not tax their lives with forethought/of grief."

Perhaps the bird is not happy. Perhaps it is utterly incapable of a sense of joy. But we are happy, and the bird has made us so. Anthropomorphic it may be, but it is also wildly, exquisitely human, and always will be, and can never be any other way.

11

Wilderness Basin:
BARRENNESS
◁ ▷

I was taken by surprise the first time I walked into the Sonoran Desert. My only previous encounter with a desert had been along the coast near Lima, Peru, one of the hottest and driest and most barren places on earth. It did nothing to disabuse me of my middlewestern notion of deserts as blazing heaps of inert sand uninhabited except by great coils of writhing, venomous snakes. (True, I never saw a snake in Peru, but that did not shake my nervous conviction that they were everywhere and ever on the prowl for just such a poor lump of flesh as me.) I expected more of the same in the Sonoran Desert, which I

142

timorously entered a little north of Cabo San Lucas at the southern extreme of Baja, California.

The terrain there is rugged; the desert floor rises sharply from the Pacific Ocean toward craggy eight- and nine-thousand-foot mountain peaks. The rains come spring and fall, bearing ten or twelve inches a year of water that drains from the landscape in rushing torrents. The tan and off-white earth is deeply cut by a confusing maze of canyons and arroyos, sandy at the bottom, rocky on the ridges. To traverse the landscape you must run the gauntlet of these ravines, which speak continuously of water in a place notable for the absence of it.

Suppose you know only two things about the ecology of deserts—that they are dry and that they come alive at night when the cold-blooded reptiles, in particular, are safe from the potentially fatal heat of the daytime sun. You set out into the Sonoran Desert after a long, lazy breakfast. The sun is already well launched when you begin, and despite your thin clothing and a bit of a breeze and a ridiculous white sombrero, you are not far beyond the first ridge when you start to think rather constantly of the incredible intensity of the heat. Knowing what you do, you expect not only a spare landscape but an empty one.

I did not find it. True, I found a landscape that was hard and dry and fiercely armored: Absolutely everything in it seemed equipped with some variety of thorn or spine, the little ones barbed like fishhooks, the biggest ones as fiendishly long and sharp as hypodermic needles. They could immobilize you, I knew that firsthand. I had fallen once onto a minuscule northern species of prickly pear cactus. Next morning my leg was stiff and tight with pain.

143

I hobbled off to a surgeon who, having been raised in Australia, showed a nostalgic affection for the problem at hand. He spent almost an hour digging sixty nasty barbs out of my knee. Twenty minutes later the pain had vanished and I was a sauntering man again. In Baja the prickly pears grew as tall as lilac bushes, their pads as big as elephant ears. I was not going to stumble into one of them. I inched along, leaning on my bamboo staff.

I found a hard, dry, and prickly landscape, but not an empty one. From the first dolorous coos of the white-winged doves floating across the cactus-covered hills, their voices reminiscent of the lamentations of the mourning doves of home, I found a place vibrantly colorful and alive. The last flaming red flowers of the ocotillo bushes blazed brightly, and here and there the trumpet-shaped flower of a buffalo gourd vine radiated a beam of brilliant yellow. Vultures soared overhead on the thermal winds, flashing the white patches on their black wings. On the bare tan earth beneath the shrubbery, the white shells of the big land snails, like the disc pond snails of the prairie marshes but four times the size, rested in drifts, a calciferous desert snow. In the distance the bell of a solitary range cow clanged. I hoped fervently that the cow would remain in the distance. I had seen the local cattle from the road, scrawny and gaunt, with a mean look in their eyes and very long, wickedly pointed horns.

For a time, my senses admitted nothing but the possibility of danger at every hand. Then I grew less fearful and, opening my eyes, was surprised to see that I was, in fact, proceeding through a forest, unlike any I had ever seen or dreamed of, to be sure, but nevertheless a forest. Although there were many places where the desert floor was completely bare, it was not possible to travel anywhere in a straight line. The tangle of thorny vegetation was impenetrably thick.

Close to the ground grew little barrel-shaped cactuses—fishhook cactuses, cushion cactuses, claret cup cactuses—and serpentine forms of familiar plants in unfamiliar guises—fleabanes, lupines, vetches, milkweeds. Above these rose the paddle-shaped cactuses, the beavertails and the prickly pears. And above these shoulder-high shrubs, including the yuccas and the ocotillos, and, in profuse numbers, the most devilish of all cactuses, the jumping cholla, so called because its spiny fruits, capable of inflicting extremely painful wounds, as I can attest, are said by those who must live with them to leap out at you, especially when your back is turned, a claim pooh-poohed by literal-minded observers but easy enough to believe anyway, as so careful a naturalist as Ann Zwinger has testified. "Balderdash," she says of the botany books. "It jumps." What is true is that the slightest sort of contact seems sufficient to entangle one of the heavy fruits in your skin or clothing, and then dispossessing yourself of it without being repeatedly pricked to the point of bloodshed will prove quite impossible. It is hard to imagine a more ruthlessly efficient means of seed distribution.

Above the many-armed jumping chollas, there are the pale trees of the desert, technically still shrubs, although sometimes in the literature called subtrees—the desert willows, the palo verdes with their yellow-green or blue-green barks, the silver-colored ironwoods, the tan mesquites with their long bean pods, all delicate of construction and feathery of leaf and very beautiful. I came also, in the sandy bottom of a wide and green wash, upon a single magnificent specimen of the elephant tree, a stubby, thick-trunked, wide-crowned tree with leaves of a ghostly green and papery bark, peeling like the bark of a birch, bronze in color on the trunk, tending toward reddishness on the branches, in the singular shade of which I spent a couple of contented hours at the height of the day.

And above all these rises the stately cardon cactus, probably the largest species in the world, resembling the saguaro of deserts farther north, but taller and more branched and sometimes covered improbably with ball moss, which supports itself on the moist Pacific air. These are the cactuses that at a certain stage of development extend two upreaching branches on opposite sides of the main trunk, like bandits sticking up their arms in surrender to the law.

You expect of a desert—I expected, at any rate—something clean and unadorned, radically simple. I found instead a place with very complicated, almost baroque, architectural lines.

When the sun was straight overhead, I sat down in the shade of the elephant tree to eat my lunch, to rest, to await whatever might appear. The shade of the elephant tree fell not from its canopy but from its fat trunk; the leaves had already curled to conserve moisture, as the leaves of desert plants do in the heat of the day. And because the thin band of shade fell from the trunk and because the sun constantly moved in its arc across the sky, the shade circled around the tree, and I shifted with it like an animated needle on a sundial.

I sat in the shade and waited. Experiencing a landscape is an act of creativity. Like any creative vision, it cannot be forced or willed. No amount of busyness will produce

146

it. It cannot be organized on a schedule, or happen by appointment. If you would experience a landscape, you must go alone into it and sit down somewhere quietly and wait for it to come in its own good time to you. You must not wait ambitiously. You must not sing to pass the time, or make any kind of effort. The solitude is necessary, the silence is necessary, the wait is necessary, and it is necessary that you yourself be empty, that you might be filled.

How contrary this is to our assumptions! We put our faith in action, in hard work, but as Thoreau said, it is not necessarily the hardest-working person who works best. We sometimes make such a noise at being busy that we drown out everything worth hearing. Bent over our labors, we fail to catch a glimpse of the thing worth seeing.

I sat for a long time in the shade of the elephant tree while the temperature climbed. The birds that had been singing noisily stopped one by one and took shelter somewhere. There was no longer even the hint of a breeze. A tremendous silence fell. I seemed to be wrapped in it, as in the heat. And then I was aware of a movement at my feet, and the desert came alive.

The motion was that of a little whiptail lizard darting from heaven knows where onto a twig. I stared at it. It cocked its dainty head, as lizards do, and stared back at me out of one eye. It looked quizzical, in the manner of lizards, curious as a young child. And charming. Curiosity is always charming. It is, I suppose, a kind of love, the love of knowing; and every form of love beautifies both the lover and the loved.

One of the mysteries is how we lose our curiosity as we grow up. I think hatred and scorn are the weeds that choke it out. The older we get, the more clearly we understand what we do not like. Finally we do not like so many things that we have no room to love anything, and that is when curiosity dies. There are two large approaches to life. One is to know your enemies clearly and to pour your energies into nullifying them, into scorn and satire, cynicism and protest, into the arts of nay-saying and emasculation. The other is to know your enthusiasms and to give your energies to celebrating them, to praise and thanksgiving, curiosity and wonder, to the arts of affirmation and lovemaking. Both approaches can be moral, intelligent, forces for betterment. But one is so much more beautiful than the other. Why should it be so easy to make the uglier choice?

I shifted position to prevent my right leg from falling asleep and the lizard fled. But I knew the pattern of the lizard now and, looking about, saw that they were everywhere, in the shadows of stones, on the undersides of twigs, in the litter at the base of the tree, exquisite creatures, streamlined, beautifully striped, small and fleet.

I could have watched them all afternoon, but I had grown less visible and in the silence and solitude my eyes and ears had been unwrapped. I became aware of insects: of an agave billbug, a big black beetle with the long curved snout of an anteater; of an abundance of ants; of an orange-headed blister beetle; of a tiger beetle crawling across a page of my notebook; of several small spiders in the foliage above me. A lubber grasshopper took flight in a startling clatter of wings. Black butterflies and yellow sulphur butterflies flitted past. An enormous wasp whizzed by. There were mosquitoes! I couldn't imagine how they might exist here, but plainly they did.

And I became aware, when I finally looked, of incredible numbers of chambers dug into the desert floor, ranging from tiny, insect-sized holes to a tunnel two inches across at the base of a prickly pear cactus. I watched the big tunnel, ten yards away, for a long time, hoping that some resident might peek from it, but in vain. I could only imagine what creatures skulked in cool, subterranean nests during the blistering heat of midday: mice, no doubt, and rats, scorpions, tarantulas and spiders, snakes, ground squirrels.

The sandy earth was littered with the scat of rabbits. I rose to stretch my legs and to move around the tree trunk into the shade again. Although I was as protected from the sun as it was possible to be and had exerted myself in no way, I was sweating heavily. When I stood up, I startled a black-tailed jackrabbit resting beneath a shrub twenty yards off. It bounded away, its huge, almost transparent, heavily veined ears held high. It seemed to be all ears and hind legs.

I settled in again. The sun had begun to climb down toward the western sea, and the birds had begun again to scatter and scoot restlessly. I noticed for the first time the round, covered nest of a cactus wren with its narrow, funnel-shaped entrance at the bottom. I got up and peered into it. No one home. The chamber was lined with downy feathers, a soft and shadowy sanctuary in the midst of a world of sharpness and glare. Back at my post, I also noticed the woodpecker holes in the spires of the cardon cactuses. In one of them, perhaps, a tiny elf owl lurked. I heard a tapping, and turned to see a gila woodpecker, red-capped and elaborately marked as so many woodpeckers are, working the smooth green furrow of a tall cactus. In the palo verdes there was a brilliant flash of scarlet, and I verified in the lenses of my binoculars the gaudy presence of a vermilion flycatcher. A pair of ravens landed briefly, their brazen bass voices, like death rattles, shattering the shimmering silence, a sound as surprising, despite their great size, as the baritone cry that a human baby will sometimes utter. The slang expression "to croak" meaning "to die" must have been invented by someone familiar with ravens. Half a dozen black-chinned hummingbirds flitted about, their wings whirring like little electric motors. Cactus wrens sang indelicately, unmelodiously, relentlessly in the bushes. Overhead the vultures continued ceaselessly to soar.

I was alone and without any kind of light in a strange landscape. Determined not to be lost in the darkness, I arose at last, reluctantly, from a wide limb of the elephant tree upon which I had slung myself as in a hammock, and started walking south, toward the ocean. I proceeded slowly and cautiously, as one must in such a place, but not timidly, as I had begun. I walked through air tinged with the faint odor of resin toward the smell of saltwater, curious to be affirmed in every fresh encounter with the abundance of life in this strange, hot and harsh, and yet oddly pleasing place.

The shadows were settling like fog in the arroyos and a chill had begun to creep into the salty air by the time I had made my way back to the place where the land-snail shells gathered like snow in the sand. I paused for a moment at the edge of the road to listen once more to the plaintive cries of the white doves, sounding like oboes in the hills. While I stood there, a red-tailed hawk landed on the pinnacle of a cardon cactus, lit from below by the long rays of the evening sun, turning orange in the gathering dusk. I watched the hawk and it me for a long time. When I grasped my bamboo stick and made my way down the desert road toward the blue sea sparkling in the distance, it did not move, but watched me go. I could feel its eyes as I went, my footsteps crunching in the gravel. Brimming with the fullness of life, I passed down the curve of the road and into a thicket of palms.

I tell this desert story because Wilderness Basin reminded me of it. A place as cold as the Sonoran is hot, as tested by extremes of climate, equally as raw and strange and forbidding. In many ways, in fact, a good deal more barren: rockier, less diverse, higher in altitude, thinner in atmosphere, steeper, windier, altogether treeless. Yet the impressive thing at close range is not what is absent but how much manages to exist and how robustly.

One sunny day John and I walked the basin as far as the base of Cloud Peak. I wish to understand now why this walk made us so happy.

It was, I suppose, uneventful. There was no moment of crisis or of testing, no flash of revelation, no surprise around the bend. We were not fatefully drawn toward anything. We walked, ate lunch in the shelter of a boulder, walked again, talking along the way, returned to camp, settled in for the night. It was a perfectly peaceful day. Hardly worth telling. Yet that day will endure brightly in memory when whole years of living have vanished into the muck of time.

Epiphanies have a way of sounding false. I must be careful about this.

We followed a deer trail running between a willow thicket and the pines higher on the basin wall, and the

deer trail followed the stream, and the stream followed the
path of the glacier. There were no well-beaten human
trails in our direction, but there was no shortage of prece-
dents either for the progress of our ascent. At treeline we
encountered a marshy little lake and, at nearly a right angle to it, one of the gigantic steps glaciers carve, a high,
steep wall of gray granite, worn smooth by wind and rain
and centuries of springtime flooding. Walking up it past
the whistling pikas along the white ribbon of falling water
was as easy and obvious as climbing the marble steps to
the Washington Monument.

At the top of the waterfall was another lake, long and
narrow, curving away out of sight, blue-green, not especially deep from what you could tell by standing along its
rocky edge and peering into it, velvety beneath the clear
surface of the water with a growth of rust-brown moss.
Nothing seemed to be moving in it. It appeared as innocent as a glass of tap water.

Along one side of the basin ran a steep cliff that fell
directly into the water. Along the other side the cliff was
higher and farther back, and the space between it and the
water was filled with talus. This was the way we should go.
Beyond the curve in the lake towered the jagged peaks,
like a row of ancient tearing teeth, at the center of the Big
Horn range, which arcs like a boomerang. We were approaching the eye of the boomerang. Above everything,
the bright sky, rising in a benevolent blue smile.

A gentle wind ascended from the plains to the west and
lofted toward the mountaintops, rippling the water as it
went. We began to pick our way over the rocks, scrambling after the wind. In the crevices grew lusty green
bunches of monkey flower, lavender with blossom. Melt-

water tinkled beneath the rocks. It was falling from the patches of snow lingering along the shadow lines of the cliff. It echoed faintly, as if the earth were hollow.

We turned the bend and then another, walking the back of a granite snake, into the narrow basin of a finger-shaped lake sheltered from the wind.

There we found birds. At the narrowest part of the lake, in the rapids, a water ouzel dived and sang. Along the shore, white-crowned sparrows, the sentinels of the alpine world, cried excitedly. Water pipits bobbed through the air. Rosy finches darted from boulder to water-bound boulder. That high, cold, austere world of rocks and water and wind *teemed* with birds.

Late in the year though it was, it sounded like spring-time, an illusion reinforced by the scattered patches of snow and ice, by the brownness of the landscape despite its flowers and greenery, by the knife-edge of the wind despite the brilliance of the sunlight. And perhaps it was not after all an illusion. It suited the rawness and newness of the place, the infancy of it, I thought, to regard the recurring interludes of growth as a long succession of springtimes, unmatured by summers, unmellowed by autumns. As a newborn baby sleeps for long intervals and briefly awakens to feed, so this high mountain tundra sleeps, briefly awakens, and is nourished.

We walked on over stones, across ledge-top bogs, around mammoth boulders fallen from the mountainsides, always near water, always toward summits, teased by the wind, the sun boring into the pores of our skin like thousands of tiny, sharp needles.

In one place we passed a den, its entrance well worn, in front of which rested the leg bones of a mule deer. The

153

bones were bare but not yet white. They showed the teethmarks of a cat and of some smaller rodent. Cracked and picked clean. A death and a tidy succession. Nothing wasted.

We walked on.

What is there, finally, to say?

We walked. We stopped in a green fell-field, hid from the wind, ate our lunch, leaned against warm granite and took warmth from it.

We walked. It was nothing, really.

"Too bad this is all going to waste," John said sardonically. We were standing at the last lake in the chain. Beyond us there was nothing but rock, ice, and sky. "Think what a decent developer could do. You could dam this and put motorboats in."

"Yes," I said. "What good is a place if you can't even use it?"

"Damn right. Waterskiing. You could have summer competitions."

"Steamers," I said. "Sternwheelers, maybe. Scenic cruises."

"Yes!" John said. "A Scandinavian theme. 'Sail the fjords of Wyoming!' 'Olde Europe in the Romantic Rockies!'"

"Package deals for North Dakotans. 'The Norway of the West.'"

"Housing developments, of course. A trailer home park at the lower end of the basin. Mountainside chalets up here."

"A revolving restaurant! On the summit of Black Tooth there. Alpine Haus."

"Ski lifts."

"A water slide."

"Gift shops."

"Helicopter rides."

"A jogging trail."

"Alpine golf."

"Fireworks."

"Tennis courts."

"A trout-by-the-pound place. Marshmallows and all the tackle provided."

"A wax museum."

"An open-air theater. Summer jazz festivals."

"You'd need a road, certainly. Maybe a monorail system. Something with a Disney theme."

John sighed. I laughed.

"It is so sad," he said. "All this just sitting here going to waste. Just think! It could be generating tax revenues!"

"Excessive tax revenues," I said. "I'm going to start a landholders association."

We walked. Back down the basin toward camp in bright sun and gentle wind, through silence, through birdsong, along whitewater falls, beside still waters.

We did not see anything one would not expect in an alpine basin. We discovered nothing previously unknown. We performed no feats of daring, set no new records. Although visitors there are infrequent, they are by no means unprecedented; we advanced no frontier.

We walked and talked, watched and listened. In our own good leisurely time. And were happy. Not wildly, deliriously happy. It was the sort of happiness that comes quietly and stays on in the mind as a template of happiness for the future.

Why? I asked myself. What did we do?

We returned to camp. John went his way, I mine. I climbed the mountainside to a high ledge and sat, watching the sun fall. The wind had died, and in the lake below rings of water formed where the trout rose to feed on hatching nymphs. I watched the circles rise, spread concentrically, dissipate.

Nothing, I thought. That's the answer.

Exactly nothing.

12

The Pass:
THE CLIFF
◁ ▷

W E began with a sense of urgency. Stormy weather was in the offing, and our route for the day was up the Middle Tensleep Creek drainage through a long, high pass and down the eastern side of the mountains to Lake Angeline. We wanted to be over the pass and out of the lightning zone before the storm struck. There was a trail for the first three-quarters of a mile, but at the point where the creek forks, the trail leads southeast to Lost Twin Lakes, a popular fishing destination. Our route was up the other fork, heading northeast toward the pass.

We made quick work of the trail. For much of the way it meandered along the green ridge of the valley through open forest, the creek often invisible but never inaudible below. In these mountains you never long escape the sound of the steady rush of water over rocks, sometimes in a roar, sometimes in a murmur. Eventually you hear it subconsciously, as you hear the sound of the surf at the ocean shore, or the lapping of the water against the rocks of a northern lake, or the whisper of the wind on the plains. It is part of the great pulse of mountain life, like a heartbeat, but it comes always to an outsider as a surprise, the shock of the familiar, like the sound of one's own heart throbbing through the tubes of a stethoscope. To the east of these mountains lie the high plains, to the south-west, the Great Basin Desert, both regions defined as much by the absence of water as anything else. It is hard to fathom so much water tumbling so relentlessly out of these mountains and amounting to so little by the time it reaches the flatlands below. And the tumble of boulders over which these mountain streams crash is a constant reminder of the work of water, of the violence in its music, of the slow but steady progress of the mountains toward the plains. From a distance the mountains seem immovable. In the heart of them, permanence is seen and heard to be a pile of rubble, just as the sound of every heartbeat forecasts the moment when its beating will stop.

We descended the ridge to the fork in the creek, paused to catch our breath, cast wary eyes at the skies, and pressed on toward the pass, free at last of the trail, happy to have entered into the illusion that ahead lay a world we ourselves were uncovering for the first time. In fact, of course, we were treading where many others had also gone, as we were reminded by the traces of footsteps showing here and there in the tundra sod. We were above treeline again, ascending gently but relentlessly. The way grew ever more rocky, the plant life increasingly sparse as we climbed, until, for half an hour or so, it was us and the lichens and the rocks and the gathering clouds.

We came up over the edge of the drainage and onto the saddle between the mountains under skies that had grown thick and gray. We hurried now, dawdling nowhere to admire the view. Perhaps this sense of needing always to press on colored my view of the place. John was setting the pace, and it was faster than I could easily maintain. At times he was five hundred or a thousand yards ahead of me, and I only wanted to catch up. Perhaps also the overwhelming grayness of the place and the damp chilliness in the air took their effect.

The grayness was not just of the sky, although here it had become again the dominant element in the landscape: We were on a wide, flat plain, sloping upward like a big board on tilt and terminating not in a view of the depths below, which had vanished, but in the sky itself. The grayness also showed in the rocks; they seem, like water, to reflect the color of the sky, and they were heavily covered with gray-green lichens. And the grayness showed in the dense carpet of mosses, short grasses and sedges, interspersed with thick, ground-hugging mats of wildflowers, none of them quite green, as plants aren't in high places. They were various pale imitations of green: gray-green, silver-green, khaki-green.

And the dampness was not merely a matter of the low-hanging clouds sodden with icy moisture—in places it seemed as if we might reach up and touch them. This wide saddle of thin earth and rock was like a vast worn-out sponge, intercut with thousands of tiny pools and pud-

159

dles of crystal-clear water, with hundreds of thin rivulets of water. The clumps of vegetation between them sometimes held our weight and sometimes not. We zigzagged, following the intermittent striations of rock.

It was an eerie place, at once impossibly lush and incredibly barren. It was thick with mosquitoes that preyed on what? Even hiking as resolutely as we did, we could not help seeing the rich population of black and gray spiders, hefty creatures, some almost as big as my thumbnail. Flies sucked at flowers, and now and then a white-crowned sparrow flitted past. Among the black and gray rocks in this monochromatic world lay, scattered like jewels left behind in haste, enormous crystals of quartz, too big to think of carrying home. And here and there we stumbled across the bones of small mammals, bits of leg, pieces of skull, in one place the horns of a mountain goat. We saw no mammals, but the abundance of bones argued for them. It was like a world suddenly fallen silent, as in the aftermath of a holocaust. In the west lightning flashed and thunder growled. We hurried on.

We consoled ourselves with the ridge above us. When we got to it, surely, we would have reached the crest of the pass. But on arriving, we found that the line of the horizon had inexplicably shifted and lay still higher; and when we got to that ridge, we pressed on, hopeful still, and it vanished and another had taken its place; and then another. It was like walking in sand, or across the desert from one mirage to the next. Neither the place we had just been nor the place we could plainly see ahead seemed in reality to have any substance. But we had to be getting somewhere. The saddle was narrowing, and two nondescript peaks had emerged, caressing fields of snow, not

great craggy peaks, not triumphant terminations of mountains, but merely higher mounds of rubble. The rumble of
thunder became more persistent.

We hurried on. We had trudged resolutely for some
time over what we judged to be the relatively flat seat of
the saddle. Suddenly it dawned on us that the water in the
runoff channels was running in our direction. The peak of
the pass, when we finally got to it, was not on a ridge after
all, but only an imperceptible tilt in the table. How far is
the east from the west? About six inches if you're standing
at the right spot about 11,300 feet above sea level in the
saddle of the Angeline Pass in the Big Horn Mountains.

I live a couple of miles from a subcontinental divide in
southwestern Minnesota, a lateral ridge created by the ter-
minal moraine of the last of the great Ice Age glaciers to
scour and shape the northern tallgrass prairies, the
Wisconsin. The divide is obvious, even mildly dramatic, if
you approach it on foot or on a bicycle, but it is scarcely
noticeable if you cross it in a car, a slight incline, vaguely
flattened on top, indistinguishable from any other prairie
knoll. It is the sort of thing you know about because you
have heard of it, not because you have first seen it for
yourself. I like to point it out to visitors, to remark casually that the water to the west of this ridge flows into the
Missouri River drainage, the water to the east of it into
the Mississippi River drainage. We are not far, about a
hundred miles, from the 100th meridian of longitude,
roughly the dividing line between the eastern prairies and
the western plains, the line where to the west the average
precipitation drops below the critical measure of twenty
inches a year.

The Mississippi River may be the cultural dividing line

between east and west, but the 100th meridian is the ecological divide; and I think of my own backyard divide as an early warning line of the imminent transition. An hour's drive past this point, I tell visitors, and seed company caps give way to cowboy hats. True as this is, the divide exists for me as an intellectual idea, not as a tangible object. I stand atop it in a rainstorm, and I cannot see some raindrops running eastward and others westward. That this happens, I accept as an article of faith.

So it is with many geological landmarks. I have stood at the equator, for example, had my photograph taken there, but I was able to see no evidence of the equator except the monument marking the spot. "Well," I said finally, "so that's the equator. How interesting." And climbed back into the bus, quite unchanged. The continental divide through the Rockies, which I have crossed in many places, has the same unreal quality. It is incontrovertibly a fact, which I do not for an instant doubt, but it is nevertheless emotionally unbelievable. No transparent physical evidence exists for it, or the physical evidence is too general to have any particular meaning.

We paused, despite the gathering storm, growling out of the west like a chained dog, at the place in Angeline Pass where the water began to flow east rather than west and marveled over the fact, so unostentatiously but observably true. We had come at last upon the kind of geologic fact that one can celebrate with one's heart as well as one's mind. The water running suddenly east down the other side of the mountain was as tantalizing as a summit, one of the rare moments in life when one has, if only for an instant, arrived.

The eastern slope of the saddle fell more gently than

the western, ending abruptly in a pile of enormous granite boulders. We started down through the boulders.

No matter how well designed, a full pack counterbalances your normal center of gravity and puts you slightly off balance, a fact you can handily compensate for in most situations by leaning slightly forward. But this posture thrusts your pack out behind you to a degree difficult to judge since you have no sensory connection with it. It is a little like being pregnant from behind, I imagine. On a steep decline, you are always in danger of misjudging the amount of space it takes to accommodate both your body and your burden, so you constantly confront the possibility of the error that squeezes you from your foothold and thrusts you forward into the abyss. Solid-looking boulders, for another thing, have a way of dislodging or suddenly tipping in unexpected directions. And they are frequently slippery. A fall in either direction—forward or backward—is given a good deal of momentum by the weight of the pack, nearly impossible to overcome. So you move cautiously, lunge about a lot, and find yourself frequently on all fours or turning around to back down a crevice or across a ledge that your pack won't allow you to descend frontally. This is called scrambling. A better word for it would be lumbering, and lumbering taken with all the energy and grace of an arthritic old skunk.

We had scarcely crawled over the edge of the saddle and begun to lumber down the wall of the cirque toward the as-yet invisible lake eighty-five stories below when the storm that had been threatening all morning fulfilled its promise. It quickly grew very much darker, a wintry wind buffeted us, and, as suddenly as a shower in a rain forest, the clouds above us opened and began to dump big, sharp crystals of sleet upon us. The sleet made the rocks slippery, and we were, in any case, unwilling to get soaked. We took shelter in a little cave among the boulders.

It wasn't, of course, a cave in the ordinary sense, not some discrete little chamber hollowed out of the surrounding bedrock by the erosive action of wind or water, but merely an accidental juxtaposition of several-ton stones, heaved and rearranged by frost and ice to make a hollow with a roof. It encompassed a little ledge on which the two of us could sit. In the rocks beneath our feet we could hear a trickle of water running, a burbling sound, faintly echoing. We sat shrouded in twilight, free from the bite of the wind but not from the scratching of the air gone so suddenly frigid, nor from the chill in our own bodies, damp with perspiration and dampered with inactivity.

We rummaged slabs of beef jerky, bags of nuts and dried fruit, bars of chocolate from our packs, and ate, not so much because we were hungry as because we had time to kill and because we knew that we needed it. It was a caretaking gesture, like stoking a furnace; at that moment we regarded our bodies as machines, as mechanical contrivances on feet, separate from our consciousness, which had requirements quite apart from our own intimate desires, a need for coolants, lubricants, fuel that we attended as dispassionately as one of us might drain the oil from the engine block and replace it with clean.

Nothing is more carefully attended in advance of an expedition than the question of food. Before we left we had examined the catalogs, made visits to the food displays at the outdoor supply stores, considered the incredible array of freeze-dried temptations in their shiny space-

164

age envelopes, foods packaged under such names as Alpine Aire, Mountain House, Richmoor, Smoky Canyon, Bear Valley, names that made you want to drop everything and begin hiking toward the mountains directly from the parking lot outside. What would it be? Sweet and sour pork? Turkey tetrazzini? Chicken teriyaki? Beef bourguignon? Shrimp creole? For a few ounces a serving we could carry all the delights of the best restaurant in town with us into the wilderness. What for dessert? Would it be Neapolitan ice cream or blueberry cobbler or perhaps a French apple compote? We studied calorie charts, calculated weights, consulted the recommendations of the experts. It was more than a person could decide. How does one know at three o'clock on an early June afternoon in Minneapolis what one might desire on an August night in the Wyoming mountains? Finally we made choices at random, took them home and cooked them on the Svea, a lightweight camping stove, one Sunday afternoon in John's backyard. "Well," we said, looking at each other when we finished, "Yes. Edible, certainly. I would say that, wouldn't you? Definitely edible." But without conviction.

We vacillated, and finally, the night before we left, went to the local grocery store and raided the instant foods section. So we came, after all, with a little freeze-dried chicken and beef, an assortment of dried soups, a lot of rice, and a hefty package of prize-winning beef jerky homemade at the locker plant in Lismore, Minnesota, the sort you would voluntarily eat in your own living room as well as under duress along some mountain trail. And when we had set out, we were reminded of what we had known all along and forgotten, as one always does. On the trail, you are as discriminating about food as your lawnmower. In the evening at camp, a bit of tennis shoe boiled with some rotting bark would taste divine. And not even in the space age has anybody ever devised a convincing imitation of an egg. It is one of the hard truths of the trail: An imitation is an imitation is an imitation.

We huddled in our dark cave, which was not quite so spacious as to allow us to sit fully upright, taking our technologically marvelous sustenance, our bodies warmed by clothes made of spun plastics, and looked out upon an ancient and inhospitable world. It was a world of cloud and rock and turbulence. Crystals of sleet clattered against stone. The wind moaned. Hiding in the recesses of these rocks we might find insects, flowering plants, a bird or two. The rocks themselves were already decomposing, particle by minute particle, beneath their wigs of lichen. We huddled in a land of permanent snows, of raging winds, beyond the trees, above the altitude at which human beings can comfortably survive for long, hunched like the ancients in a primordial cave. But we were by no means beyond range of tenacious life.

For as long as we have been able to scheme, it would seem, we have been devising strategies for counting our own superiority over the rest of life. We were the last and best act of creation. Then we were the lords and ladies of a universe centering upon the earth. Then we were the highest and most glorious link in the Great Chain of Being. Then we were the latest and most intricate achievement in the long story of evolution.

The conceit of the present age is the least convincing of all. Whatever the nature of life, the argument goes, echoing a theme of the Enlightenment, the proper study of humans is humankind. And the thing that is unique about human life, it is said, is that it is peculiarly moral, or has, at any rate, the potential to be lived morally. Oranges and butterflies and fruit bats are trivialities, and people who are interested in them are trivial, lacking in a properly human sense of seriousness and purpose, because oranges and butterflies and fruit bats are merely objects—living objects, it must be conceded, but still, individually at least, lives of no particular consequence. What does it matter if the world has one less butterfly or orange tree? If, indeed, it has one less species of orange tree or fruit bat? Human life is what matters, and with respect to human life the critical questions are social, and the critical social question is moral: How can I induce or inspire my neighbors to behave better? To take any other view of life is to be some sort of wimp, bent on avoiding pain; is, in fact, to be amoral. "A German who is an expert on butterflies, and has found a new species on the eve of September 1, 1939, is much more content than a moralist was that night," one proponent of this view said recently by way of summing it up.

There are lots of arguments against this stance of the "even so" variety, so familiar by now as to be tedious. All life is interdependent. Earth is a fragile spaceship on which all the parts count, even if they are only spare parts. Wild things are all potentially of strategic or economic benefit to humankind. The plant you destroy today may have been the one that could save your life from cancer or from starvation tomorrow. Consider Aldo Leopold's famous dictum: "The first rule of intelligent tinkering is to save all the parts." All of life constitutes a gene pool, a repository of historical information that may someday

167

prove vital. Life itself is sacred and ought to be honored in all its forms, high or low. And so on. These arguments are by now part of our intellectual creed. Almost everybody accepts them.

But it is possible to profess this orthodoxy and still to believe that human life is superior to every other kind and to behave on that assumption in ways that are disastrous to the rest of life, either innocently, out of the distortions of view that come from looking at the world through human eyes alone, or arrogantly, out of the distortions that come from overestimating the strengths or wisdom of human culture and imagination. I was furious when I first read that casual dismissal of the German scientist. Someone interested in butterflies wouldn't or couldn't, it was being asserted, understand the moral implications of Nazism. I spent a sleepless night over it, and I find, a year later, that it still makes me angry. What angers me is its arrogance, an arrogance with consequences not only for butterflies and other "trivial" creatures but also for human life, moral consequences.

Consider our own history. We came to this continent holding the firm conviction that human life was at the center of God's plan for the earth and with a high Christian sense of mission: first, to turn the American wilderness to useful purpose, that is, to utilitarian human ends, to cultivate and tame the wild garden, to subject it to our dominion, as we, it was understood, had been called to do; and second, to convert the native Americans to the true faith. But, we found, the native Americans were set in their ways; it came to seem proper, even, to kidnap their children and to hold them hostage until they should convert; and in the meantime, what more powerful evidence of their fallen state existed than that the native Americans had lived, perhaps for centuries, on this continent in a state of nature, without ever having made any serious effort to transform the wild earth into a tame human garden? They seemed quite prepared to live life in the context of nature, to exploit its resources without transforming them, indeed to see their own lives as continuous with the rest of life. They were, plainly, savage; and by this we did not mean merely that they were uncivilized, but that they were, somehow, less than human, that they were some sort of life intermediate between humans and animals, and that they were therefore, in fact, a species of lower animal, meant to be tamed like the rest of the wilderness. "The animals, vulgarly called Indians," Hugh Henry Brackenridge, the author of the first novel of the American West, wrote in 1782, meaning to be sympathetic.

If it proved necessary, as, alas, it sometimes did, to destroy some kinds of life in order to fulfill God's plan for human supremacy, then the destruction must also have been a part of the divine plan from the beginning. And if the kinds of life we needed to destroy included some communities of native Americans, then we destroyed them in order to save them, and that, too, was God's will. So we earnestly believed.

The view was expressed plainly by John Winthrop, Governor of the Massachusetts Bay Colony, in 1629:

> . . . the whole earth is the Lord's garden, and he hath given it to the sons of Adam to be tilled and improved by them. Why then should we stand starving here for the places of habitation (many men

spending as much labor and cost to recover or keep sometimes an acre or two of lands as would procure him many hundreds of acres, as good or better, in another place,) and in the meantime suffer whole countries, as profitable for the use of man, to lie waste without any improvement?

And it was affirmed as late as 1830 by President Andrew Jackson in his second Annual Message to Congress:

Humanity has often wept over the fate of the aborigines of this country, and Philanthropy has long been busily employed in devising means to avert it, but its progress has never for a moment been averted, and one by one have many powerful tribes disappeared from the earth. To follow to the tomb the last of his race and to tread on the graves of extinct nations excite melancholy reflections. But true Philanthropy reconciles the mind to these vicissitudes as it does to the extinction of one generation to make room for another . . . Philanthropy could not wish to see this continent restored to the condition in which it was found by our forefathers. What good man would prefer a country covered with forests and ranged by a few thousand savages to our extensive Republic, studded with cities, towns and prosperous farms, embellished with all the improvements which art can devise or industry execute, occupied by more than 12,000,000 happy people and filled with all the blessings of liberty, civilization, and religion?

Sometimes the belief was stated more bluntly, as in this

170

Fourth of July toast at an army garrison in 1779: "Civilization or death to all American savages!"

I don't see the moral distinction between such belief and fascism. The fundamental flaw is the same. It begins with the arrogant conviction that human life is, after all, all that really matters. This conviction inevitably invites distinctions between human life and animal life: The fate of a species of butterfly is a trivial matter; the fate of a cultural or racial group of humans, on the other hand, is a moral matter. Once this distinction is admitted, refinements are also admitted. Are some kinds of humans, after all, more human than others? The Puritans said yes; Christians are more human than savages. Hitler said yes; Aryans are more human than Jews. It is a repugnant and ultimately dehumanizing judgment, but it is perfectly logical. And the only way to correct the logic is to correct the fundamental assumption, namely that human life is superior to the rest of life. "Humanity is exalted," the biologist Edward O. Wilson said, "not because we are so far above other living creatures, but because knowing them well elevates the very concept of life." Perhaps the German scientist did go to bed on the eve of the Nazi invasion of Czechoslovakia more content than the moralist of the writer's imagination. Perhaps he did so because he knew that in finding a new species of butterfly he had struck the kind of blow for life that would ultimately defeat, on genuinely moral grounds, the degenerate premises of fascism.

We human beings remain in some part wild, despite all our centuries of refinement, against whatever we might do about it. It is, most of the time, an embarrassment, which we are nevertheless drawn toward, as toward an uncouth

171

and seedy but nevertheless charming uncle who insists on appearing at inconvenient moments. In our most serious moments, our wildness is an unfathomable intellectual puzzle. Plainly, we are animals, but just as plainly, we are also something else, something more than, or different from, animals. The story of the banishment from the Garden of Eden is evidence of how long we have puzzled over this problem. When Adam and Eve fled the garden, they were embarking on a life outside nature. We have wandered in limbo ever since. Sometimes we have seen our wildness as sinful and sought to repress it by the authority of belief. But this authority has proved tenuously effective, at best, and we continue to seek another answer.

For a long time we had an admirable solution in the Great Chain of Being, the idea that all life was organized hierarchically by degree of perfection, beginning with the lowest and meanest form of existence and culminating in God. Each gradation in the chain represented the smallest possible distinction of perfection, and every possible distinction was represented by some form of life; if even one possible link were unrepresented, the chain would be broken, and the strict order of the created universe would collapse into chaos. Humans occupied the link in this chain just above the highest animal and just below the humblest of the angels. The solution offered humans supremacy in life here on earth and at the same time explained the mysterious connection between humanity and the rest of earthly life; we were different not in kind but in degree.

But the Great Chain of Being depended absolutely upon a static nature. It assumed, and had to assume, that God had created, from the beginning, a world of perfect order, that every species of life existed from the beginning and must continue to exist forever. The discovery of fossils, the incontrovertible evidence that now-vanished forms of life once flourished, killed the whole grand idea, and we have yet to think of a workable substitute, an intellectually and spiritually satisfying explanation for our dual natures, our wildness and our otherness.

After the collapse of the Great Chain the temptation, against which Thoreau and the whole Transcendental movement rebelled, was to discount our wildness, to see ourselves as distinct altogether from nature. Thoreau made it the contrarian work of his life, a labor he never fully completed, to search for the wildness in himself, to fathom it, and to draw the connections between it and his life as a pencil-maker, dutiful son, man of letters, surveyor, and citizen of Concord, Massachusetts. He insisted that the rest of us do the same. Attentive as he was to the task—as his life wore on, he grew ever more methodical about it—he never managed quite to find what he was looking for. "The true harvest of my daily life," he said, "is somewhat as intangible and indescribable as the tints of morning or evening. It is a little star-dust caught, a segment of the rainbow which I have clutched."

He told a parable of his frustration: "As I came home through the woods with my string of fish, trailing my pole, it now being quite dark, I caught a glimpse of a woodchuck stealing across my path, and felt a strange thrill of savage delight, and was strongly tempted to devour him raw; not that I was hungry then, except for that wildness which he represented." Wanting to snatch and devour the woodchuck is the story of a defeat, of an unsatisfiable longing to taste wildness firsthand and so, perhaps, to come to some understanding of it. But more than understanding, Thoreau sought, I think, certification; he longed for some sign of the authenticity of his wildness, which he loved, he said, no less than goodness. He sought admission into the society of which the woodchuck was a part; in this sense he envied the woodchuck, and was sometimes prepared, he admitted, to kill to satisfy his desire.

This made him uneasy. His desire, he said, was to live chastely and simply, to live morally, as human life requires. He perhaps succeeded farther in this direction than most of us, but not far enough to satisfy himself. He could not, for one thing, entirely conquer his desire to fish, something he was skilled at. "I have found repeatedly, of late years, that I cannot fish without falling a little in self-respect." Still, he was thankful for his years as a hunter and fisherman. They had brought him, he said, a little closer to nature. He recommended, for this reason, that every boy should learn to hunt and fish. (I think in all his two-million-and-some words he never used the word "girl.") "We cannot but pity the boy who has never fired a gun; he is no more humane, while his education has sadly been neglected." But he expected boys to outgrow this instinct, as they do other childish habits. One of the sad and insurmountable requirements of our otherness, he believed, was that we must pass, as an embryo passes through the stages of development (he used the phrase "embryo man" to describe a boy), from life in the wild into civilization. The "beautiful and winged life" he called this passage in the memorable penultimate paragraph of *Walden,* seizing on the metaphor of the metamorphosis of an insect.

He may have loved wildness as much as goodness, but Thoreau nevertheless saw a clear distinction between the two. He made, therefore, a distinction between love of nature and sentimentality. "I like better," he said, "the surliness with which the woodpecker speaks of his woods, handling them as indifferently as his axe, than the mealy-mouthed enthusiasm of the lover of nature." And he once said critically that his friend and mentor Emerson unfortunately loved more of nature than he knew of it.

"Though there are more ways to kill a cat than by stuffing him with cream, that is, nevertheless, one way," naturalist Joseph Wood Krutch said. I suppose, in the same manner, that there are many ways to avoid seeing nature, but surely seeing it as nice is one of them. Every path through the woods is littered with bones, and not one of those bones relinquished its flesh voluntarily.

The deep longing that Thoreau felt to discover and to fulfill the wildness at the heart of his civilized soul, and his search, pursued like a lover, for the sometimes harsh and uncompromising regions beyond the merely pretty, continue to have currency. Each generation strives again to find some message in the dark and inscrutable wilderness.

The storm did not last long, half an hour, perhaps, long enough to give us a good rest and to prime us for the descent to the lake. The sleet stopped. A bit of sunshine flickered from behind the clouds. We emerged from our hiding place, shouldered our packs, cinched their straps, adjusted our hats, and resumed our shuffle down the mountain even more carefully than before because the sleet had made the stones slippery.

We quickly came to a point of decision. The lake

175

opened into view, a quarter-mile-long emerald-green leaf, shaped somewhat like that of an elm, obviously deep and frigid even from our perch eight hundred feet above it. It was held in the U-shaped embrace of a high, nearly sheer wall. The glacier that carved the cirque was small and inconsequential, but the cirque itself is a lovely example of the geologic form, an almost surgical bite of rock out of the side of the mountain. The last remnant of the glacier melted at about the turn of this century, but a permanent snowfield remains, a shroud of white wrapped halfway around the upper reaches of the cirque wall and extending in a narrower tongue back toward the pass. It has the shape of one of those fossil shark's teeth that one finds washed up on southern Florida shores along the Gulf of Mexico. We had arrived at the top of this snowfield and then climbed around the northern edge of it to its base, from which a little waterfall plunges several hundred feet through a chimney into the lake. We were on a ledge several feet wide, peering down the wall into the waters of the lake, high enough so that we could just barely distinguish the forms of two fishermen trying the waters at the foot of the waterfall.

The wall along the northern shore of Lake Angeline deteriorates into a ridge of boulders, which, we could see, it would be an uncomplicated, if not easy, matter to scramble down. But we would have to climb back toward the peak to the north of us to gain access to it. It looked, on the other hand, as if we might be able simply to jog down the narrow ledges and tables of the cirque's face. The angle of the wall was so steep, however, that we could see the way for only fifty or a hundred feet at a time. We might descend four hundred or five hundred feet, dis-

cover ourselves up against an insurmountable obstacle—
we had no ropes or technical equipment—and find that
we had to retrace our steps all the way back to the snowfield and then climb toward the northern summit and
down the ridge after all. A fall on the ridge could bring
serious injury, but certainly nothing more. Falling from
the cirque wall burdened with full packs and unprotected
by any equipment would likely prove fatal. What to do?

We vacillated. We studied the long climb we would
have to make to get to the ridge. We stared down the
cirque wall toward the lake. We looked at each other,
shrugged, and set off down the wall. It would be, if nothing else, an adventure.

There were many places where the way was obvious and
easy, where we had achieved a grassy ledge several feet
wide and sloping inevitably toward another ledge, and we
could proceed confidently. Still, we advanced cautiously,
mindful of careless slips. But there were many other places
where the way was narrow, and the rocks wet and slippery, where we faced the wall, gripped it where we could
with our hands and inched our way down, considering the
consequences of each step before we made it. There were
places where we thought we were defeated; where the next
line of attack was not at all obvious and we were almost
ready to turn around and go back up the cliff; where, in
fact, we did turn back until the sight of another possibility
suddenly opened to us. Finally, three-quarters of the way
down, we did come up against a dead end.

We were on the south side of the waterfall. There was
clearly no way to continue unless we crossed to the north
side. We had another of those talks that consist not of
words but of glances. Then we crossed the waterfall on a

loose bridge of pebbles not quite so wide as the sole of one of our boots. The pebbles held. From there we crossed a narrow plateau where a bit of tundra had taken hold, scrambled a couple of hundred feet down a chimney that had not been apparent from the other side of the waterfall, and emerged upon the shore of the lake.

Perhaps two hours had passed, but we were oblivious of them. We turned away from the lake and looked up the wall we had descended. "Look!" we said, as if we had just discovered it. "That's what we just climbed down!" And then we laughed heartily, altogether delighted with ourselves.

Most of one's life is spent in a kind of daze, in a swirling world of confusions and counterattentions. You work with half your mind on the task at hand. At the same time, your left knee aches, you are conscious of the desire for another cup of coffee, and you remember the appointment you intend to keep in an hour. Somewhere in your subconscious a daydream is taking shape. You hear the noises of the machines and people in the background. You start a sentence, a conversation, or a walk down the street, and something intervenes. You start again. And again. In such a world, you are aware of the slow grinding of the hours, sometimes of the interminable minutes.

There are very few extended moments in any life when time stops, when external or secondary considerations fail to intervene, when all of your energy and thought is directed toward a single effort. Sometimes, perhaps, you get lost in the make-believe world of a book or carried away in a flood of melody for half an hour; or you face a crisis of health that erases every other consideration; or you make a speech and your only thought is for what you mean to say. These moments are always memorable for their single-mindedness of purpose; they stand like mountaintops in a life. Our descent down the face of the Lake Angeline cirque was one of them.

13

The Talus Field:
THE WAY DOWN
◁ ▷

W E were camped on a flattened, gravel-bound fell-field perhaps twenty-five yards square, one of the hayfields of the pikas. It was intricate and subtle, a world in miniature. I plodded through it feeling uncharacteristically gigantic, clumsy, grotesquely out of scale. A fell-field, one of several distinctive alpine tundra communities, is characterized by its flatness, its base of stabilized gravel, and its primitive cover of soil, dry and rocky. The name comes from the Gaelic word "fell," meaning "stone." A fell-field is a stonefield. It is estimated that, on the fertile plains far below, it takes a hundred years to create an inch of soil. The inch or so of soil here had taken, in the slow-motion world of the alpine tundra, at least several centuries to accumulate.

The strength of a fell-field community is that once it has been established, it may remain stable for hundreds, perhaps even thousands, of years. Its weakness is that, once disturbed, it is equally slow to recover. A study of a fell-field community in the Colorado Rockies suggested that erosion damage along a footpath began within two weeks of its opening, that the vital cushion plants had been damaged to the crown within eight weeks, and that full recovery along the path after a single season's use took more than twenty years.

Two factors are at work. For one thing, *everything* on the alpine tundra proceeds slowly. Plant growth is excruciatingly slow—it may take a decade for a healthy plant to achieve its first flowering. But so is decomposition. A cigarette pack that decomposes in a year in the lowlands, Ann Zwinger reports, will take several years to decompose at high altitude, and a metal can or bottle top will not disintegrate for at least a century. Then there is the factor of scale. A crushed cigarette pack is a large object in the miniature world of the alpine tundra, and so is a bottle top. The shade from either is sufficient to smother in a matter of weeks the life of a mature plant. "Fifty to one hundred years of plant growth can be snuffed out by a beer can," Zwinger writes in *Land Above the Trees*, the best available account of life in the alpine tundra communities of North America.

Here, out of the way though it is, was a place already showing the scars of thoughtless use. A discarded beer can bobbed in the clear waters of the lake just beyond the outlet of the stream. Among the shoreline boulders lay a rusting fishing reel, discarded where it had broken. Just below our tent site were two big fire rings of blackened rock, despite the regulations against them; the fires lighted in them had been made with wood sawed out of the krummholz thicket that sheltered the picnic place, wood it might take a century or two to renew; and all around the rings was scattered the debris of old lunches, tin cans, candy wrappers, cigarette filters, plastic bags.

It is, I thought, a form of incontinence, this devil-may-care attitude toward beautiful places, as unthinking, perhaps as involuntary, as the wetting of a diaper. But every weary parent of a toddler eventually consoles himself with the thought that no able-bodied child goes to college in Pampers; there seems no similar triumph of maturity over trash incontinence. It is an infantilism that regularly endures long beyond a seemly age. Confronted with the evidence of it, I felt uncomfortable even about the relatively benign damage that my own lugged boots did as I trampled across the tundra.

Looking at a fell-field forces one back to an old paradox: Wherever the stage is grandest in nature, the details of its performance are proportionately reduced. You climb to the top of a mountain. The higher you climb, the broader the reach of the horizons within your visual grasp and the more compelled you are to fall to your knees to come within sight of its life forces. Every factor at work in shaping the life forms of a fell-field is a withering one: Here the winds blow hardest, the soils are thinnest, water is scarcest, temperatures are coldest, the radiation of the solar light is most intense. Life triumphs in even such a place, but only by laying low. This is a world in which a full-grown willow tree may stand as high as your index finger.

Of all the plants in this scrubby world—perhaps forty species survive in the fell-fields of the northern Rockies— none are more basic than the lichens. They were the first plants to venture out among the stones a long time ago. They were able to do so because they demand next to nothing except an intermittent source of at least a little water, some sunlight, and pure air—only industrial pollution totally defeats them. Wherever the earth is at its most extreme, wherever it is hottest or driest or coldest or windiest, the lichens take hold and bring forth life.

The lichens have sometimes been described as a retrogression, as an organism of last resort. In a small way they advance the prophecy that the rough places will be made plain. They decompose the rocks that play host to them and so begin the long process by which barren rock becomes soil. In this, as in so many respects, they are an oddity. Most species conspire to preserve their environment rather than to tear it down.

Lichens are not high on anybody's list of the critical species. Perhaps the most noticeable contribution they make is an aesthetic one; they bring color to the severe landscape of high and rocky places. They come in a vivid array of hues: black, pale gray, orange, yellow and green, widely intermixed. The vast patches of them among the rocks soften and enrich the barest and least hospitable of places. And some of them—for example, the intensely green foliose lichen that grows on trees in the northern Rockies, looking like fronds of coral cut in jade—are strikingly beautiful.

183

Almost everybody has learned in some elementary biology lesson that the lichens are a classic example of symbiosis, that a lichen is not one form of life but two, a fungus and an alga, which somehow in an ancient age discovered the mutual advantage in sharing resources, the alga its ability to manufacture carbohydrates, the fungus its skill at collecting and holding water and certain minerals. But the spectacular success of this arrangement has eluded the mythmakers who give us our metaphors for life. We are steadfastly committed to seeing the process of life as a competition. Everywhere we look in nature, we see battles for survival, wars for territory, contests for domination, the fight for possession of limited resources. We speak in these terms not just about ourselves but about all of life, plants as well as animals. We say that in a given ecosystem this or that plant is dominant, that one plant replaces another by invasion, that the transition from one kind of community to another is a succession, a term that calls to mind the progressions of royalty. We talk about the food chain, a hierarchical order in which something bigger or more aggressive is always consuming something smaller or more passive. The language of biology is often as violent as that of geology is romantic. But this is not because the facts of biology lead inevitably toward violent or combative conclusions. The instances of cooperation in nature surely equal those of competition. For every predator-prey story there is a lichen story.

Nicolette Perry in a fascinating book, *Symbiosis: Close Encounters of a Natural Kind*, catalogs known types of cooperation between unrelated species. Perry reports that algae are very adept at cooperative ventures and have forged alliances with many organisms, trading their capacity to

184

photosynthesize for secure housing and mobility. The green hydra (*Hydra viridis*), for example, a long tubelike freshwater creature, ingests unicellar algae called chlorellae and absorbs them into the inner layer of its transparent body wall. There the algae photosynthesize, sharing the surplus oxygen and carbohydrates they produce with their host, which contributes to the effort by swimming about to find for the algae the best sunlight. The very simple freshwater protozoan, *Paramecium bursaria,* is a one-celled animal that eats by surrounding a particle of food and digesting it. It, too, ingests chlorellae, which escape into the cytoplasm, migrate to the transparent outer wall of the paramecium's cell, and set up shop. It is not understood how so rudimentary a creature as the paramecium can distinguish algae from the other one-celled organisms it consumes, an astonishingly sophisticated achievement, but it happens. The same sort of relationship, with a couple of refinements, exists between algae and the flatworm, *Convoluta roscoffensis*, a creature of the North Atlantic. The algae not only, in this case, photosynthesize, but also convert the flatworm's wastes into reusable food, and the flatworm, in turn, cleans the algal colony in its body of dead cells and regulates its population. The flatworm takes in algae accidentally and subsists by ordinary foraging if it doesn't chance upon the right algae, but the little sea slug, *Elysia viridis*, purposefully seeks out a particular species of seaweed that contains suitable chloroplasts, penetrates the seaweed's cell walls, and sucks the chloroplasts out.

The most spectacular association of this kind, considering its results, exists between certain unicellular algae called dinoflagellates and several species of marine polyps.

Again the algae photosynthesize food and convert wastes into usable food in exchange for secure housing. The dinoflagellates also produce more oxygen than they and the polyps together can use, and, as a by-product of the recycling of wastes, they intensify the collection of calcium in the bodies of the polyps. These calcium deposits harden when the polyps die, and out of the accumulation of many millions of them, coral reefs emerge. In the meantime, the surplus oxygen that the algae give off helps to support the rich fauna of the reef, and these animals, in turn, keep the reef waters clean and unpolluted, a necessary condition for the polyps. So the whole spectacular ecosystem of a coral reef can be said to be one grand, and extremely complex, instance of symbiosis.

The other half of the lichen team is a fungus, and the fungi are similarly involved in a variety of other symbiotic relationships. At least one of these relationships is critically important to all of life on earth. Dense forests, which are responsible for the production of much of the world's supply of oxygen, thrive because of the symbiotic association of trees and fungi. One factor inhibiting forest density is competition among trees for adequate root space. This problem is solved when fungi attach themselves to the root tips of the trees in a forest and spread cobweblike nets of tissue, much more finely veined than the tissues the trees themselves are capable of producing, into the surrounding soil. In doing so, the fungi greatly expand the total capacity and efficiency of the trees' root systems, allowing much denser forests than would otherwise be possible. The fungi, for their part, get the safety of being connected to a strong tree and a share of the sugars the trees produce.

Some species of orchids have become so dependent on the root-extension abilities of fungi that they no longer develop root systems of their own. And all orchids are dependent upon fungi for successful seed germination. Orchid seeds are so tiny that they do not store enough food to last until the new plants are capable of manufacturing their own. Instead, associated fungi provide a nutrient-rich medium for orchid seedlings and augment the root systems of the young plants until they have a chance at independent survival. The fungi benefit, again, from having a stable place to live and by getting a share of the surplus sugars their host plants produce.

Ambrosia beetles burrow in wood and live on wood fibers, even though they can't digest cellulose. They survive by planting fungi in their chambers. Fungi can break down cellulose into digestible carbohydrates, but not from intact wood. So the beetles chew the wood up into pieces the fungi can manage and the fungi break it down into carbohydrates the beetles can digest, and both prosper. The relationship has become so close that, by now, ambrosia beetles can't even reproduce without the fungi; their larvae won't pupate without a substance synthesized by fungi.

Termites are also fungus farmers for the same reason, and some varieties of wood wasps plant a bit of fungus with their eggs, so that when they have hatched, the larvae will have a ready source of food.

There are variations on this theme of almost every imaginable sort. Ants guard colonies of aphids and the caterpillars of certain butterflies in exchange for the honeydew they excrete. Crabs offer sea anemones transportation in exchange for the protection of the anemones' fierce stingers. Shrimp clean the gills of fish; fish the mouths of hippopotomuses; birds the backs and wounds of cattle and of whales, and the mouths of crocodiles. One party gets sanitation, the other a reliable supply of food. A blind species of shrimp digs holes for its companion fish to hide in, and the fish in turn guides the shrimp in its search for food. Lizards in New Zealand keep bird nests free from parasites in exchange for a place to lay their eggs. In Southeast Asia and Africa the Black Throated Honey Guide, a bird, guides honey badgers to beehives. The badgers tear the hives open and eat the honey; the birds clean up the grubs, to which they would not otherwise have had access.

These relationships are not just exotic but often fundamental. Most plants need nitrogen to survive. The legumes capture it in root nodes, but it can't be used by plants until the symbiotic bacteria in the nodes first convert it into ammonia. Without this cooperation, many plant communities would be nitrogen-starved. Ruminants are able to digest grass only because it is first broken down by anaerobic bacteria that live symbiotically in one of their stomachs. Many plants are dependent upon symbiotic insects for pollination. Where would we be without nitrogen-fixers, without cattle, without flowering plants? We would be back, at least, to the age of the dinosaurs, far beyond the first pale intimations of human life.

All this, of course, begs the question of cooperation within species. Mating, the nurturing of young, territorial defensiveness, schooling, flocking, hiving, herding, swarming, bunching, cloning, the forming of packs, colonies, hibernacula. In how many ways do living things band together for their own benefit? Essayist Lewis Thomas once remarked that the surest sign of life on another planet would be evidence of a committee. "We do not have solitary, isolated creatures," he said. "It is beyond our imagination to conceive of a single form of life that lives alone and independent, unattached to other forms."

Still, we favor the stories of struggle and conquest. Why? Because biology is as much a product of culture as any other intellectual enterprise, and because the bias of our culture runs strongly in that direction. The junior high school principal rises at the orientation meeting to welcome his new charges and their parents. "We want all of our students," he says, "to be involved in extracurricular activities. Successful people have always participated in extracurriculars." We cannot presume that he is an educator of catholic tastes, tolerant of the deviant interests and preferences of his young charges. He does not say that success in life is learned on the playing field. He does not need to. We understand perfectly well what he intends. Life as a ball game: What are its lessons?

Life is a contest. That much is given. It is a competition with a certain outcome: One side will win, and the other will lose. But there is no point in playing a game one does not expect, or at least hope, to win. Chance plays its part, but the presumption of the game is that chance can be conquered by superior skill or character: by clever strategy, by training that has overcome deficiencies of ability, by determination, fortitude, turning the rules to one's advantage. A game in which chance always has the upper hand would hardly be interesting or worth playing. The winner is the team that has rearranged the terms of the playing field, one might say the environment of the game, to suit its own purposes. The world is what we make of it; that is one of the lessons of the parable of life as a ball game.

The world of the game is a world of, by, and for rules. There is plenty of room for intelligence in the game, but none for the sort of creativity that institutes a new order. Good gamesmen do not make leaps of faith, dispute the judgments of superiors, or let their emotions get the better of them.

The game is unambiguous: The play follows foreordained patterns, lasts a measured amount of time, and results in a mathematical score. If everybody would play by the rules, one is given to understand, all the rest of life might be equally tidy.

In the game, wit sometimes outplays brawn, but not for long. Size and strength win eventually. Market hogs, sex objects, and athletes are all measured by their physical statistics. In life, a child learns from the game, one gets what one wants by taking it.

And the game is the fountain of eternal youth that we have so long sought. In the game, the winner is the one with youthful vigor; there are few aged victors in sport. The game is a way of denying aging, which is a way of denying death. It is not surprising, therefore, that the adult professionals of spectator sports should continue to live as children, should train in camps and be headquartered in clubhouses, should be segregated by sex and housed as buddies, should live according to rules and curfews set down by parental owners and coaches, should dress as children, should keep childish names—how many grown athletes answer to such names as Timmy and Jimmy and Bobby, names other men leave behind early in adolescence?—and, when they leave the world of the game, should enter the real world primarily as emissaries to other children, as visitors to the children's wards of hospitals, to clubs and camps for children. In the world of the game one need never grow up.

When a plant flowers, when it comes to maturity, we say that it blooms. And when the seed of the flower has come to maturity, when the plant is in old age, we say that it has ripened. But we see our own aging as a deterioration, not as a blooming or ripening, not as a beautiful fulfillment. We see our own ripening as a termination, not as a continuation of the life we would cling to forever. It is one of the many ways in which we distinguish ourselves from nature.

To see life as fundamentally a competition is, similarly, to view it in terms of the game, to read into it our own youthful expectations. It is more than a denial of progression and process in nature; it is a vision of the otherworldly life of nature, partly a lament that it is a world we cannot enter and partly a denial of that lament, a declaration of independence from the savage ways of nature, of allegiance to the civilized world of humanity in which life is played by the rules.

The violent language of biology comes out of science, but it is an expression of culture, a statement not of fact but of belief, more a description of how we see than of what we see. The truth of the lichens, at any rate, is quite unlike the truth of the game; it is evidence of what may be accomplished in a forbidding world by laying low, biding time, and sharing resources.

Above the lichens in the Angeline fell-field rose an astonishing variety of flowering plants, considering the par-

191

simonious character of the setting. I counted twenty-seven species in my unmethodical survey. I found the tiny blossoms of the fragrant alpine forget-me-not, one of the cushion plants characteristic of high altitudes, so called because they grow in tight clumps very close to the earth, conserving heat and moisture, and gathering strength against the fierce winds of alpine regions by locking together. The forget-me-nots look gray, as do so many alpine plants, because their leaves and stems are covered in long, white hairs, another heat- and water-conserving device. And like all cushion plants, the exposed carpet of foliage covers a dense and comparatively massive structure of shoots and intertwining roots that provide anchorage against the winds, food storage for the long months when the climate is inhospitable, and the infrastructure, as an engineer might say, for extracting as much water and nourishment as possible from the thin and rudimentary alpine soils. Bits of old leaves, grains of soil, particles of rock collect in the spaces between these elaborate structures, creating organic islands in this domain of rock and ice. And the plants themselves, rising two or three inches above the surrounding surfaces, foster at ground level a new microclimate, slightly warmer and damper than the exposed surfaces nearby, in which somewhat taller plants may take root and prosper.

But ingenious as the strategy of the cushion plants is for taking hold on the alpine frontiers the lichens have opened, the forget-me-not comes by its name for other, more subjective reasons. Its flowers, among the earliest of the alpine spring, are as diminutive as everything else in this scaled-down world, but there is nothing in the least modest or retiring about them. They are as aromatic in their own way as lilacs, and vibrantly blue in color. The word "shocking" is customarily applied to a particular shade of pink, but the forget-me-nots might as appropriately be said to be shocking blue; a shimmering, almost fluorescent color of the purest blue imaginable, reflecting simultaneously the blue of cloudless skies and the blue of deep ice, but alive, as pulsating with life as a blue eye; and in the center of each daisylike blossom shines a flaming yellow sun. The sight and smell of a carpet of them on a remote reach of alpine tundra is, in fact, unforgettable.

Many of the plants growing in the fell-field repeat the survival strategies of the forget-me-nots. They grow in cushions, shapes streamlined to deflect wind in the same way that an airplane wing does; moss campion is the circumpolar and classic example of the type. Or they grow in mats, as the sandworts and dwarf clovers do: Their low, spreading branches send down roots at every point where they touch earth, so that the plants are anchored at many points, like miniature banyon trees. Or, like the saxifrages, they grow in rosettes, their leaves spread out radially from the central taproot, an arrangement that allows the leaves to huddle very close to the ground, with no vertical separation and within efficient range of their water supply. Rosette forms are practical in places, like the alpine tundra, where there is no shade to interfere with photosynthesis.

The plants may be spongelike, as the lichens and club mosses are. Like the cinquefoils and the buckwheats, they are frequently covered with fine hairs that deflect the intensity of the strong alpine light. At high altitudes the light, particularly where it is reflected by snow or rock, might otherwise damage plant cells. Some plants have a reddish cast, as the leaves of some trees do in the spring, a further protection, it is thought, against ultraviolet rays. The hairs, situated to protect the stomata through which a plant breathes, also reduce water loss and capture and conserve heat. The hairy plants, in effect, produce their own hothouses. Some plants—the spring beauties, for example—are succulent, like many desert plants: Their fleshy leaves are coated with a waxy substance that retards evaporation.

Aside from these plants, there are the grasses and sedges, their long, narrow leaves well designed for maximum solar exposure and minimum water loss, their sturdy, flexible stems capable of withstanding the abuses of the winds, their modest flowers dependent only upon the winds for pollination. The grasses and sedges appear similar at first glance, but they are actually members of different families, most easily distinguishable by their stem structures. Grass stems are hollow, jointed tubes, a design affording great strength with very little weight; they tend to be the tallest plants in the fell-field. The water-loving sedges grow in the dampest niches and have solid stems, often triangular in shape. Both are durable and extremely hardy, as they must be to survive on the tundra.

All of the species that grow in the alpine regions of the northern Rockies are perennials. (Indeed, of the approximately three hundred alpine species found anywhere in the United States, only one is an annual.) The growing season is too short and unpredictable for the luxury of annual reproduction. All are slow growing; many of them take a decade or more to reach mature flowering. And many of them depend upon vegetative rather than sexual reproduction: They produce rhizomes, bulblets, corms, runners, underground bulbs. Sometimes lichens spread when a piece of an established colony breaks away and is carried by the wind to a new location. Vegetative reproduction circumvents the uncertainties of the fickle alpine summer, and it speeds the spread of plants that otherwise operate in slow motion: An offspring tied to the parent plant and benefiting from it for food and water has a clear advantage over a young seedling that has to produce its own sustenance.

The fell-field was gray-green with foliage and brimming with flowers: blue, yellow, white, purple, green, brown, all showing against brown and gray rocks in which the quartz and the mica glittered, against the emerald greenness of the tarn, against the blue sky billowing with white clouds. The wind blew, but in opposition to nothing. I thought, looking at the scene, of one of those vast medieval tapestries that hang in the windowless galleries of museums. It was like finding, when you stepped forward, that the cloth images had suddenly and miraculously sprung to life.

14

Medicine Mountain

◁ ▷

AT the summit of Medicine Mountain in the northern arc of the Big Horns, there is a construction in the shape of a wheel, built of stone. It is not clear who built it or why. Its history is shrouded because the people who established it as a sacred place are lost in unwritten time and the Crows who came after them, about the year of our independence, it is thought, never heard its story or were told it and forgot it. Nobody knows how, exactly, the circle of stones with twenty-eight spokes and seven cairns was intended to be used. Evidence grows, but not conclusively, that it was, at least in part, a celestial observatory. Astronomical evidence dates it as early as the twelfth century. Archeological evidence, however, dates it only to the late eighteenth century. If the archeological date is correct—it is based on tree ring analysis of a piece of wood excavated from one of the cairns—it could not have been very old when the Crows first encountered it, and it is puzzling, therefore, that its story should have vanished. But vanish it has.

One thing is clear: It is a sacred place. To this day the ancient rites of the native Americans are celebrated there, and it is generally agreed that worship of some kind has been practiced there for at least a couple of centuries. You would think it was a sacred place even if it were not marked as such, even if the wheel had not been built there. Some places are like that; they feel holy. You can't explain it. You can't point to evidence, cite data. Some things in the world wither and die in the face of too much scrutiny—poems and string quartets, for example—but this does not mean that they do not exist. Holy places are the same. They exist, but there is no use asking how or why or by what means. The summit of Medicine Mountain is one of them.

I had left my friend John behind—he had appointments to keep—and had gone on alone, headed farther west. I was not yet ready to take my leave of the mountains. Or perhaps they had not yet released me. So I approached the summit of Medicine Mountain alone one morning. It was gray and windy, raw, on the mountaintop. In the west, dark clouds growled menacingly. They hid the distant ranges, the Tetons, the Absarokas, the Beartooths.

My aloneness traveled with me that morning like a companion. It walked beside me, benign and peaceful, calming me and affirming me in my silence. I had not spoken a single word that day to any other human being, and I was glad, now that I approached Medicine Mountain, to be under no obligation to speak, to exclaim, to take account of any presence save that of the mountain.

All holy places command us, if only for a little while, to keep silence. I suppose that to be speechless is to go back to the beginning of things, back to our own individual beginnings when we knew nothing but the cry for help, and back to the voiceless beginnings of life on earth when the waters of the primordial soup churned and the winds raged, and nothing heard or saw. In speechlessness begins awe for life.

The mountains in the vicinity of the wheel are of a different sort than the ones I had been walking in. They are lower—about ten thousand feet in elevation— rounder, softer. The hard gray granite has given way to a soft yellow limestone, and the mountainsides are green in summer, not only with pines but with gentle and aromatic cedars. In the moist crevices of the green valleys, groves of silvery aspens grow. The tops of the mountains are bald, like the heads of old men. They are covered not with boulders but with a fuzz of wispy grass, like the last hairs of men growing bald. They have old-mountain names: Bald Mountain, Sheep Mountain, Medicine Mountain.

It is a region of small caves. The entrance to one of them lies scarcely a hundred yards from the wheel. It is a place to hide and in which things lay hidden.

At the same time, it embraces three visible worlds. To the west, you can look a mile down into the basin below. The Big Horn River winds through it like a piece of string, and you can see towns the size of toys. It is high enough so that you begin to feel diminished before the world, and this is good. This feeling of diminishment is the beginning of reverence for life. Still, the face of the mountain falls precipitously in a sheer limestone cliff just beyond the upper edge of the wheel. High as you are, you have the sensation that it would be only a short leap into the lap of the plains. You imagine that you might stretch out your arms and take flight like an eagle and soar to a resting place in the sagebrush. Here you belong simultaneously to the mountains and to the plains, and this is good. You feel empowered with choices, and in such empowerment is the beginning of joy for life. Yet the great dome of the sky rises all around you. Beyond the mountains and the plains stretches the third world, the unimaginable world of the universe. You feel the mysterious void, and this, too, is good. In mystery begins thankfulness for life.

I approached the wire fence that encircles the medicine wheel, saddened by the reminder that even in such places we somehow manage to act as if nothing were sacred.

I walked around and around the wheel, very slowly, pausing to consider it from each new angle. I noted the daisies blooming in the grass, the pika that fled from one of the cairns as I approached, the ladybugs soaking up the warmth of a stone, the charred remains of some recent ceremonial fire. It was a monument, like all monuments. What distinguished it, I thought, was the purity of its setting, so spare and austere, so high and silent, so grandly inclusive of sky and plains and mountains, a place conjoining the whole world of the people who came here to worship.

The Bighorn medicine wheel is one of forty or fifty similar structures so far discovered on the northern Great

Plains. It is the largest and best known of these, a roughly circular pattern of stones, about eighty-two feet in diameter, laid out on the surface of the ground. At the center of the circle lies a cairn in the shape of a broken doughnut, about ten feet around, and from it twenty-eight lines of stones, irregularly placed, radiate out to the rim. There are six further cairns here and there along the rim, five of them situated on the circle and the sixth a few feet outside it. Except for the central cairn, the construction is modest in scale, there being generally no more than one or two courses of stones, and the stones being roughly the size of footballs.

The first white person to see the site was probably a gold prospector from nearby Bald Mountain City, a mining camp of the 1880s, which was succeeded in the 1890s by the boom town of Fortunatus. Rumor had it that the Indians knew of a fabulous lode of gold somewhere on or near Big Baldy, as the mountain was called. But nobody ever found it. "Money flowed freely," the Federal Writers Project guide to Wyoming reports dryly, "and everyone prospered but the miners and investors."

By 1895 the first printed reference to the wheel had appeared in *Field and Stream* in an account of a hunting expedition, the author likening it to the "Calendar Stone of Old Mexico," a guess more accurate than any to appear for the next eighty years if current scholarship is correct.

The first scholarly examination of the site was undertaken in 1902 by S. C. Simms of the Field Columbian Museum. Simms, an anthropologist, questioned Crow tribal leaders about it. None had actually seen the site, but a few of them had heard of it from their fathers. They told him it was an ancient holy place but professed not to know its origins, saying only that it was made "by people who had no iron." There was a bleached buffalo skull at the site when Simms visited it, near the center cairn facing east toward the rising sun.

The wheel was photographed in 1902 and 1915 and mapped in 1917. These records have satisfied subsequent investigators that the site is authentic and that it has not been significantly altered since.

In 1922 anthropologist George Bird Grinnell noted the similarity of the wheel to the floor plan of the Sun Dance lodges of the Plains Indians and suggested that it was a representation of such a lodge, built, perhaps, by the Cheyennes.

A thorough, not to say persnickety, assessment of the site was undertaken in 1958 by the Wyoming Archeological Society under the direction of Don Grey. (Persnickety: the construction, Grey argued, should not be called a medicine wheel because it is not literally a wheel, for one thing; and for another, because the definition of a medicine wheel then in academic vogue prescribed something with spokes radiating from a central point, and in this case, the spokes radiate from the outside wall of the center cairn, not from the middle of it. Nevertheless, he said, he might *call* it a medicine wheel, given historical precedent, so long as a medicine wheel was understood to be "a compound polargram constructed upon the earth in loose stone, wood, or earth." I am trying not to giggle.) The investigators made a new map of the wheel, and excavated down to bedrock all of the cairns and about a third of the spaces between the twenty-eight spokes in the wheel. The excavations produced nothing particularly revealing: a few stone artifacts, a few pottery shards, some bone fragments, and nine beads. The central cairn yielded a piece of buffalo bone and the information that a two-foot deep pit had been dug into the limestone bedrock there. In one of the outer cairns, wedged into the stones, the archeologists found a piece of a tree limb. An analysis of its rings suggested that it dated from approximately 1760. Therefore, Grey concluded, the site could be no more than about two hundred years old.

This conclusion stood until 1974, when an astronomer, John A. Eddy, proposed an entirely new way of looking at the site. In a report published in *Science*, Eddy suggested that the real significance of the medicine wheel had been missed because earlier investigators had concentrated on the wheel and its rims. In fact, he said, the importance of the structure lies in its cairns.

Eddy guessed that the cairns were markers for astronomical observations of some sort. He set out to test this hypothesis in 1972 and 1973. An examination of the site persuaded him that the observations had to be connected to the summer solstice since it is snowbound and generally inaccessible during the winter solstice. Indeed, shortly before the summer solstice in 1972, boot-deep snow fell there, and four days before the solstice in 1973 a late storm halted traffic on the nearby highway. But these snows demonstrated the practicality of the site. While the storms left the mountainsides at lower elevations deeply covered in snow, winds swept the medicine wheel site bare within two or three days. Still, Eddy conceded, "the choice of a cold and arduously reached mountaintop in preference to the equally usable nearby plains must be justified on other grounds—possibly mystical or purely aesthetic."

Eddy found confirmation of his hypothesis on that cold solstice day in 1972. A sighting from the cairn he labeled E through the center cairn marked the solstice sunrise, and a sighting from the cairn he labeled C through the center cairn marked the solstice sunset, not exactly, but close enough. The statistical odds, he calculated, that any two of the cairns placed by chance would align with the solstice sunrise and sunset are about one in four thousand.

Two questions remained. How might the other four cairns have been used? And at what time in history would the markings have been exact?

As for the cairns, Eddy found answers for three of them. From cairn F, the largest of the peripheral markers, the builders could have sighted the star Aldebaran rising over cairn A; Rigel over cairn B; and Sirius over the center cairn. These happen to be the three brightest morning stars rising near the path of the sun in the summer sky over the Big Horns. And they would have been important stars to someone using celestial sightings to mark the calendar.

Although it is not true now, in earlier centuries Aldebaran made its first rising with the sun just before the summer solstice. Its appearance would have been important because the sun moves rather slowly along the horizon at the time of the solstice, making it difficult to mark its occurrence exactly. But the first yearly rising of a star is rather easy for a practiced observer to pinpoint to within two or three days. So the first appearance of Aldebaran would have signaled quite precisely the solstice day.

In the centuries when Aldebaran served to mark the solstice, furthermore, Rigel made its first yearly appearance exactly one lunar month later, and Sirius first appeared exactly one lunar month after that. (I mean lunar month here in the sense that the Indians did, as including only the twenty-eight days in each synodic month when the moon is visible.) With the first rising of Sirius, in other words, the two high summer months of the alpine season would have passed, and seeing it, nomadic hunters in the mountains would have known that it was time to pack up and head back to the plains for the winter. Probably they made their descent along the well-marked travois trail that passes within easy distance of the medicine wheel.

As for dating when the wheel might have been constructed, the same difficulties arise as in deciding when the precise day of the solstice has occurred. But, again, these difficulties are not present with respect to Aldebaran. Eddy calculated that the Aldebaran alignment could have been made any time from about 1500 to about 1900. The most likely guess, he said, is that cairn F was built about 1700.

Since then another astronomer, Jack Robinson, has proposed a possible use for cairn D, the one that stumped Eddy. A sighting from cairn F through cairn D, Robinson proposed, would have been useful from about 1050 to about 1450 in locating the rising with the sun of another very bright morning star, Fomalhaut, which would have made its first appearance one lunar month before the summer solstice. It could have been, then, one more observation useful in pinpointing accurately the time of the solstice. If Robinson is correct, obviously, the wheel would considerably predate 1700, an idea, I think, that Eddy would not resist. In fact, Eddy was the first scholar to suggest that the medicine lodges of the Plains Indians may have been patterned after the medicine wheels and not, as is usually presumed, the other way around.

Were the Plains Indians good enough astronomers to make all of this credible? "The answer is surely yes," Eddy wrote. "There should be little doubt that any people who lived by the sun would intimately know the dawn, and that any who lived at the mercy of the seasons would know as well the solstices."

There remains the matter of the twenty-eight spokes and the ring of stones that connects them. The ring might be simply ornamental, and the spokes have one obvious use in calendar keeping. They could have been markers for the days of the lunar month.

Recently anthropologist Robert L. Hall has suggested that all of the speculation about the wheel may be right, that it is *both* a representation of a medicine lodge and an observatory, and that the site has significance even beyond these interpretations.

The twenty-eight spokes have both practical and ritual connections. Twenty-eight, for example, is the number of days in a month as the Plains Indians counted them. Each of these days had a particular symbolic significance, Black Elk, a holy man of the Oglala Sioux, explained:

. . . two of the days represent the Great Spirit; two are for Mother Earth; four are for the four winds; one is for the Spotted Eagle; one for the sun; and one for the moon; one is for the morning star; and four are the four ages; seven are for our seven great rites; one is for the buffalo; one for the fire; one for the water; one for the rock; and finally one is for the two-legged people. If you add all these days up you will see that they come to twenty-eight.

Hence the twenty-eight poles in a ceremonial lodge. Again, the buffalo has twenty-eight ribs, upon which the Plains Indians depended for their lives. The number of these ribs was not something that might have escaped their notice. Again, in Plains culture, the sacred numbers were four and seven. Four for the winds, the ages, the quarters of the earth, the seasons. Seven for the seven days, the seven rites, the seven cardinal directions (north, south, east, west, up, down, and here). And, of course, the product of the sacred numbers is twenty-eight.

Even if the spokes in the wheel were merely ornamental, there would have been twenty-eight of them, automatically, instinctively, even as an orator in our own culture rises in debate to make three points.

What particularly attracted Hall's attention, however, was not the spokes or the rim of the wheel but the shape of its cairns. They are all roughly round, but each has an opening, and the openings appear to be placed at random. The cairns do not mark the directions, and they do not open in ways consistent with their use as guides to celestial observation. What could they mean?

To Hall, the cairns looked keyhole-shaped, reminiscent to him of similar shapes in the ritual constructions of other native American cultures. They reminded him of a shrine on Chicoma Mountain in New Mexico, the earth altars of the Omaha, the keyholed-shaped prayer symbol of the Pawnees, and the Cahokia woodhenges at the site of the great pre-Columbian agricultural city east of St. Louis on the Mississippi River flood plain.

206

And the wheel in its totality was suggestive not only of medicine lodges, of Pawnee earth lodges, and of Cheyenne tipi encampments. It reminded Hall, as well, of the netted hoops of the Piegan Indians of Alberta, Canada, and of those used in the hoop and pole games of the Plains Indians.

These are two sets of images with the same implications. The keyhole images, Hall contends, are all variations on the structure that the Pueblos called the earth navel. He quotes Alfonso Ortiz, a Pueblo by birth and an anthropologist by training, on the significance of the earth navel: "It functions as a scared center in two respects. First, it is a point at which one may communicate with the spiritual underworld, and second, it serves to gather in blessings from the three world levels and directs them, through the open end, to the Tewa villages." In the village where Ortiz was born, further, the earth navel was the site of an annual ceremony of renewal. At the beginning of the growing season, seeds from all of the food plants important to the village were planted in the earth navel in a ritual intended each year to reawaken nature.

The netted hoop images, on the other hand, recall the spiderweb, a natural trap with meaning in the rituals of many Indian nations. The spiderweb, the Indians noted, caught not only prey for the spider but also moisture, because the dewdrops condensed on it, and the sun itself, trapped in the drops of dew. So it symbolized the rain and the sunshine of the annual rebirth of the earth in spring. It was also used as a symbol in the buffalo fertility rites of the Plains Indians. A ritual game was played with a netted hoop and pole, in which the pole represented the buffalo bull and the hoop the cow, and penetration of the hoop by the pole was a metaphor for fertilization.

It is consistent with what we know about Indian culture, Hall argues, to suppose that the wheel on Medicine Mountain had a variety of uses. Perhaps it sustained the observations necessary to determine the coming of the summer solstice, when the blessings of the sun were thought to be most powerful. Perhaps it had connections with the Sun Dance rituals, which were meant to honor dead chiefs. But it is also likely, he says, that the wheel was a world center, an earth navel, for the nations occupying that region. If so, the cairns would be properly understood as having both the passive purpose of marking celestial phenomena and the active purpose of catching the blessings of the earth and directing them to the nations that worshipped there. Their openings, in this case, would be seen not as random but as pointing to the home grounds of the tribes. And the spokes and rim of the wheel would be understood as recalling not only the medicine lodges but also the webs of the fertility rites.

The argument appeals to me, in part because the site of the Bighorn medicine wheel is so spectacularly well suited to such a grand purpose. From it one really does feel connected with every part of a vast homeland. But it is an argument that no one, least of all me, is in a position to settle now. What is not written down is eventually lost. The world that the wheel represents has vanished. We can imagine it, well or badly, but we can never again know it.

Perhaps, therefore, all this is moot. But I think not. I think two things, on reflection, about my visit there. I am, for one thing, touched by the sentence with which

Dr. Eddy's path-breaking report ends. "With the encroachment of a white civilization on the northern plains in the 19th century," he wrote, "the Indian's requirement for a natural calendar could have vanished, taking with it certain astronomical traditions." *Taking with it certain astronomical traditions.* I think of all that some prehistoric peoples knew about the stars, and of all that most of us now don't know about them. It reminds me that a culture can get a lot more urbane without growing one iota richer. And I think of Hall's argument. *It would be consistent with what we know about Indian culture to suppose that its artifacts had both practical and spiritual significance.* That, I think, is an argument that no anthropologist a millennium hence will ever be moved to make about us. Let it be said: We knew the difference between the spiritual and the practical. And let the question ring: And what good did knowing it ever do us?

BOOK

3

15

The Work of the Devil
◁ ▷

I left Medicine Mountain, winding my way down the steep road into the basin. The question occurred to me as I stood on the rim of Devil Canyon two thousand feet above the Big Horn River in north-central Wyoming. Why are so many of the really spectacular places in this country assigned to the devil?

Partly, I know, the answer lies in a perverse habit of mistranslation. Indian place names sometimes referred to the Spirit, or to spirits, just as white place names often pay homage to saints. They were holy places. But our view was that any spirit the Indians worshipped must be a devil,

213

so we named their holy places after the devil. But there is more at work in these names, I think, than simple racism.

Devil Canyon is not actually a discrete canyon but a particularly deep and dramatic bend in the Bighorn Canyon, which the Big Horn River cuts through the foothills of the mountain chain of the same name on its way to the Missouri River. The rimlands are arid and austere. Along the waterways a cottonwood or willow sometimes takes root, but on the hills and uplands the fawn-colored and pale-yellow earth, if you can call it earth, baked to an unyielding hardness, supports only a sparse cover of gray-green rabbit brush, snakeweed, and sage. It is the province of grasshoppers and sand-colored lizards, of a small band of wild horses, fleetingly seen, of an occasional scraggly goat or elegant pronghorn antelope, wary and insatiably curious at the same time.

But perhaps I exaggerate the intensity of the life in this place, on the beaten track to Yellowstone National Park, but little noticed or visited. Even the cactuses shun it. Mainly, as the Montanans say, it is the land of the big sky, of clouds and sun and moon and wind. Here it takes something like a canyon to drag your attention down to earth again. The clouds gather in the west over the Absarokas and the Wind Rivers, great craggy peaks in a landscape where you may sometimes be beyond mountains but never out of sight of them. The clouds accumulate in billowy banks, looking like ranges of mountains themselves, and march across the elliptical basin in which the Big Horn River runs, pulled along by the perpetual exchange of air between the cool alpine regions of the Big Horns to the east and the sweltering basin to the west. They forever threaten rain but seldom deliver it, passing overhead

merely as a visible sign of the palpable winds. In sufficiently hot places rain falls without reaching the ground;
the raindrops tumble out of the clouds, evaporate on their
way down, and return as vapor to the clouds again.

There was a time when the study of clouds had more
than meteorological significance, when we found philo-
sophical and aesthetic as well as practical meanings in
them. This time extended from the late eighteenth century, from Goethe, say, into the early years of our own
century, the span of the Golden Age of natural history.
But the time for reading messages in the clouds has passed,
a casualty of our lost sense of natural history.

All those contemporary nature programs on television,
in particular, have radically distorted, have trivialized, I
think, our sense of what natural history is. We tend to
regard it now as a pseudoscience, like astrology, as an as-
semblage of odd or amusing or romantic facts about life in
exotic or remote places. It carries the same quaint con-
notations and appeal as missionary work, a certain anthropomorphic and xenophobic contentment with our
own lofty superiority. Heathens and hyenas are both lower
forms of life, curiosities with whom we may be safely involved intellectually but not emotionally. They are oddi-
ties we may learn about without learning from. But
natural history is a distinguished, if now a languishing,
branch of literature, not of science. Its subject is not the
strange and wonderful ways of The Plant Kingdom or The
Animal Kingdom or The Wild Kingdom, as if natural life
were lived in some fairytale principality. Natural history is
about places, real places, and in a broader sense it is about
place. The serious natural historian, for example, wonders
not so much how bats employ sonar soundings in naviga-

tion, although this may be useful to know, as how bats and human beings are related, what our mutual dependencies are, and how an acquaintance with bats helps to define our own place in the world. Where do we fit in? What are our limits? Our responsibilities? Our debts to the rest of life? These are the real questions of natural history. They are, ultimately, questions of morality.

Morality is a practical response to vulnerability. It is our defense against weakness, against the things we fear, particularly in ourselves. It is also a mark of maturity. We are born with certain fundamental fears: of the dark, of falling, of sudden loud noises. Many of our fears, however—including such universal ones as the fear of snakes—develop as we mature and continue to intensify over time. I am using the word "fear" here, of course, in its dictionary sense to mean the emotion stimulated by an awareness of danger. I do not mean fear in its macho connotation, as a form of timidity or cowardice. Within reasonable limits, a healthy quotient of fear is a rational and grown-up response to life, in no way inconsistent with the self-confidence that maturity also demands.

We are passing through what one can hope is only a phase of childishness. One of the proofs of this is that we are, as a people, in a relatively fearless frame of mind. Any nation that can seriously entertain the notion of a state of technological invulnerability to the weapons of war, the premise of our Star Wars program, is a nation with a childish innocence about history, about human nature, and about danger.

Despite all the doomsday talk of environmentalists over the past twenty-five years, we remain equally as innocent, as blissfully fearless, about nature. I heard a striking expression of this innocence not long ago at a conference on farm policy. The man in charge of the University of Minnesota's College of Agriculture was speaking forcefully against a bogeyman, or a group of them. He had falsely characterized the people who question the appropriateness of the industrial model for agriculture as opponents of research, as people who would stop the quest for learning and turn back time. He asked us to consider what the primitive past was like. The vision he offered was arresting for its intensity and passion. It was a time, as he saw it, of harsh and tedious physical labor, unrelieved by any glimmer of human joy, unrewarded by any material comfort. This much of the argument was routine. Anyone who sees limits in the uses of technology can expect to be accused sooner or later of wanting to relieve the populace of the benefits of electric lights and running water. But the speaker went a good deal further than that. He asked us, most vividly, to imagine a time when farmers lived at the savage edge of the dark wilderness, beset on every side by the unimaginable terrors of nature. Listening to him, even I shuddered.

The scientist's implication was clear, although he did not himself draw it; his vision was ideological, not reflective. Science had brought to farming, he was telling us, not only physical and material comfort, not only longer, happier, and softer lives, but freedom from wildness. He would concede, no doubt, the continuing unpredictabilities of weather and pestilence, but he was asking us to believe in security of a larger kind, to accept the premise of a world in which the enveloping wildness has been tamed. But we have not mastered nature, nor are we likely to, and we are no more free now to live in disregard of it than we ever were. We may have lost our awe of it, but its power remains, and to the extent that we are unmindful of that power, we are less, not more, secure. The historian Phillip Ariès has suggested, for example, that fear of death intensified after the onset of the industrial age, when we began to leave our agricultural past for life and work in settings at some distance from nature. With industrialism, we had put the wilderness behind us, but we had also removed ourselves from everyday confrontations with the fact of death, and the stranger it became to us, the more frightening the prospect of it seemed.

The moral necessity of which natural history speaks, the necessity to find our place in the natural world and to live within its limits, will seem relevant only when we maintain a sensible fear for the future of life and a healthy doubt of our own ability to foresee every circumstance vital to its prosperity. We are, in our present state of mind, like children gamboling on a precipice, secure only because we are ignorant of the depths.

In the time when clouds were taken seriously, this was, really, the point. Emerson's remark was representative: "The sky is the daily bread of life." What one found in clouds was a powerful statement of the mysteriousness of life, an affirmation of its unfathomability, a sustaining sense of wonder. The word "fear" once had two meanings. It meant the emotion one feels in the face of danger, but it also signified reverential awe, as in the phrase "the fear of God." That the second meaning has become archaic hints at something more than a slight impoverishment of the language. It marks a shift in perception, the devaluation of an emotion. Lacking a proper sense of fear, we are unable to experience fully that most wonderful of emotions, the feeling of awe.

The greatest appreciation of a natural landscape in American letters is John C. Van Dyke's brilliant and not quite forgotten book, *The Desert*, first published in 1901. Van Dyke was not a naturalist by training but a student of art, as so many great natural historians have been. He saw the same virtues in the desert landscape as in modern painting. He experienced there a world in which form had given way to purity of line and color, in which beauty had superseded function. His book marks the end of an era; it is, so far as I know, the last major work of natural history to devote an entire chapter to sky and clouds.

"What is it," he asks in that chapter,

that draws us to the boundless and the fathomless? Why should the lovely things of earth—the grasses, the trees, the lakes, the little hills—appear trivial and insignificant when we come face to face with the sea or the desert or the vastness of the midnight sky? Is it that the one is a tale of things known and the other merely a hint, a suggestion of the unknown? Or have immensity, space, magnitude a peculiar beauty of their own? Is it not true that bulk and breadth are primary and essential qualities of the sublime in landscape? And is it not the sublime that we feel in immensity and mystery? If so, perhaps we have a partial explanation of our love for sky and sea and desert waste. They are the great elements. We do not see, we hardly know if their boundaries are

219

limited; we only feel their immensity, their mystery, and their beauty.

Sublime. There is another word that has gone hopelessly out of fashion. Van Dyke is dated by his resort, twice, to it. Once everybody knew what the sublime was. It appeared in capitals. The Sublime. It made sense when there were still things to fear in the fullest and now archaic sense of the word.

The sentence immediately following the passage I have quoted is also revealing. "And quite as impressive as the mysteries are the silences."

Devil Canyon along the Big Horn River is as much a place of silences as of clouds and sky. You stand on the rim of that wide and nearly formless place, immersed in the blue of the firmament. At your feet the narrow walls of the deep cavern, gray precipices of soft limestone tinged with splashes of Indian red rock, plunge toward the gray-green river below. The fall is so precipitous that it grabs at your belly when you peer into it. The water is deep. You can tell that by the intense purity of its unwatery color. And the river is powerful. It has left this gracefully curving cavern as a sign of its strength. But what is unearthly about it, awesome, fearful, is its ghostly silence.

The river seems not to run at all. Its surface is level and glassy. There is no sign of a current. It speaks in no voice of any kind. The wind sounds gently against your eardrums. Now and then an unseen pigeon coos from a perch around the bend. The river, you know, is boring relentlessly into the mantle of the earth, is running restlessly toward the sea. But not a drop of water seems to move, not a grain of stone gives audible ground. It is as if you

had suddenly gone deaf, as if the wind and the pigeon
were figments of a dream. Here is a mystery past compre-
hension.

After I first published this observation, an illuminating
letter came from Dr. Donald B. Lawrence, a botanist by
profession. He wrote:

> Fortunately, Lib [his wife] and I have lived long
> enough to have seen Big Horn River free and unfet-
> tered. When we first saw that great canyon on 13
> July 1947, the river had not yet been silenced by the
> hand of man. It roared with a mighty current of
> white water, gnawing its way to the sea. It was mag-
> nificent, and still more awe-inspiring in those days!
> We have not had the courage to look at it since con-
> struction of the Yellowtail Dam which backs up the
> water for forty miles to form "Yellowtail Reservoir"
> or "Bighorn Lake," depending on the map you look
> at.

Of course! I had made the mistake one so often does, of
taking the present moment for granted, of trying to comprehend something without taking into account its history. I had forgotten that eloquent warning of Black Elk's:
"A man without history is like the wind on the buffalo
grass."

But when I reflected on it, I thought that the history
reinforced the interpretation. In an important sense, the
canyon has always been silent. Even when its white waters
roared, it did not make any sound that we could fully in-
terpret. Our own capacity for language creates the void
that divides us from the voiceless things of the earth. But

the river was not always tame. In losing its roar, it has lost its wildness, and in losing its wildness, it has become less fearsome, and in losing its fearsomeness, it has grown less awesome. Its power survives, although pent up. One day the river will conquer the dam and be free, and wild, and fearsome again. It will prevail. But its power now lies hidden, and therefore unaccounted. We have temporarily discounted it and so hidden from ourselves its real nature. What we have done to the river, we have done to the earth. In subduing it, we have tamed our fears. But it is still a wild world, and in the wilderness there is nothing more dangerous than to be unafraid.

One might marvel at the canyon, even tamed. But we don't. It is the work of the devil, we say. We shrug our shoulders and walk away. There are hundreds of other places like it on our continent, devil's canyons and towers and tables, badlands, hell's holes and half acres, places silent and sublime, mystifying and disregarded.

A few hundred miles away, rangers in teams were directing hordes of traffic to one of six clogged parking lots at Mount Rushmore. No talk of the devil in that puny place. I, in the meantime, had Devil Canyon entirely to myself.

Not far from Mount Rushmore is another silent and mysterious landscape. It is called Hell's Canyon, but you won't find it on any tourist map. It, too, is unvisited, except by a few neighboring ranchers and a few Sioux Indians, who have maintained a sweat lodge there in memory of its long tradition as a sacred place. But Hell's Canyon is about to be redeemed. Honeywell Corporation has bought

6,200 acres of it as a testing site for conventional munitions. It'll be good for the community, Honeywell says. Economic development.

Perhaps they'll rename it. Peace Alley. Blissful Valley. Something like that. In the world we live in, it would make a lot of sense.

16
Lost
◁ ▷

I should not have been so impatient. I arrived in Cody, Wyoming, on a Saturday afternoon. Cody is a bustling tourist town at the southeast corner of the fabled wilderness region of northwestern Wyoming, the country that encompasses Yellowstone, the world's first national park; the Tetons; the beautiful mountain valley called Jackson Hole; and the Absaroka and Beartooth mountains, rugged ranges, the former volcanic in origin, the latter the result of a twenty-thousand-foot uplift of Precambrian bedrock. The town was jammed with weekend traffic and, at five thousand feet, low enough in elevation so that one felt the full heat of the August sun. I had been traveling for several days in the sagebrush basins of central Wyoming, and I was eager for freezing nights again, for fields of snow, for streams of icy mountain water. Every minute I spent at populated elevations seemed to me wasted. I restocked my pack at a grocery and dashed through town in search of topographical maps. I was headed into the Beartooths, I knew not where. The Forest Service office was closed for the weekend. The mountaineering shop had run out of maps and the clerk there didn't know where else I might find them. They were hard to keep in stock, he said. He suggested another shop down the street. It, too, was closed. I abandoned Cody and headed for Cooke City, a tiny mining town that advertises itself as the gateway to Yellowstone. Every sort of souvenir imaginable was for sale in Cooke City, but no maps. I retreated from Cooke City and headed east on the Beartooth Highway for Top of the World Store and Motel, a little general store so far from nowhere that it, all by itself, merits a legend on the U.S. Geological Survey maps. There were no 7.5 minute maps in stock there either, but the young man behind the counter said he did have 30 minute maps.

"Fine," I said. "I have five days. Where would you go if you were me?"

"Five days?" he said. "I'd go to Martin Lake."

"Fine," I said, "I'll go to Martin Lake. Give me the maps." The clerk produced them.

"Have a good time," he said. "Just be careful of the bears. Although they usually aren't up that high, except when the trout are spawning."

I thanked him, and in twenty minutes had found a campground to spend the night, tempted though I was to

225

set out on foot in the hour before dark. It was August, and, I would soon see for myself, the trout were spawning.

I set out confidently the next morning. The trail was wide and smooth and very nearly level. The sun was brightly shining and the temperature coolish and comfortable. It felt good to have a pack on my back again. Early on I met two or three other hikers returning from treks, stubby with week-old beards and walking briskly, as one does on the last leg of a foot journey. I greeted them more enthusiastically than they did me. A brief climb up a steep ridge and Beauty Lake came into view. My map seemed to suggest that the junction in the trail that I was looking for would come before Beauty Lake, but its scale was such, I told myself, that no doubt it was merely deceptive on this point. Here the trail divided. I took the fork to the right, not bothering to consult my compass. And why should I? I was on a clearly marked trail, and I plainly could not go far wrong. So I set off, after a bit of rest, in what, so far as I am now able to tell, was a northwesterly direction, convinced that I was headed north.

The trail climbed steadily past a string of tiny lakes. I might have thought this odd too, since I was presumably headed toward Becker Lake, a long lake shaped like a woman's high boot, the sort of feature one couldn't possibly mistake for anything else. The map showed no intervening lakes. But I put the nagging doubt that was beginning to arise out of mind. Anyway, it was a beautiful walk, which had already carried me, as I had hoped, above treeline and into a region of lush alpine meadows where the grasses rose almost to prairie height.

At Horseshoe Lake, named obviously for its shape, the trail suddenly headed sharply southwest. Confused, I gamely followed it, and soon encountered Beartooth Butte, a distinctive, castle-shaped mountain of sedimentary rock, 10,500 feet high and flat-topped. It had been hidden by a ridge, which, it now turned out, I was circling. In the north I could see Lonesome Mountain, to which I would eventually become attached in several ways, and beyond it the high granitic Beartooth Plateau and the snow-topped peaks of the Beartooth's highest summits. To the south I had a splendid view of the high, dark, sharply etched and snow-covered Absarokas. Immediately ahead of me rose the butte, heavily eroded to show its classic sedimentary lines, a beginner's lesson in basic geology. I did not, however, recognize any of these features by name. It was beginning to occur to me in a quite conscious way that I no longer knew where I was. But I remained convinced that if only I kept going, everything would eventually come clear.

I kept going, and before long the trail forked again. This development was entirely unexpected, and it made me angry. The trail had personally betrayed my confidence in it, I thought. I got out my compass. It indicated that if I followed the right-hand fork in the trail, I would be headed northward again. Fine, I said to myself. I want to go north.

And then I deliberately put the matter aside. I was not going to let my day be ruined by a bit of confusion. I rummaged around in my pack, came up with some lunch, and settled down on a rock to enjoy it. I was seated beside one of many little streams that flowed from this high place into the valley below. In the damp sod, the elephant heads were brightly blooming. The fragrance of bluebells, which I remembered fondly from Florence Canyon, was

227

back. And the meadow was dotted with a tall, thorny, purple-flowered thistle, an elegant, statuesque plant I had not seen before but recognized from reading about it. It is commonly called elk thistle because it is a favorite early summer food of the elk and of black and grizzly bears. The Indians gathered its roots and stems too. Peeled, they are said to have a sweet, delicate taste. The elk thistle is also sometimes called Everts' thistle, and behind that name there is an incredible story.

Everts was Truman C. Everts, a hapless and apparently disagreeable man for whom a mountain in Yellowstone Park is also named. Although immortalized now both in the name of a frequently visited mountain peak and of one of the showiest plants of the West, he began and ended his life in total obscurity. He was born in Burlington, Vermont, in 1816, the son of a ship captain who took him along when he was still a child on several voyages into the Great Lakes. As a young man Everts married, and had at least one daughter, later celebrated as one of the most beautiful women in the West. Aside from these bare facts, nothing is known about his life until he was forty-eight.

Somehow, at that age—the year was 1864—he managed to fall under the patronage of the Lincoln administration and was appointed assessor of internal revenues for the Montana Territory. He served until 1870, when President Grant came to office with his own patronage obligations. Out of work, Everts lingered in the Montana Territory for a few months, hoping to find some other position. None materialized, and by midsummer he had decided to return to the East, but before he did, he signed on with Major General Henry D. Washburn for an expedition into the country now encompassing Yellowstone Park, which had not yet been thoroughly explored by white men. Washburn was surveyor general of the Montana territory, a post he had sought in hopes that the fresh mountain air would restore the health he had lost in the Civil War.

The Washburn expedition left Fort Ellis on August 22, 1870. The party included nineteen men, forty mules and horses, and a dog named Booby and was provisioned with rations for thirty days and a pavilion tent. Everts got himself into trouble almost from the moment the expedition left camp: He gorged himself on berries the first day out and was so sick from them on the second day that he couldn't move. Washburn left him to recuperate at the Bottler Ranch, although it would have been better for everyone if he had dismissed him, as he deserved, and sent him back to Fort Ellis. On the twenty-fourth of August, Everts was well enough to travel again and caught up with the expedition at a camp below Yankee Jim Canyon.

By the ninth of September he had separated from the company again, this time accidentally, and he would never rejoin it. For some days, Everts said in a highly romanticized account of his subsequent ordeal for *Scribner's Monthly*, the going had been very rough. The expedition had been traveling through dense forests, frequently encountering huge, impenetrable windfalls of trees. When the company faced such a barrier, it had developed the practice of splitting up, each person separately seeking some passage. It was not unusual, Everts said, for the men to lose temporary contact with each other during these searches. And so, on September 9, he thought nothing of it when, late in the afternoon, hunting for a way around a windfall, he fell out of touch with his companions. "I rode on," he said, "fully confident of soon rejoining the company, or of finding their camp."

Nightfall came, and he still had not found the company. "This was disagreeable enough, but caused me no alarm. I had no doubt of being with the party at breakfast the next morning. I selected a spot for a comfortable repose, picketed my horse, built a fire, and went to sleep."

Everts was in the Yellowstone forest somewhere between Grouse Creek and Sunrise Creek, not far from Yellowstone Lake. He got up at dawn the next morning and headed in what he supposed to be the direction of the lake, expecting that the expedition would have camped on its beach for the night. The way was through dense woods, and all signs of the previous day's trail seemed to have been obliterated. Finally he came to an opening from which he could see the surrounding countryside in several directions. Everts dismounted to survey the situation and consider his route, leaving his mount untethered, as he had always done in such situations. While he was deliberating, the horse suddenly bolted and disappeared into the trees, leaving Everts with nothing except the clothes he was wearing, a couple of knives, and a small opera glass.

Everts spent half a day in a desperate search for his horse, posting several notes along the way in case any of his compatriots should be looking for him. By the time he had given up hope of finding the horse, it was too dark to resume his search for his companions, and he resigned himself to spending yet another night alone in the forest, this time without food or fire or blankets. He still, he said in his account for *Scribner's*, did not think that he was permanently separated from his company. Nevertheless, he felt the first stirrings of terror.

A night must be spent amid the prostrate trunks before my return could be accomplished. At no time during my period of exile did I experience so much mental suffering from the cravings of hunger as when, exhausted from this long day of fruitless search, I resigned myself to a couch of pine foliage in the pitchy darkness of a thicket of small trees. Naturally timid in the night, I fully realized the exposure of my condition. I peered upward through the darkness, but all was blackness and gloom. The wind sighed mournfully through the pines. The forest seemed alive with the screeching of night birds, the angry barking of coyotes, and the prolonged dismal howl of the gray wolf. These sounds, familiar by their constant occurrence throughout the journey, were now full of terror, and drove slumber from my eyes.

After a sleepless night Everts retraced his steps of the day before, finding, to his despair, that his notes had not been discovered. It was beginning to be clear to him that he was seriously lost. Still, he said, he consoled himself with the thought that Providence would not offer him a challenge he did not have the resources to meet. "There is life in the thought. It will revive hope, allay hunger, renew energy, encourage perseverance, and, as I have proved in my own case, bring a man out of difficulty, when nothing else can avail." In Everts' case, at least, it was true.

He continued in the direction he imagined his companions to have gone and about midday arrived at Heart Lake near a geyser basin. It was, he reported, an exquisite place, the lake "of beautiful curvature," the beaches wide and sandy, a lofty mountain—Mount Everts, named by Washburn a few days earlier—seeming to emerge directly from the depths of the waters, and teeming with wildlife.

Large flocks of swans and other waterfowl were sporting on the quiet surface of the lake; otters in great numbers performed the most amusing aquatic evolutions; mink and beaver swam around unscared, in most grotesque confusion. Deer, elk and mountain sheep stared at me, manifesting more surprise than fear at my presence among them. The adjacent forest was vocal with the songs of birds, chief of which were the chattering notes of a species of mockingbird, whose imitative efforts afforded abundant merriment.

All the same, Everts was not amused. "I was in no humor for ecstasy."

Very quickly, the situation grew much worse. Everts began to hope for the appearance of an Indian who might rescue him, confident that the defenselessness of his situation rendered him quite safe from attack. Indeed, to his wonderment, a large canoe soon appeared on the distant horizon of the lake, sailing rapidly in his direction. He hurried off to meet it, but when it drew near, it turned out only to be a big pelican, which rose from the water and flew away. "This little incident," Everts said, "quite unmanned me."

It so unmanned him, in fact, that he crawled, stricken with depression, into a thicket of pines and fell asleep, only to be awakened some time after dark by the blood-curdling scream of a mountain lion. Terrified, he leapt from his bed and scrambled as far up a tree as he could get. The cat approached and paced and growled at the foot of the tree in the very place where he had been sleeping. Everts tried screaming back at the lion, but it would not go away. Finally he fell silent, and so did the lion. The silence, he found, was even more terrifying than the pacing and growling. After what seemed an interminable spell, the cat emitted one last screech and disappeared into the forest. Everts was so exhausted from this encounter that despite his terror, he climbed down from his perch and went to sleep again in his old bed.

But before the night was out, a snowstorm swept in on gale-force winds. Everts, whose clothes were already torn to tatters, was soaked. In order to keep warm, he buried himself in the earth and covered himself with a thatch of pine boughs. Washburn's party, realizing by now that Everts was hopelessly lost, sent out a search party the next day, and Washburn and one of his men got to within half a mile of the place where Everts lay, but they were forced to turn back when one of the horses broke through the crust covering one of the hot springs in the region and was badly scalded on the legs. The whole company searched for Everts for four days under almost impossible conditions. It continued to storm—more than two feet of snow fell over the next week—obliterating every trace of him. The searchers marked their trail with blazes and left behind a few small caches of food, although they themselves were running dangerously short of food.

Washburn was finally obliged to abandon the general search and to move his party on, but he did leave behind three men to continue the effort for a few days.

Everts, in the meantime, had become badly frostbitten, and his feet were already beginning to fester. In an effort to keep warm, he moved to the hot springs and built a little hut of pine branches over the crust of one of them and lay down there. The steam coming up through the crust kept him quite cozy—"parboiled," in fact, he said—but this arrangement led soon enough to a new disaster. While he was lying there one night, he broke through the crust and scalded his hip in the boiling water. From that moment on, he said, he lived in constant pain.

Still, he would not be defeated. He managed to capture a small bird with his hands. He was so hungry that he tore it apart and ate it raw. During a lull in the storm, he suddenly realized that he could make a fire with his opera glass, and for a time he was sustained by the boiled roots of the thistle that was abundant there, the thistle now known as Everts' thistle.

Somehow he had managed to lose his knives, but he fashioned a new one from the tongue of a buckle on his vest. With this, he cut apart his tattered boots and made a new pair of slippers bound with bark thongs. He had a linen handkerchief, which he unraveled. Some of the thread he used to mend his clothing, and the rest he attached to a pin he found in his jacket, which he had bent into a fish hook. Thus provisioned, he awaited the day when the weather would break and he could make a new attempt to reach Yellowstone Lake.

The nineteenth of September dawned clear and sunny, the opportunity Everts had been praying for. Lame and in great pain, he set out to find Yellowstone Lake. That was the day the three searchers Washburn had left behind arrived at Heart Lake. Finding no sign of Everts, they finally gave up the effort and turned back toward Fort Ellis. Everts failed in his attempt to reach the lake and returned to Heart Lake on the twentieth, thus for the second time narrowly missing rescue.

He lingered for two days, nursing his burns and his feet and subsisting on thistles. By this time his burns were so inflamed that he could only sleep sitting up. Nevertheless, on the twenty-third of September he set out again, determined to find his way out of the wilderness. On the twenty-fifth he reached the camp the Washburn party had made at Thumb Lake, three days after they had left it. He had lost one of his slippers by now, and he hoped to find food and some means of fashioning another piece of footwear in the remains of the camp, but the best he could come up with was an old fork and a half-pint yeast tin, which he made into a drinking cup. Despairing but not defeated, he set out on the trail of the Washburn party. When evening fell, he built a fire and, to protect it from the fierce winds, erected a shelter of pine boughs over it and settled down to sleep. In the night the shelter caught fire, and the fire spread into the surrounding forest. Everts tried to slap it out. He now had a badly burned hand as well as rotting feet and a festering hip.

Still he persevered into the bitter alpine October, shoeless and in rags. He lost his opera glass, and took to carrying an ember from the last fire with him to the next evening's campsight, but one night a snowstorm doused the flames, and he was altogether without heat. He pressed on. Washburn's expedition returned to Fort Ellis

on September 27, and on October 2, the three-man
search party also returned with the news that there was no
sign of Everts.

A group of sympathizers got together a reward of six
hundred dollars for his recovery, and two men volunteered
to hunt for him until winter storms should make the effort
impossible. They were George A. Pritchett, a handyman
and packer, and John Baronett, also known as Yellowstone Jack, an English adventurer who had been a sailor, a
prospector, a soldier of fortune, an Indian fighter, and a
guide, among other things. Baronett knew the Yellowstone wilderness well, having prospected it for gold in
1869.

On October 6 the two were approaching the divide between Blacktail Deer Creek Plateau and Crescent Hill in a
cold sleet when Baronett's dog picked up the scent of
something, a wounded black bear, Baronett thought:

. . . and looking across a small cañon to the mountainside, I saw a black object upon the ground. Yes,
sure enough, there was Bruin. My first impulse was to
shoot from where I stood, but he was going so slowly
I saw I should have no difficulty overtaking him, and
crossed over to where he was. When I got near to it,
I found it was not a bear, and for my life I could not
tell what it was. It did not look like an animal that I
had ever seen, and it was certainly not a human
being. It never occurred to me that it was Everts. I
went along close to the object; it was making a low
groaning noise, crawling upon its knees and elbows,
and trying to drag itself up the mountain. Then sud-

denly it occurred to me that it was the object of my
search.

His rescuers described Everts as weighing about fifty
pounds, the balls of his feet worn to the bone, the flesh of
his scalded thigh rotted away to the bone, his fingers
curled up like the claws of a bird, inarticulate and irrational. Everts remembered a somewhat different scene a
year later:

> Groping along the side of a hill, I became suddenly
> sensible of a sharp reflection, as of burnished steel.
> Looking up, through half-closed eyes, two rough but
> kindly faces met my gaze.
> "Are you Mr. Everts?"
> "Yes. All that is left of him."
> "We have come for you."
> "Who sent you?"
> "Judge Lawrence and other friends."
> "God bless him, and them, and you! I am saved!"

Baronett, in any case, picked him up and carried him to
a campsite, built a fire, spoon-fed him some tea, and, the
next day, carried him to a trapper's cabin fourteen or fifteen miles away. Pritchett rode first to Fort Ellis and, fail-
ing there, on to Bozeman in search of an ambulance
wagon and a doctor while Baronett stayed behind and
nursed Everts, among other ministrations feeding him a
pint of rendered oil from the fresh fat of a bear to unstop
his digestive system, which was clogged with uncooked
thistle roots. Ten days after his rescue Everts was well
enough to travel, and less than a month later, on Novem-

ber 5, he went under his own power to a banquet in his
honor in Helena. It could not be said that he was a man
of limited will.

But the will to persevere, however remarkable, would
not seem to be the key to a successful life. After his great
adventure, Everts stayed on in Montana for a time as part
owner of the trading store at Fort Ellis, married again, and
eventually made his way back East, where he sired a son,
Truman C. Everts, Jr., and, at the age of seventy-six, a
daughter, dabbled at farming, held a minor sinecure in the
Post Office Department, and ultimately died at the age of
eighty-six, penniless and forgotten.

Even his rescuers had no soft spot in their hearts for
him. As soon as he was able to talk about it, Everts began
maintaining that he did not need to be rescued, that he
could have found his own way out of the mountains, and
when Baronett, some years later, paid a courtesy call on
him, Everts, far from expressing any gratitude, received
him coldly. Baronett went away saying he wished he had
"let the son-of-a-gun roam."

I got up from my rock set in its forest of Everts' thistles,
shouldered my pack, which seemed heavier than usual,
and headed up the trail running north. In an hour Beartooth Butte was out of sight, and the trail had dwindled
from a wide and well-worn one into a grassy and sometimes indistinct path. As it grew more and more indistinct, I grew correspondingly more distraught. I knew that
I had taken a wrong turn somewhere, but I wasn't yet
ready to admit it. I continued on. Eventually the trail disappeared altogether. I was not carrying an altimeter, but I
didn't need one to know that I was losing altitude. I was

below treeline again, in a region dotted with small, marshy lakes, ponds, really, although none were so shallow as to support water lilies.

Late in the day, as I was standing near one of them studying my map to see if I could find anything resembling it, a couple of hikers appeared over the hill, headed south. When they passed, I inquired casually whether they knew the name of the lake, thinking that if I had the name, I might be able to orient myself. No, they said, they didn't. I thanked them, unwilling to pursue the matter. This is male behavior of the sort that has, on occasion, driven my wife nearly insane. There is no shame in the world, it seems to me in my most irrational moments, greater than admitting that you are lost, and I could not bring myself to admit it even now, when the fear of it was beginning to assert itself in the nerve ends of my skin. If I asked too many questions, those strangers would figure out that I was lost, and then where would I be? So we bade each other good day, and they disappeared over the horizon, seeming to know where they were going, while I continued unsuccessfully to try to make out my position on the map. Well, I told myself, I'll walk a little farther and perhaps something will turn up. I did and nothing turned up. I had two maps, one for the Wyoming part of the wilderness, one for the Montana portion, and I no longer knew which to look at. I had no idea which state I was in.

The light was running out. Already the long shadows of evening were beginning to stretch across the slopes. I decided to proceed only until I could find a reasonable spot to camp for the night and to head back in the morning while I was still fairly confident I could find my way.

I had been walking among lakes all day. Now, of

course, they vanished. Not so much as a puddle of water appeared in the next half hour. I was beginning to be not despairing but angry again when finally, nestled below a rim of rock and spruce, a kidney-shaped pond appeared, a lovely blue-water pond supporting a community of cattails and reeds at its shallow edges and, in the narrow neck of the kidney, a floating island of lily pads and feathery water plants. It looked a perfect place to settle for the night, and my mood immediately lightened.

There was no site close to the lake to set up residence, the land around it being composed entirely of a spongy bed of peat, but I found a dry outpost among the spruce trees on higher ground, prepared a place to sleep, and changed from boots into soft-soled shoes. When I went down to the edge of the pond to collect water for my supper, a spotted frog stared up at me for an instant from a perch on a stone in the water, then disappeared with a strong kick of its hind legs into the cover of the water plants. It seemed a talisman of welcome, this chance encounter with a spotted frog in the subalpine country of the Beartooths. Amphibians are not numerous in this country. There is the spotted frog; rarely, in protected ponds, the boreal chorus frog; in the high ponds of Colorado a mountain salamander. The reptiles are even less well represented. Occasionally one might find a wandering garter snake, more rarely at lower elevations a rattlesnake. But, in general, cold-bloodedness is a severe handicap in this forbidding country, rendering it reptile- and amphibian-sparse, a fact I have seldom, I admit, regretted.

Supper was an unadulterated misery. In the tundra country of the Canadian arctic regions, one species of mosquito swarms and attacks in such formidable numbers that arctic hares and reindeer, literally in danger of being sucked to death, are driven out of the lush meadows and into the mountains by them, and it has been calculated that an unprotected human being, standing among them, would be exposed to about nine thousand bites a minute, a rate sufficient to drain half of an average man's total blood supply in an hour. Perhaps I was not set upon by quite so many mosquitoes as that, but this is a concession I am able to make only in the calm and insect-free repose of my study. I slathered myself in repellent until I felt oiled for an orgy, a bitter reminder of how solitary my state was.

The stench of the repellent nauseated me, but it seemed to induce little modesty in the mosquitoes, which swarmed around me in a dense, black cloud, lunging and biting at merry will. When I breathed, I sucked them up my nostrils. When I opened my mouth, they took it for an invitation and crowded in. They drowned in my cocoa and cooked in my stew. In the beginning I fastidiously fished them out of my cup, but while I was fishing for the dead ones, their living colleagues landed on my exposed fingers and stabbed viciously in search of my veins. Eventually I abandoned this hopeless effort and, deciding that turnabout is indeed fair play, I ate and drank as many of them as came my way, figuring that I was, after all, reclaiming my own blood.

After an attenuated supper, the foul taste of mosquito repellent lingering on my tongue, I went down again to the pond to collect water for the morning. As I came around a big granite boulder into view of the shoreline, something exploded at the middle of the pond. I turned to see an enormous bull moose, his huge rack held high, a trail of water plants dangling from his mouth, galumphing out of sight.

I watched him go with a sudden and not entirely explicable melancholy, a sadness, it would turn out, that was not to leave me for several days. I was, of course, frustrated at having lost my way, although not dangerously so, I was confident. I really was driven nearly to despair by the unrelenting mosquitoes, which made it impossible for me to sit anywhere, to think, to do anything except keep moving. I missed my family, whom I had not seen in weeks. I missed the familiar comforts of home. I missed hearing music, having the company in the evening of a good book, the sound of laughter. I missed hearing even the sound of my own voice, which, except for an occasional word with a clerk or greeting on the trail, I had not exercised in many days. I tried it out tentatively, and it sounded strange and disembodied. Anyway, I felt foolish about using it so pointlessly.

But the melancholy sound echoing most deeply in my mind was that of the moose crashing through the water in a wild attempt to get out of my sight. It played again and again in my mind. I regretted that I had not suspected the moose's presence, wished that I had been less intent on finishing my evening chores and more alert to the possibilities of the pond, that I had come down stealthily to the water, prepared to be surprised, open to the potential of a chance meeting of this kind. Had I come upon it unawares, I might have found a hiding place among the rocks and so have kept company with the moose for a time. I desired its companionship, and it was indifferent to mine. The moose put me up against the incontrovertible fact that although I might visit this place, still in some

important way I would be forever outside it, always a
stranger, always the one to be avoided, bringing up the
tail end of things, like the clumsy schoolboy I once was,
miserable whenever it was time to choose sides for a game.

My grandmother had little interest in words and none,
so far as I know, in painting or any other kind of orna-
ment. She cooked by boiling and blanching, did not raise
flowers, avoided jewelry, and was content with the plain
white walls of her house, except for a plastic plaque that
hung near the dinette set in the living-dining room.
"Earth hath no sorrow that heaven cannot cure," it said.
The words were framed in a garland of roses. I thought, as
a boy, that it was an incredibly beautiful expression. It
reminded me of a hymn that we sang often at church:

> I'm but a stranger here,
> Heav'n is my home;
> Earth is a desert drear,
> Heav'n is my home;
> Danger and sorrow stand
> Round me on every hand;
> Heav'n is my fatherland,
> Heav'n is my home.

We believed that, I myself believed it, as devoutly as
anything. Earth was a rough spot, dangerous, unfair,
cruel, to be gotten over, endured, on the way to heaven.
In part, of course, we needed an explanation, an excuse,
for lives without wealth or status or influence. As Jesus
might endure the humiliation of living as an infant to
fulfill the promise of God, so we might suffer the indig-
nities of earth to achieve the glories of our final destiny.

We might be nobodies here, but the day was coming when the somebodies of this earth would find the tables turned.

But there was a good deal more in our sense of alienation than that, something more encompassing than religious dogma, a feeling that had been building in us as human beings for millions of years, perhaps, or at least for the thousands of years since we had become rational and literate.

I understand the feeling to be not unlike the melancholy of fame. The sacrifice of fame is intimacy. The more widely known one becomes, the less one is a person and the more an object. Friends and neighbors withdraw out of sympathy and consideration, and increasingly one comes to live in a world of strangers, of casual contacts, one-time meetings, comes to be adored, revered, sought after but never known in the sense that one yearns to be known, intimately, by a few others. The paradox of fame is that the better you are known, the less anybody knows about you. Life becomes a kind of prison, which one lives behind walled houses, venturing out in the company of guards, or wearing dark glasses and disguises. One becomes a stranger to the world, lonely and sad.

Our sense of ourselves in nature has taken the same path. Once, a long time ago, we saw ourselves as indistinguishable from nature. In our animistic world, trees and worms and bears, no less than human beings, had souls and were bound together with us in a common existence. Life then was hard and short and uncertain. We were cold and hungry and beset by fears of many kinds. But we were not, I think, in the modern sense quite so lonely, quite so afflicted with the sense of alienation, from life we say, but really from nature.

244

It has become by now, of course, taboo to think of the rest of life in human terms. We must not see parallels or lessons in nature in the quaint way that we did as recently as Victorian times. Animals, we know, do not think or feel or reason, and it is childish to think of them in this way, even in analogy or metaphor. Butterflies are butterflies; bears, bears; roses, roses. That leaves us exalted, famous in a sense, but also isolated, and somehow diminished.

"Anthropomorphizing: the charge of my critics," Loren Eiseley wrote in his journal.

> My countercharge: there is a sense in which, when we cease to anthropomorphize, we cease to be men, for when we cease to have human contact with animals and deny them all relation to ourselves, we . . . cease to anthropomorphize ourselves—to deny our own humanity. We repeat the old, old human trick of freezing the living world and with it ourselves. There is a sense . . . in which we do create our world by our ability to read it symbolically. But if we read it symbolically, aloof from ourselves and our kindest impulses, we are returning to the pre-Deistic, pre-Romantic world of depraved Christianity—where man saw "fallen nature" with the devil slipping behind each tree. Modern anthropomorphizing consists in mining nature down to its ingredients, including ourselves.

But Eiseley himself, a man given, one senses from his books, to an innate melancholy, admitted that he was not able to mine nature in this way. He wrote to his friend Hal Borland:

I felt it necessary to offer some kind of choice to man, but in reality, like yourself, I am deeply depressed about the human situation. I do not fear our extinction. What I really fear is that man will ruin the planet before he departs. I have sometimes thought, looking out over the towers of New York from some high place, what a beautiful ruin it would make in heaps of fallen masonry, with the forest coming back. Now I fear for the forest itself.

How should I learn to live in the same world with the moose? I did not know. I came down to the edge of the water, and it fled from me and never looked back. I watched it go and felt rebuked.

At dawn the next morning, I crept down to the pond on all fours and hid behind a boulder of granite, hoping in vain that it would come again to feed on the lilies glinting with frost. I asked of it a certain intimacy, and it spoke to me only of great distances. It was then that I began to feel truly lost.

17
Walking in Clouds

◁ ▷

I turned myself around, retraced my steps, got going in the right direction and eventually found Martin Lake, but not blissfully. From my notebook:

Martin Lake
8:30 P.M.
After an afternoon of storms and a trek across country, boulder-hopping most of the way to, miraculously, my destination.

Solitude can teach you your dependencies as well as your capacity to be independent.

I have often dreamed of setting off across country

247

and wandering forever, but I know now I could never do it. I have been incredibly homesick the last few days and despite moose and spawning trout and spotted frogs and thundering mountain streams and breathtaking high country vistas and meadows full of flowers, all I can think of is going home.

I hope I can remember that the next time I want to leave it.

My melancholy had deepened with every false step I had made in three days of confused wandering. It rained constantly. It was bitterly cold. The mosquitoes were unrelenting, as if neurotically desperate to get in one last fill of blood before winter. I was pursued for a day and a half by a merry band of teenagers, whose every scream of delight cut through me like an arctic wind. The spawning fish reminded me of bears. Every turn I took was the wrong one. Every stone in the trail tripped me. Every ascent up a ridge seemed interminable. Every descent seemed maliciously difficult.

I was in the country a thousand feet below Hellroaring Plateau and feeling appropriately hellish. Coming the wrong way around so-called Golden Lake, on the bad advice of a fisherman, I squeezed onto a ledge too narrow to accommodate me and was forced into the frigid water six feet below, somehow landing upright on a submerged rock and so saving myself from drowning. I trembled afterward violently for an hour, in part from fear, in part from incipient hypothermia.

I had worn holes in the inner soles of both boots and walked in pain, despite the layers of moleskin and gauze in which I had wrapped my feet. In the half hour before I

entered the rebuke to myself in my notebook, I had tried
to make a fire, but the kindling was too damp and the
wind too strong, and afraid of using more matches than I
could afford, I had abandoned the effort with a curse.
Martin Lake might be lovely—in fact it was so full of
trout that their feeding ripples made it look as though it
were boiling, and from the lake a chain of gurgling waterfalls fell through a succession of pristine ponds—but I was
damned if I would admit it. All I wanted was out.

In any case, the lake wasn't altogether lovely. Around
the bend from my campground, a horse had recently died,
of some disease it seemed. It didn't look injured in any
way, and I could see no sign that it had been shot. Whatever, its owner had carried away the saddle but had left
behind the blanket, which was smothering a patch of
meadow flowers; and the horse itself had either stumbled
into the water and collapsed or had been dragged down to
the water after it had died on the trail nearby; its carcass
was now lying half submerged in the lake, bloated and
beginning to stink like a packing-house settling pond. A
thicket of flies swarmed around its exposed head, from
which a milky eye bulged grotesquely. Was there, I asked
myself furiously, any place on earth where one might escape the endless trail of litter and garbage? At least the
horse would eventually rot, although I wondered how long
it would take in this frigid environment. I didn't ask myself how I would propose to remove a horse that had died
on me from the middle of a wilderness.

I slept fitfully, the night being so cold that even in all
my clothing and buried in my mummy bag I could not get
warm, and in the morning I drank my hot cocoa sullenly
and set out bitterly for home. I did not intend to spend

another day, if I could help it, in any godforsaken wilderness refuse heap. The access to Martin Lake was through a narrow canyon. In the effort of climbing it, I found myself warmed again. The day was almost as cold as the night, and very gray, but once I was moving, I did not mind it. I found the darkness of enshrouded morning as comforting as an old blanket. The day suited my mood, humored me by glowering back, and was strangely intimate. It seemed as if I were walking in a long but very narrow hallway, which stopped ahead in a gray screen of dense cloud. I climbed steadily until, in the vicinity of Arrowhead Lake, at an elevation of about 10,400 feet, I entered the cloud. I could see for no more than a couple of hundred feet in any direction, and the dampness of the cloud brushed against my warm cheeks like a soft and soothing cloth. The air had ceased altogether to move. The sound of my own feet plodding against the rocky incline of Lonesome Mountain, toward which I was headed, thundered in my ears. They sounded like my own heartbeats coming through the tubes of a stethoscope.

On the pass into the Golden Lake basin I found gentians blooming among the rocks, members of the species *Gentiana algida*, cream-colored flowers splashed with lavender, shaped like the bowls of champagne glasses. *Algida* is the Latin word for cold; arctic gentian is the common English name for the plant. Gentians are herbs. Their roots and rhizomes have been employed in many places to soothe ailments of the stomach. But they are bitter herbs, bearing bitter news. When gentians bloom, on my own prairies as in these mountains, the news is published that winter cannot be far behind. They emerge just as the other flowers are folding, a brief blaze of glory before the ice. Often they are brilliantly blue, the blue of Dresden china, and shimmer with electric intensity against the browns and russets and wine colors of autumn. But the cream and lavender blossoms of the arctic gentian, nestled in downy rings of green leaves, manage to be quite as spectacular in the stern alpine tundra. After the bloom, the leaves will turn vividly orange, and before a month has passed, all this country will be locked in the wild embrace of the long winter.

The gentians are among the wildflowers that summon you to your knees. I fell to mine before them, feeling a new sadness in the face of their delicate beauty, the sadness of another year passing, of another cycle in things coming so softly and brightly to a close, an emotion I supposed I shared with everyone who had once walked this way in the end-days of summer.

I approached the base of Lonesome Mountain. Its summit was wrapped in inscrutable cloud, but it was recognizable still by the massiveness of its slopes, climbing steeply into the mists. Its name, I suppose, derives from its solitary position on what is otherwise a high plateau, a lob mountain of sorts in a forest of rocks, but I saw it now, by virtue of its name, as a kindred spirit, lonesome, like me, in something more than name alone. I felt comfort simply in drawing close to it, one place in this wilderness that I was certain of, that would not lead me astray. I drew a strangely animate warmth from its flanks.

I mounted the ridge connecting the mountain to the steep cliff of the drainage divide on the east, descended it on the other side to Albino Lake, in which ice floats all year, a climb of three hundred feet, a descent of four hundred, like a long scramble over a garden wall out of forbid-

251

den territory and into the street. At the far end of the lake, people were fishing. I did not want to meet them. I was suffering the sort of loneliness that begs to be indulged.

So I left the trail and went a little way across the meadow to the place where three giant boulders of granite, erratics left behind in the sweep of the glacier, stood like maiden sisters, tall and faceless, on a knoll. From the top of the most distant of them a raven croaked noisily. Sleet had begun to pelt from the clouds, cutting and cold, and a wind sharp as a razor blade swept through the canyon from the north. I huddled in the shelter of the maidens, hoping to blot up the thin warmth stored in them, and scrounged for lunch: beef jerky, a chocolate bar, and a sublime apple, sweet and juicy.

It was after noon, but the temperature was still in the thirties, and the clouds had not yet begun to lift. I sat dreamily in the lee of the rocks, listening to wind and ravens and watching sheets of water dancing on the surface of the lake. There was a kind of twilight, a strange yellow light, the color of the air in a big city during an inversion, but coming from no visible source. It was as if the air itself were glowing with a phosphorescence, like the light of the organisms that sometimes glow at night in the sea.

The cliff rising across the lake disappeared into gray mists, and where it was visible, it, too, glowed in soft twilight colors, pink and purple, a rosy tan, a powdery black the color of coal dust. It did not look like rock. It looked like something made of foam and spray-painted in drawing-room colors, or hung in a sheet at the rear of a gigantic stage, an enormous, billowy tapestry of tie-dyed

252

linen. Looking at it through the cloud, it did not seem possible that it had substance. It looked as if you would sink into it if you set foot upon it. And in the diffused light the grasses and flowers all around similarly glowed in shades of gray-green and butter yellow and baby blue, gauzy plants clinging listlessly to life, like flannel cut-outs ornamenting a nursery.

The lake was the color of gray flannel and silky, like the lining of a businessman's suit, and it looked deep and clammy, impenetrable, an arrangement of mirrors, perhaps, over a treacherous pit. But it, too, glowed with a mysterious light, which seemed to emerge from its depths, a crown of light, a halo, that hovered just above the water, a luminous viscosity.

The raven flapped away. Someone down the shore, beyond sight, screamed. I crawled into a frost-driven crack in the rocks, a cave of sorts, and the sound of the wind fell away. The sleet stopped. It seemed to grow darker. I could hear the sound of my own breathing, the rustle of my clothing whenever I stirred, but everything else was suddenly as quiet as an empty house in the middle of the night. I had been, I realized, searching for the silence, begging for it, for the calm eye at the center of the storm raging inside me, and here, where I was unprepared for it, it floated down upon me like an autumn leaf.

I have known on other occasions in my life the eloquence of silence. I have been admonished by it, instructed by it, loved by it.

One spring evening when I was a boy of twelve, my mother and my sister finished the supper dishes and announced that they had to go out. The announcement alarmed me more than it is easy to tell. In our household, nobody ever went out in the evening. Where would one go and what would one do? The women were mysterious about this. No explanation was forthcoming. Furthermore, my mother spoke in a formal tone I had never heard from her before, as if she were making a stage exit, which she was. So my father and I were left alone in a house brimming with silence and darkness, and the night stretched out endlessly before us. We sat in the living room in the yellow circle of light from a table lamp. Moths drummed on the window screens behind us, trying to get in. The clock ticked. We had been planting an orchard, and, after an awkward time, we turned to a discussion of the varieties of apples. I cannot imagine what the two of us had to say to each other on the subject, although I remember that Haralsons, improbable as it sounds, figured in the conversation. In any case, the subject was soon exhausted, and the chorus of crickets in the grass beyond the open windows swelled.

Finally my father cleared his throat. "Your mother wanted me to talk to you," he said. He was staring into the darkened bedroom door at the opposite end of the room, beseechingly, as if an angel might appear there at any moment and absolve him of his awful responsibility. "About sex."

My God, I thought, it's worse than I feared.

Father took a deep breath. "Remember," he said, speaking very rapidly, "it's more powerful than you think!" Spent from this effort, he lapsed into silence. Eventually he needed to go out to check on the sheep, which had previously fended well enough for themselves in the evenings, and I felt a powerful compulsion to gaze at the stars. But it stands as the only speech I remember in its entirety, and the echoes from it have reverberated through the rest of my life.

"Silence," Shakespeare wrote, "is the perfectest herald of joy: I were but little happy if I could say how much."

At the University of Minnesota, on another spring day, I heard the poet John Berryman fail to lecture on *The Illiad* to a room jammed with students. He sat down at a table, as was his custom, put on his reading glasses, lit a cigarette, which he held at bottom of the space between his trembling index and middle fingers in the way that drunks do, and began to read to us from the poem in his dark voice, oddly powerful coming from such a frail man, paying as much attention to the stops in the lines as to the accents. He read to us the scene in which Hector and Andromache say farewell to each other. Hector is destined to die and Andromache to be hauled into slavery, and both know this by premonition. When he came to the end of the scene, Berryman was weeping and so, unexpectedly, were we. He made no effort to hide his grief, running from an ancient pen across the long centuries through a modern language into our hearts. He did not even brush away his tears. We sat, stunned, until he got up and left the room without another word, and then we, too, gathered up our books and emerged into the cruel sunshine. I hurried to my office (I was editor of the student newspaper) and locked myself in, and it was an hour or two before I could see anybody. It was the first time, I think, that any of us had ever been taught what literature is all about.

"And silence," Oliver Wendell Holmes said, "like a poultice comes / To heal the wounds of sound."

Later still, I was at a noisy party one night in Washington, D.C., one of those dinner affairs one attends in the dismal line of duty, when I was seized by an odd and overwhelming feeling of panic, a breathlessness. I needed to get out of that place immediately. I located my wife and insisted that we leave at once. She was puzzled and chagrined: It was very early; perhaps the meal had not even been served; but she came. We hailed a cab and were entering the front door of our house, a house we shared with others, when the phone began to ring. The call was for me. It was my mother calling to say that my father had just died. He must have died, I realized as I pieced events together later, at almost exactly the moment when, some twelve hundred miles away, I was overcome by nausea at a party. I am not superstitious, and I have not wanted to make anything more of this than what I record here as a matter of fact.

The other people in the house—this is the thing I wanted to tell—realized that something terrible had happened and lingered near the telephone. I told them the news. I wanted more than anything to be alone. I said nothing, but what I desired must have been written in my face, because within the minute, everybody had quietly retreated to the upper stories of the house, leaving me to the silence of the main floor, and the time and the silence worked their mysterious balm. Sometime after midnight I put some recordings of Bach on the record player, and by dawn I felt equipped to catch the next airplane home.

"The silence sank," Samuel Coleridge wrote, "Like music on my heart."

We often imagine that the problem in our lives lies in knowing what to say, or in exorcising the festers of what remains unsaid. But the more serious difficulty is in know-

256

ing what not to say and how not to say it. This is a uniquely human predicament. Speech, as Loren Eiseley has pointed out, is not altogether the invention of our imaginations, unlike the management of fire, for example. Fire as a tool did not exist until we thought of making it one. The thought was one of those great leaps across the chasm into humanity for which we were not in any biological sense prepared. Nothing in the mechanics of the human body predestined us to the alchemy of the blast furnace. But we were biologically adapted for speech long before we made sonnets of it. Our mouths and tongues and throats were suited in their construction for the making of sound. In learning to sing songs we have not transcended our biology but only fulfilled it. Our words may soar, but the word was implicit. "In the beginning was the Word." In the sense that speech is not, strictly speaking, our own invention, it is also something over which we have incomplete control, just as we preside imperfectly over the rest of nature. So we have the obligation to use it sparingly, judiciously. We remain uncertain of its ultimate consequences. No other essence in nature is similarly burdened. No mountain or tree or snake is ever forced to choose between silence and speech. Annie Dillard tells the parable of a man trying to teach a stone to talk. The stone might teach us something: It might teach us how to keep silent.

I have been writing about a particular kind of silence, the one we keep in the presence of others, the complex universe of silences we maintain by convention, judgment, and temperament. But there is another more difficult, more terrifying silence than this, the silence we are sometimes required to confront within ourselves.

Once in a schoolroom when I was a boy we students were gathered in a circle playing a game of musical chairs. The phonograph needle ground against the vinyl and we all dashed round and round the chairs until the music suddenly stopped and we plunged toward our places. It was very noisy and merry. There came the moment when the music ground to a halt and I was left standing alone. The music started again and I found myself immobilized and terrified. The fear has traveled with me since. I had been suddenly, inexplicably, transmuted into a spirit floating high above the children in the draft of warm air near the tin ceiling. I saw everything clearly: the high-ceilinged room; the gas stove at the back of it; the long, empty rows of school desks; the south light streaming through the tall windows; the circle of chairs and the children around them; our teacher poised at the phonograph; the stone water cooler behind her desk. I heard everything: the needle scratching in its groove, the screams of the children, the teacher saying "Paul, is something wrong? Don't you feel well, Paul?" I saw myself standing there and heard myself answering "No, I'm fine, really I am." But I was lying. Because there were two of us. There was the me who was seeing and hearing everything without feeling any of it. And there was the physical manifestation of the boy I recognized as myself but did not any longer know, a stranger standing in an alien classroom. I was dizzy with the fear that the two boys could never again be connected.

I had temporarily lost all sense of myself. It was as if I had precipitously perished and had been granted one last look at the ghost of my former self before I was swept away into the void. The sensation did not last long, a few seconds, I suppose, but I think that in some way I was never the same person again. Certainly I was badly shaken at the time. I had grown weak in the knees and light-headed, had turned pallid and begun to sweat. It was thought that I was about to faint. I was made to sit at my desk and to put my head between my legs until the color returned to my cheeks, and then I was sent home for the day.

I had come face to face in that early trauma with the awful mystery of my own existence. I had momentarily seen myself from the outside looking in and did not know who I was. I had no idea where I was or what I was. I was floating in a void and what I saw when I looked into myself was a void, a vast and somehow tangible silence drifting in the great and intangible silence of the universe. Jesus' disciples asked him once who he was, and he said, "Who do men say that I am?" It was the quintessentially human response to the question, the prophet in his least godlike moment.

Perhaps this youthful vision does not now visit everyone, but there was a time on this continent when boys who wished to become men were universally commanded to seek it. A boy would leave behind the village and travel into the wilderness to some remote place, high and sacred, leaving behind his tools and the trappings of civilization in quest of a vision. He would stay in the place he had chosen for days and nights without eating or drinking. He would find the void in the universe and locate it inside himself and, so emptied, await a dream. The dream would tell him who he was. It would honor him with a vision of himself, a name, and a conviction for the future, the equipment necessary for a fully adult life.

I imagine that an Indian youth returning from a vision

quest felt as suddenly at peace as I did that noonday when I sat silently in a cloud at Albino Lake and found again my bearings, when I located myself in the mists of the mute mountains as a creature with a voice. "No man in the middle of a desert or on top of a mountain ever fell victim to the delusion that he himself was nothing except the product of social forces, that all he needed was a proper orientation in his economic group, or that production per man hour was the true index of happiness," Joseph Wood Krutch wrote in *The Desert Year*. "No such man, if he permitted himself to think at all, ever thought anything except that consciousness was the grandest of all facts and that no good life for either the individual or a group was possible on any other assumption. No man in such a position ever doubted that he himself was a primary particle, an ultimate reality."

I got up from my perch among the three rocks that looked to me like sisters and shouldered my pack. The sisters had come down in the ice and would stand there immutable until the ice moved them again or the winds and rains and frosts of the centuries should heave them apart and the lichens should grind them into dust. I myself will long since have returned to the dust, but I shared with them once for a brief and silent moment their outpost above the icy lake, of my own volition and in full and glorious consciousness of the occasion, in the consciousness of words. I set out again on the trail, and by the time the sisters had fallen from sight, the cloud had lifted and the sun had begun to shine.

18

Appointment with a Trout

◁ ▷

I descended into the pines and then climbed again, steeply, along a moaning cataract. I climbed until, turning to look behind, I could see, stretching southward toward the Wind Rivers, the whole long range of the Absarokas, the Mountains of the Ravens, jagged black teeth capped with crowns of snow, like a great jaw yawning out of the green forests. I was headed toward a pair of high-country lakes, Wall Lake and Snow Lake, that huddle in the shadow of the cliff of Beartooth Plateau. I was going there for no reason at all except that I had been ready to abandon these mountains and then been redeemed by them in a cloud, and now I wanted to walk a little farther in thanksgiving. I did not know when I set out that I had an appointment to keep with a trout.

I found Wall Lake puddled on a glacially carved table, its contents spilling into the valley below, as from an overfilled dinner plate, across a granite rim shrouded in shrubbery. Ten feet below the rim, the falling water screamed, but above it the world was as silent as ice. The table looked like a dining table after the guests had gone home and the hosts had turned out the lights and retired exhausted to bed, leaving the cleaning up for the morning after. The lake spread like a wine stain on the cloth and everywhere across it great boulders of granite lay like dinnerware where they had been carelessly dropped, some still standing upright, some tipped over, some leaning precariously against each other. Everything was decadently disheveled and disarranged, as if the guests had been too drunk to care. Perhaps, I thought, the party had gone out somewhere for music and dancing. There seemed the faint echo of laughter in the sunlit air. And then I saw the glossy green growths of moss in the running waters and the apple-green lichens growing like bacterial molds on the rocky tableware, and I thought, No, there was some emergency, a fire in the kitchen, maybe, or the sudden eruption of fighting in the streets, and everybody fled in fear, and nobody has ever returned. There was an atmosphere of panic over that tumultuous table, the randomness of some great violence. And surrounding it, the deathly silence. I looked and saw that it was not a table at all but a graveyard, in which every monument had been upset.

The impression was of haste, but haste in nature is like ease in art; the stronger the impression, the less likely it is to be true. I was at the end point of a tiny glacier, a field of ice that had formed in the accumulation of the snows of hundreds or thousands of years until finally it had begun to slip forward of its own weight, carrying whatever it had been clutching when the earliest snows had settled into the first ice. For whatever reason, the ice had stopped here and dissipated, leaving behind its debris, like the line of gravel and discarded beer cans at the edge of a snowplow drift when the city winter has surrendered to the warm and fierce winds of spring.

I made my camp on a mound of fallen gravel where a few spruce trees hunched like victims of osteomalacia. In the slope of the moraine I found a ledge of stone that made a high-backed chair and settled onto it to soak up the soothing sun. There is happiness in sunlight, literally, as any denizen of dark winter can tell you. I felt as happy as a lizard basking on a rock. I imagined that I could feel the blood thinning in my veins and running away to the damp ends of my feet. I could have sat forever in that sunlight, I think, until I had dried away to the bone and the bones had bleached as white as the tongues of snow sticking out from the dark caverns among the disarranged boulders. I could see my skull, heaved into the grass by some frost, flashing the grin of death into the heavens.

But a hawk soared on a thermal wind over the wall of Beartooth Plateau, and, following it, I saw that storm clouds were gathering again in the west and beginning their march in my direction. The mountains would not be long in sunshine. I wanted, while there was still the light for it, to search the waters of the lake for some sign of companionable life. So I rose slowly from my stone throne, my sinews already having begun to stiffen, and

made my way through drifts of flowers and a flutter of insects to the boulder-bound shore of the frigid basin.

I cannot begin to say what is the fascination in piles of
stone, but I am drawn to them as if by magnetic force. If I
am driving down a highway and see any accumulation of
rock, a cliff line or a stony hill or a rocky shore, my bones
begin to ache for the chance to climb them. I am never
more content than when I have submitted to their beckoning. The shore of Wall Lake was, for me, therefore, a
place made in heaven, a tumble of boulders as big as trac-
tors and full of crannies and corridors of every imaginable
sort, a fantastic toyland, and I was the babe in it. I began
to crawl and climb, to slide, to crouch, to leap, making
my way steadily around the labyrinthine shore, intending
to go all the way around, but in no hurry to get there. I
had soon altogether forgotten the lake.

Perhaps an hour later I came out from among the rocks
at a place where a single boulder made a wide, flat ledge
that dropped straight down into a deep channel of water,
a place where the lake circled around a tiny island of boulders. The distance between the island and the ledge was
too wide to leap, I decided, after considering the matter
carefully and from several angles. It was, I suppose, a distance of a couple of yards, although the deepest part of the
channel was much narrower than that, only a couple of
feet, the waters on either side of it harboring piles of
barely submerged rocks, too slippery, I thought, to chance
a wading. So I gave up the idea of achieving the island
and was standing there regretting its inaccessibility when I
had a rare communication with a creature from another
part of the universe.

The sun had disappeared momentarily behind a cloud,

and I had worked up a sweat. I was suddenly chilled and had reached down to zip my jacket when, out of the corner of my eye, I caught a dark image at the entrance to the water channel. I turned quickly to get a better view. By that time the swiftly moving creature was directly below me. It caught sight of me in the same instant that I had located it, and then it did exactly what I was doing. It stopped short and stood motionless.

The creature was a brook trout perhaps fifteen inches long, its lithe and dappled body admirably discreet among the patterns of shadow and light in the sparkling depths of the rocky channel. I gazed at it with the advantage of my binocular eyes, rescued from their myopia by a pair of plastic lenses that had been darkened to cut the glare of the sun overhead. It stared back at me out of its single left eye, its right eye facing the opposite wall of the channel, but with the keen vision of a trout. I felt the piercing power of its eye and was reduced by it to self-consciousness. The difference was not so much of acuity as of habit: the habit of looking. In the trout it came instinctively; it was a matter of nature, a requirement of survival, that it should be alert to every visual clue in its watery world, to the passing of every shadow, to every hint of movement, to every sign of an event beyond the confines of its habitation as well as within it. That the trout should have spied me, standing high on a rock above it, was evidence that the boundaries of its conscious existence extended beyond the viscous seal of the lake, that it lived somehow in two worlds, both in the water and out of it, that its universe included a territory it would never know directly, but only by the implication of the dangers emanating from it. I, on the other hand, equipped though I am with powerful vision, wide of angle, stereoscopic, dis-criminating of depth and color, have not depended, for the most part, upon the salvation of sight, and so I have had to learn to see. I have had to make the habit of look-ing when it did not originally exist, of seeing in discrimi-nating patterns rather than in confusing detail, of remembering to include the information at the peripheries of my vision. I have had to practice the discipline of look-ing, have had to learn how to concentrate on the visual symbols that reach my eyes when I am walking, to pay attention to them when my instinct was to walk blindly, to see everything indistinctly and indiscriminately.

We sometimes have the habit of seeing as children and then we lose it, as we lose the gift of imagination; we lose at the same time the talent for seeing the world mythically rather than literally. One goes walking with a child and suddenly the barren path is shown to be alive with spiders and butterflies and egg cases, with snakes and toads, with life in a hundred dimensions that otherwise would have passed unnoticed. The child in me is more like the trout than is the man I have become. The eye for wonder of the child approaches the eye for survival of the trout. How much of the art of survival do we lose, I wanted to know, when we lose the capacity for wonder?

I stared at the trout, and it stared back at me. What did the trout see? I wondered. And then I thought that it saw a bear, that this was not an encounter between a human and a fish but a confrontation, from the trout's point of view, between a fish and a grizzly. I had become, for a moment, the animal I most feared in this wilderness. I had become hairy and massive, and the nails on my fingers had grown sharp claws, and I could feel myself wanting to ex-

266

tend an arm, to reach suddenly into the water, to spike the trout in the belly in one swift jab, to scoop it up dripping from the water, to tear it apart in my long canine teeth, to gulp it down, the fresh taste of sweet water and fish oil on my tongue.

But I remembered that a grizzly is as nearsighted as I am without my glasses, that if I were standing on that ledge unaided by the technology of my species, I would not in fact have seen the trout at all. And I realized that the trout would in some sense know this, would know from instinct or experience that as long as it remained motionless in the deep channel of the water, it was invisible to me, the bear. I thought of myself as the observer, but, from the trout's perspective, the roles were reversed. The trout was observing me from a watery invisibility. I was the innocent one in this encounter.

I wondered if the trout was sensible to the progress of the seasons, if it was more than usually wary of shadowy figures like mine lurking over the water because others of its species were spawning in a shallow basin at the opposite end of the lake. I had seen them as I was climbing, and they had scattered into the depths of the lake at my approach. Did the trout, I wondered, make the connection between spawning time and bear time? I had no way of knowing, except that this particular trout moved, or failed to move, in expectation of the bear I had now become.

I thought, in fact, standing there, that I could feel the presence of another bear not far off, could smell its foul breath in the wind, that I was being observed from behind as well as from depths of the water, over which a dark cloud had now fallen, bringing a sudden chill to the air. I

267

felt that the bear even now was seeing me not as a human being playing the part of a bear at the edge of the lake but as an elk or a mountain sheep, that I stood there, like the trout, threatened by the complicated dependencies of our lives, and that the longer I held my place, the less conspicuous I might become. The trout counted on appearing to be a shadow in the water, and I counted on seeming to be a shadow among the rocks. We were, for that brief moment, partners in a ruse. We played our parts automatically, without fear or conscious thought, reacting in our bones to the challenge of the moment. Perhaps the bear I sensed was really myself, the breath I smelled was my own. I did not know, in that moment, the difference between myself and the bear, or between the world of the trout and the world in which I lived and had breath. In that single pause on a rock above a channel in a mountain lake I had been invited by the gaze of a brook trout to join its universe. I have long sought such an invitation.

I was the first to flinch. I shifted the weight on my legs, glanced away for an instant, and when I had focused my eyes again on the channel of clear water among the castaway rocks, the trout had vanished, as silently, as stealthily as it had first appeared, leaving behind in the place where it had hidden from the bear in me an emptiness that water alone could not quite fill.

19

Seeing the Elephant

◁ ▷

BY the time you reached western Nebraska on the Oregon Trail, by the time you had encountered its first great landmark, Chimney Rock, the landscape had turned hard and bitter. You were at the edge of the acrid desert, and the spring had worn into summer. The trees had vanished: Not a spot of shade fell from horizon to horizon. Good water had grown hard to find. The water in the naked marshes was nauseatingly alkaline. It gave you miserable attacks of diarrhea. It made the oxen bloat and die. Sometimes you couldn't find a place to camp at night away from the stench of their rotting carcasses. The alkalai dust stuck in your nostrils and collected in your

269

lungs. You knew the claustrophobia of not being able to catch your breath.

Somebody in your party had probably already died, had fallen under the wheel of a wagon or caught cholera along the polluted Platte, collapsed from exhaustion or fallen victim to the careless gunshot of a wagon mate. The trains set out loaded like armada, their organizers fearful of Indian attack. The Indians didn't attack; the wars with them came after the westward movement. Anyway, they had subtler methods. They would greet you at a river crossing, help you ford, ask a little food in return, and disappear in the night with your best horses. So the voyagers, loaded to the gills with ammunition, got gun-happy and, more frequently than one might guess, accidentally killed and maimed each other.

The slow progress across the prairies, twelve or fifteen miles a day, had become a drudging routine. By now it seemed as if you had been traveling forever. You made the miles pass by counting gravestones and praying for a diversion, the sight of a buffalo, the relief of a cottonwood tree, anything to break the monotony of the way ahead.

And now you had entered the sagebrush country, sparse in forage for the horses and mules, abounding in rattlesnakes, where coyotes barked and wolves howled in the night and the heat of the midday sun radiated from the scorching earth like the embers of an old fire.

The farther west you traveled, the less distinct the trail became, the less reliable the advice of fellow travelers, the more recklessly you were inclined to try ill-fated shortcuts. Soon you would be beyond the Platte and after that you might have only the vaguest idea how to proceed. You might know that you wanted to continue westward until you came to some other kind of country, some green mountain valley or the sea, and nothing more. The landscape itself offered fewer and fewer clues. There was the endless line of distant hills and mountains, the gray-green monotony of the arid flora, the continual parade of clouds from which no rain fell, the unceasing undulation of the earth like the waves of the sea, each new wave identical to the last.

Perhaps you undertook the journey in hope and determination, sustained by the promise of gold or of a farm at the end of the trail. Perhaps you traveled in desperation, saw the trip as the last or best hope, as the inevitable choice among the one or two available. Perhaps you didn't know why you went, simply had the itch to be a part of what the newspaper writers back East were calling the nation's manifest destiny. Perhaps you followed out of wifely duty, indulging a husband's dream in which you could not share. Whatever the reason for going, you were certain to meet fear along the way. There were so many things to fear:

Every strange noise in the night;

Every twist in a river's current;

Every sharply angled hillside upon which a narrow wagon might overturn;

Every nightfall;

Snakes lurking in the grass;

Wolves and bears;

Every bird bursting unexpectedly from beneath your feet;

Every moment when you remembered that you were unlikely ever to see again the relatives and friends you had left behind;

The midday heat;

Every fresh grave along the way;

Every fever or festering wound;

Every round of rifle fire heard over the next horizon;

Every juncture in the trail, that you might not have chosen the right way;

Thunderstorms;

The possibility that no water would be found tomorrow;

The possibility that you would run out of breast milk to supply the baby.

But fear is its own antidote. You face a fear long enough and you learn to accept it. This is why you can get into an automobile in the morning and drive to work along the freeway without a paralyzing and altogether sensible fear of dying. Oregon Trail travelers had a wonderful name for it. They called it seeing the elephant. You got to a certain point in the journey and you said that now you had seen the elephant. It was a metaphor, one historian has suggested, with origins in the circus: Once you had seen the elephant you had seen all the circus had to offer.

As a nation, we have been both too constantly on the move and too relentlessly utilitarian to think very deeply about the qualities of place. But even we now and then recognize some particular place as having unique powers, as possessing magical charms and persuasions. Independence Rock is one of them. Headed home after my own long wanderings, I made yet one more detour to visit it, the national shrine to wanderers.

There were other celebrated landmarks along the Oregon Trail. By the time its travelers had arrived at Independence Rock, they would already have passed, among others, Courthouse and Jailhouse rocks, Chimney Rock and Scottsbluff, but these were notable more for their physical than for their spiritual qualities, impressive in size, as visual links with the world back home, and for their instant recognizability, not for anything they might say in themselves to the people headed west. Courthouse and Jailhouse rocks do look remarkably, from a distance, like a pair of familiar county government buildings. Chimney Rock, aside from its towering height, reminded travelers of the obelisk on Beacon Hill in Boston; it presented a nostalgic encounter with the civilized East. And Scottsbluff was both, by the narrowness of the pass through it, a kind of gateway into the semiarid West, a point of no return and, by the impression it gave from a distance, an apparition of Europe. It looked like a pair of enormous castles somehow raised and then abandoned upon the wild plains.

Independence Rock is something different. It is not especially big; it covers about twenty-five acres and is 193 feet high at its peak. It reminded travelers of nothing in the East or in Europe, was reminiscent of nothing except itself. Diarists saw it as a mammoth egg half buried, a turtle, a bowl turned upside down, a sleeping hippopotamus, a whale. To me, it looks like a petrified brain; and it is one, in a way. It is the bald granite peak of an old mountain, its base buried in the wash of debris that accompanied the geologic revolution that formed the Rocky Mountains, a monument to the impermanence even of mountains in the vast scale of time.

Independence Rock came to mean what it did, I think, because of two felicities of timing. First, it lay at the point along the trail where familiarity had finally overcome fear, where the journey west had ceased to be a journey and had begun to seem its own occupation. By the time you reached it, you had probably already seen the elephant. Second, as it worked out, travelers could expect to make Independence Rock by the Fourth of July. So it came to be a temporal landmark as well as a physical one, and the temporal symbolism was doubly rich: One could simultaneously celebrate the nation's independence and the independence one was individually seeking. The rock offered itself as a faith stone, as an occasion for reaffirming the promise of the West.

You affirmed that faith by a ritual act as old as human culture. You approached the rock and made your mark. Some people stood at the very base of the rock and scrawled their names in charcoal or paint and they washed away in the first rain. Some scratched their names along the most exposed surfaces of the rock, eager, perhaps, to be visible, and the scratchings wore away in the rains of decades. Some carved their names deeply, taking a whole day at it, and in seventy-five years the lichens had begun to cover them. Some chiseled their names in bold, deep letters, adding curlicues and flourishes, and more than a century later their marks endure. They have gained at least this much immortality. By 1855, this being America, you could hire a Mormon, actually, to do the job for you at one to four dollars a name.

When the explorer John C. Fremont visited the rock in 1842, he carried the practice of inscription to a new height: "I engraved on this rock of the far West a symbol of the Christian faith . . . a large cross, which I covered with a black preparation of India rubber well calculated to resist the influence of wind and rain." But the symbol did disappear, probably in a blast of gunpowder set off by a

274

party of a thousand emigrants gathered there on July 4, 1847. And when Fremont later sought the presidency, his cross helped to defeat him. He was Catholic; therefore, his etching was a defilement of a national symbol; and it was used to turn him against Protestant voters.

On the late August day when I paid my own visit, I had spent the morning in pursuit of antelopes and lizards on a sagebrush range. I had gone on foot to get some idea what it might have been like to travel that country in a wagon, had walked its yellow earth, rich in minerals but poor in humus, had felt its heat in the soles of my feet, had climbed and descended its labyrinth of arroyos and hills, never seeming to come any closer to the long line of blue mountains to the north and west. By midday, although the air temperature was only eighty-five degrees, my pocket thermometer registered almost one hundred degrees at ground level. The only shade was cast by the brim of my hat, barely adequate to reach my eyes, into which my sweat ran; and by the woody stems of the sagebrushes and the paddles of the pear cactuses, shade enough for the tiny lizards that abounded there, cocking their heads and staring at me out of one eye.

I climbed Independence Rock late in the afternoon when there was already some purple in the mountains visible on every side and the shadows in the hills were beginning to cast the landscape into relief. I had approached it around a bend in the highway; the instant I saw it, I knew what it was. I tried to measure the pleasure of my own sense of having arrived against the great joy that Oregon Trail travelers must have known upon encountering it: something familiar and anticipated in the midst of so much that was strange, new, unexpected. I thought I could feel vicariously, even across the space of a century, the relief, the momentary rush of calm, the excitement, of turning around the bend in the valley and seeing the rock and knowing that you were two-fifths of the way West and all was well. "Cold chills come over me and tears would flow in spite of all my efforts to repress them," pioneer Harriet Sherril Ward wrote upon coming around that bend in 1853.

People lingered there for a day or two, made friends with fellow travelers. In such circumstances friendships come easily. There would have been music, dancing, conversation around campfires late into the night. There would have been stories about the trip, the beginning of the fabrication of a memory of the trail, the first telling of events one would alter, embellish, polish through a hundred more tellings in the years ahead. New alliances would have been forged, fractious trailmates parting ways and joining new companies. Teams fragmented by death, fights, or second thoughts would have been merged into new traveling units. There was time for rest and repairs, for swapping lore, for pooling information about the way ahead. Perhaps there was a message from home or from a friend who had passed earlier; the rock was used as a bulletin board. And there would be time to climb Independence Rock, hammer and chisel in hand, to make your mark or the mark of your family on what the Jesuit missionary Father P. J. De Smet, who signed it in 1840, called "the great registery of the desert."

I climbed the rock. It was steeper than it looked from the parking lot, but you could ascend it simply by walking up the dome over a surface almost as smooth as a city sidewalk. From the peak of the dome, submerged though I was in the taller relief of the countryside around me, I felt the familiar force of a mountaintop. The place had a summit's constricted sense of space in the context of so much visible landscape.

There were five other persons on the summit when I arrived, an enthusiastic family of vacationers scrambling here and there and calling to each other. "Here! Look here! Here's one from 1847!" "I've got an 1842 over here! Come quick, John! Get a picture of it!" "Oh, wow! Look at this one!" I tried to get out of their way, to stay on some unoccupied corner of rock, out of the way of the incessant clicking of the motor-driven camera, but it was almost impossible. They were everywhere at once and, it seemed, getting noisier and noisier all the time. I suppose I ought to have been amused at their shaky, typically American, sense of history—"What do all these dates mean, Mom?" "They are the dates when these people died, Terry."—or thrilled that a group of young children could be so excited about a historic site, or charmed by how much they seemed to be enjoying themselves. But I did not feel anything of the sort. I felt about them the way one does about the revelers in the next hotel room at 2:30 A.M. when one is struggling to sleep before an important meeting at 7 A.M. I wished they would all shut up and go away. Eventually they did. I watched them climb down the rock, wondering what they knew about the elephant, whether any of them had ever seen it. And then, regretting the harshness of my mood, I sat on a point of rock and waited for the spirit of the place, the spirit I had briefly caught on achieving the summit, to return.

The shadows began to lengthen radically. The first tinges of the color salmon began to show in the western sky.

In the prelude to twilight, the ruts of the wagon wheels, still showing faintly in the patch of grass just north of the rock, emerged vividly, two dark-green scratches in the silver-green vegetation. I imagined that I could hear the wheels of wagons clattering and creaking over those ruts, the cries of drivers shouting to horses and mules, drawing them into a circle along the Sweetwater River below, commanding them to halt: "Wagons ho!" I imagined that I could smell the smoke of campfires, that I could see children playing, that I could hear the crowing of caged roosters, that I was surrounded by the evidence of a temporary village taking shape in the valley below.

But it was, in fact, very quiet. Occasionally a car passed on the highway shining now like a silver ribbon, but noiselessly, like a phantom. There were still a few visitors in the parking lot reading the signs explaining the geology of the rock, but they, too, were beyond hearing. I got up from my perch and began to wander across the summit, inspecting the names inscribed in its face. These were the names of survivors, not of casualties, but looking at them had the same overpowering effect on me as looking at the names inscribed on the black marble wall of the Vietnam Memorial in Washington, D.C. There were no names with which I could make any personal connection. I was looking for no name in particular, the name of no relative or historical figure, for no particular date or place of origin. I wandered vaguely and without precise purpose, simply letting the names and dates and places accumulate, the array of national origins, the expanse of years, the rich melody of the names themselves, names like Obadiah and Jeremiah, Elias and Ezekial, Ruth and Elizabeth, Opal and Beulah, names speaking in the calico colors of another age. I saw names washing away in the rains of a century, names chipped away in a hundred years of freezes and thaws, names slowly being engulfed in the advance of lichens, names carved with bravado to last for the ages, and still enduring. For every name I saw, I knew that another hundred had already faded away and run down the side of the ancient mountaintop to become part of the meager soil in which the sagebrush desert now took root. There was defiance in those names and pride, determination and hope, resignation and prayer.

I saw in those names the beginnings of many other names, of a new generation of names born in the West, the names of mountains, of lakes and streams, of fledgling towns, of roads and passes, of children born along the trail, or on new farms, or in mining camps, and destined to make of a wide and nameless place a new and richly designated one. It is how we lay claim to anything, to a place, or a plant, or a person, or an idea: We give it a name; and it is, perhaps, a uniquely human handicap that if we do not know the name of a thing, we cannot know anything else worth knowing about it.

The power of the Vietnam Wall is that, in just this sense, it names a war, names it as precisely as such an experience can be named, and makes it possible for us to know the full extent of its meaning. Independence Rock worked on me in the fading light of an August day when the merciful shadows of evening were falling. Here was the westward expansion given a name, the American dream of independence translated from concept into a knowable place, a place with a name, the place of the elephant. I wandered among all those names on Independence Rock, skirting around them, preserving them from the impact of my feet, as one avoids the mound behind a gravestone, and while I was wandering among them, seeing over and over again the juxtaposition of a name, a place and a date, July 4, 18–, the weight of their accumulation rose like a bubble in the well of my throat, and it did not burst until I was long down the road past the monument, headed home through the oil fields, a new dream as capricious as the last, and had switched on my headlights to see my way across the wide, empty plains. I had been walking in mountains, in search, I suddenly understood, of my own elephant.

20

Walking Home

◁ ▷

It was early November, more like spring than fall. The sun had just set. The air was cold and clear and crisp. It smelled freshly washed. Friday evening in a small prairie town. The streetlights switched on.

On half a dozen evenings a year the wind fails and the surface of the lake glasses over, often an ominous sign, portending a radical change in the weather. It was such a night. The seasons here take their leave petulantly, like overtired children being banished to bed. "It's not fair," they seem to scream. "I'm the life of the party and now you won't even let me stay!" After the brawling comes the quiet moment of resignation, and then in storms the new.

281

Friday night. Shopping night. The stores stay open late. Game night. The football players prepare to do battle. End of the work week. The beginning of an interlude, a transposition of keys.

I locked my office door and walked out into the mild night, crossed the parking lot, moved down the quiet commercial street, past the darkened windows of empty storefronts, past yellow windows where restless store clerks circled like fish in aquariums, past the bakery window where the trays of sweet rolls and birthday cakes were draped with sheets of newsprint, past the furniture store: OUR OWN MEN DELIVER THIS LOVELY FURNITURE IN OUR OWN TRUCKS. YOU WILL BE GLAD THEY DID.

Past the antique shops, the rooming houses with vacancy signs in the porch windows, the remnants of the old power plant, dismantled when the city began to buy its power from Wyoming, past the World War I howitzer aimed ambiguously out across the water. So many scraps of things, mostly unfinished: incomplete sets of Depression glass; immigrant rooms smelling of babies and hot plates; the power plant gone like every other kind of power except guilt and, perhaps, envy; the remembrance of wars but not of their glory. "That old cannon outside our house," somebody had said at the luncheon the day before, "what in the world is that anyway? Does anybody remember where it came from?" Nobody remembered, exactly. The man who had been counted on to know such things wasn't there to ask; he had moved on, dismissed after a quarter of a century by the new corporate owners.

I came down to the edge of the lake near the place where warm water from the power plant once discharged into it. The force of the discharge carved a basin into the

282

lake bottom there, and in winter it kept the ice away and the water healthy, a function now performed by aerators. It is a favorite fishing hole. On almost every summer night a flotilla floats at anchor there, and a village of anglers waits in the sundown stillness for the strike of a walleye. The lake yields fish of many kinds: walleyes, bass, perch, crappies, catfish, bullheads, carp, suckers, buffalo fish. The suckers and the buffalo fish stick to the murky bottom and seldom take an angler's bait, but periodically the sportsmen's club or a commercial fishing crew seines the lake and harvests them. They come up in the nets by the ton, lunker fish, fat and glossy, an astonishing abundance of life from the secret underworld of the lake. Crowds gather to see the spectacle of the fish lying passively on their sides in the big wooden shipping crates, their exposed eyes, glassy as pearls, staring straight up into the unaccustomed brilliance. I wonder what they see and how it feels to be stacked like cordwood, scale upon scale, in the big boxes, and what the fishes make of it, if anything at all.

Over the arching bicycle bridge, strong enough to support small tanks, as the rules for building it with federal money required. For a time it seemed an outrage. There was much muttering and shaking of heads about the stupidities of bureaucrats. But outrage cannot be sustained. Somehow it always leaks away, like the air in a balloon. The sturdy beams of the outrageous bridge have begun to weather and gray; nobody passes it anymore and reddens at the thought of it. The bridge surmounts the dam, the connecting point between the lake and its former twin, which was drained a century ago so that it wouldn't inconvenience the progress of the railroad. Perhaps somebody back then was outraged at the sacrifice of a lake to the dictatorial whims of a railroad company. Maybe not. Maybe the world looked boundless and indestructible then at the edge of the grass wilderness. If there was any outrage, it quickly dissipated. Now the lake is not only lost but forgotten. It is beyond consideration like everything forgotten; there is no death so final as the death of a memory.

Beyond the bridge the open lake and an unobstructed view of the western sky. Is there a place in the world where the local sunsets are not a point of parochial pride? There was nothing brilliant about this particular sunset, but it was awesome in its own quiet way. The horizon darkened as it does only at sunset: the shadow of the clouds made visible at the ends of the earth. Above it, a thin strata of wispy clouds and the contrail of a jet. Patches of baby pink and pewter gray and baby blue, delicate but striking, washed together as if applied with a watercolorist's brush. The same colors repeated in the same patterns in the gray mirror of the placid lake. Harmonious colors, wrapped around the landscape like a soft blanket. And the quiet, a wilderness stillness. Noise closes in an environment; silence opens it. The lakeshore had grown vast and wild in the fading light of the day.

Around a bend in the shore, headed west, in the comfortable direction. Walking east, as naturalist John Burroughs remarked, always feels somehow left-handed.

Past the park where the Okabena apple is commemorated, an early winter-hardy species developed on the shores of this lake for this harsh climate. Two plants above all others symbolized civilized life for our pioneer ancestors: pines in the cemetery and apples in the or-

284

chard. We have an abundance of both kinds of trees now along the wooded and settled shore of the lake; I suppose this means that we have become civilized. The Okabena apple tree growing in the park is a young specimen not yet bearing fruit, or I might have gathered some for my pockets, thinking of Thoreau, the apple's most devoted fan, who spoke with particular fondness of a certain blue pearmain tree growing as if wild at the edge of a swamp. "If," he said, "I am sharp-set, —for I do not refuse the blue pearmain, —I fill my pockets on each side; and as I retrace my steps in the frosty eve, being perhaps four or five miles from home, I eat one first from this side, and then from that, to keep my balance."

When I reached the patch circling away from the city and around Mudhole Bay, it was already dark. The evening star had arisen, and the sky was lightest again at the ring of the horizon. I passed the children from the boarding school having their cigarettes in the privacy of the darkness. Beyond them, a cottontail rabbit bounded across dry leaves into a chokecherry thicket. I could see nothing of it but its white tail. A few months earlier I had turned this same corner at dawn and counted fourteen cottontails strung out along the path, feeding in the dewy grass. The old ones scattered, leaving their babies, slow to sense danger and slow to react to it, innocent and defenseless. How many of the fourteen, I wondered, still survived?

It is especially pleasing to walk in the first darkness. Night falls like a sigh. In temperate places, the restless churning and chattering of the day ceases, the music fades. Until the moon sails into view, even the endless hunting ends. Diurnal creatures have bedded for the night. The crepuscular creatures never make a stir anyway. It is their need to be inconspicuous that has turned them into habitués of the twilight. The nocturnal creatures are beginning to rouse themselves from their naps, but the night is long and urgency beside the point. It is the most tranquil of times, that first hour of night, the hour of benediction, and to walk then is to receive its blessing.

I passed the patch of horsetails, passed the open water of the cattail marsh where the Canada geese land in the springtime, shattering the long silence of winter, passed the peninsula where the catbird nests, came under the high limbs of the old cottonwood trees, whose leaves tinkle like water in the summer breezes.

A thicket of chokecherries clutches the steep bank of the bay there, and the canes of wild raspberries grow in the understory. It is a favorite nesting place of songbirds; when the leaves dropped a month ago a dozen nests came into view. The squirrels make their big, sloppy nests higher up in the crooks of the cottonwoods. Even in the darkness I could make out the shapes of three of them.

At the edge of the water, the black willows take root and arch over the bay like witching sticks. It was with the forked branch of a willow that my grandfather demonstrated the art of water witching. I tried it, but proved not to have the knack for it. Grandfather also showed us children how to make whistles and flutes from young, green willow branches. And their pliability made them our first choice for the manufacture of bows and slingshots. Later I discovered that chewing their inner bark could cure a headache, and learned to watch for their yellow catkins as one of the earliest signs of spring, and shared a peace pipe packed with a tobacco that included, among other ingredients, willow bark, finding the tobacco as excellent as the ceremony was moving.

I stopped at the place where, a few days earlier, I had watched a beaver sizing up one of the willows for the fall harvest. It waded the shallow water beneath an overhanging limb, passing under the tree twice before it stopped, stood on its hind legs, using its broad black tail as a prop, and, stretching as high as it could, nipped with its long yellow teeth at the underside of the tree trunk. A few chips of bark fell into the water and began to float toward shore. The beaver lost its balance, splashed down into the water on all fours, stood again, and chipped away a second time at the tree. But it was clear that the core of the trunk was beyond reach of the beaver, and soon, apparently, it reached the same conclusion, slipped back into the water, and swam away. I stopped, watched, listened, but there was no sign of the beaver now.

Nearby there was a muskrat feeding bed at the outlet of a drainage tile that runs enough in winter to keep the ice in the bay open for a few feet. (Perhaps the muskrats themselves also help to hold back the ice.) In the wintertime you could go there and see the shells of freshwater clams, a favorite muskrat food, scattered across the ice, as if the muskrats had been tossing them like toys. And in the mud at the edge of the bay, you could sometimes see the tracks of a mink, hunting, perhaps, for clams too, or for the muskrats. Once in broad daylight on a sweltering summer afternoon I saw a mink there scrambling across the asphalt path and into the grass, as startled by me as I was by the sight of it.

I walked on around the edge of the bay to the place where a half-submerged cottonwood log sticks out of the shallow, muddy water. In the summertime one can some-times catch the wary mud turtles basking there.

The bay is bordered by a park. Last year the caretakers stopped mowing it. It is just beginning, after decades of domesticity, to go wild again. The first season saw a lot of brome grass and not much else: a few goatsbeards, in one low place a stand of docks, a few sprigs of wild mustard, some Queen Anne's lace. It will be fascinating in years to come to see what volunteers to grow there and how it changes the character of the place. The earliest event that anybody noticed—and it was widely noticed by the towns-folk—was that for the first time in years, two broods of ducks were raised in the park. On summer evenings there were sometimes a dozen people at a time standing along the path watching the mamas swimming in the bay, their broods of peeping ducklings in tow. Normally the path is an exercise lane. People jog, bicycle, walk briskly there. Everybody who passes is on some program of self-improve-ment and in a hurry about it. But for a month or two a few ducklings changed all that. The pace around the bay slowed. People came simply to watch, and whispering and pointing, they passed on the news: Something wild was going on within the limits of the city. They passed it like news of the unearthing of a long-buried treasure, which it was.

I walked in the still darkness through the campground, the most barren place along the bay, and came to the wooden footbridge over its outlet. The ditch widens a bit just at the footbridge and rounds a curve. A thick bed of cattails grows there, and red-winged blackbirds nest in it. Between the cattails and bay, the water runs in a narrow channel, shallow and thick as a stew with mosses and algae and duckweed and little water invertebrates and microscopic organisms of a hundred kinds. Sometimes children fish for bullheads from the bridge. Often a duck swims by. At dusk in the fall, there is always a muskrat swimming somewhere from one bank to another, its hairless rodent tail dragging straight out behind to rudder it, its eyes just above waterline, alert to everything that passes.

I crossed the footbridge and entered the street again, passing the hundred-foot-high cottonwoods where the crows like to gather, passing the tree where the orange shelf fungus grows. I have made a wonderful mushroom soup from it, dark and tangy with the taste of sulphur. I passed the place where, a few days earlier, I had found a little shrew, black as midnight, lying dead along the edge of the road; passed the fishing hole where my son caught his first walleye; passed the rocky shoreline where the crayfish live; passed the ancient willow in which the starlings flock.

I came around the curve of the lake, heading east toward Whiskey Ditch, a drainage ditch recently barricaded in stone and concrete and fencing wire to keep away the muskrats. As I walked, cheers rose from the football field across town and drifted my way. I came to the footbridge over Whiskey Ditch, where the rabbits used to winter in dens beneath the shrubs until the town fathers had the shrubs removed. A beaver had recently moved this way up the lake and had begun to cut down a couple of apple trees in the park. I wanted to see whether it was at work. The moon had come up. Its long silver rays glistened on the water.

I mounted the footbridge and, looking over the edge,

found my beaver. It was lying face up in the deepest part of the ditch channel, its face frozen in a grimace, its golden teeth glowing in the harsh light of the moon. It was secured at the chest in the powerful jaws of a steel trap, killed instantly, no doubt. Well, I thought, there will be cheers for more than the football team in Worthington tomorrow.

I turned then and headed toward the yellow light pouring from the windows of my gray house, so tight and secure against the world, wondering at the wildness persisting still beyond its walls despite everything.

In the morning, a cold winter rain was falling.

Acknowledgments

▷ ◁

More people, of course, make a book possible than any writer ever knows, but I am particularly grateful for assistance in the making of this one to: Jeanne K. Hanson, my agent, whose idea it was in the first place; Carlann Scholl, who read and criticized the manuscript at every stage of its creation and did much of the research for it; John Scholl, my walking partner; the staffs of the Nobles County, Minnesota, Library and of the Worthington Community College Library, who served far beyond the call of duty to search out and import hundreds of books and technical papers; Jeff Johnson and Dan Kelly, two wonderful editors who have taught me much; Diana and John Cross, who introduced me to the Nebraska sandhills; Gordon and Patti Howard, my hosts along the Oregon Trail; and my wife, Nancy, and my children, Laura and Aaron, who have tolerated both my long absences and my preoccupations during composition with grace and good humor.

291